SOVEREIGN
of the
ISLES

SOVEREIGN
of the
ISLES

How the Crown
Won the British Isles

Iain Milligan

UNICORN

Published in 2020 by
Unicorn, an imprint of Unicorn Publishing Group LLP
5 Newburgh Street
London
W1F 7RG

www.unicornpublishing.org

Text © Iain Milligan
Images © see page 280

ISBN 978-1-913491116

10 9 8 7 6 5 4 3 2 1

Printed by Latitude Press Ltd

Contents

List of maps

✠

England

The Channel Islands

Scotland

The Isle of Man

Wales

Ireland

Timeline

✠

825   Victory of Egbert of Wessex over Beornwulf of Mercia at Ellendun

843   Kenneth MacAlpin conquered the Picts and became king of the whole of the mainland of Scotland north of the Forth

937   Æthelstan's victory at Brunanburh, by virtue of which he became the King of the whole of England

1018   Battle of Carham, bringing Lothian within the kingdom of Scotland

1034   Duncan succeeded to the throne of Scotland, bringing Strathclyde within his kingdom

1066   Norman Conquest of England

1106   Henry I of England defeated his elder brother, Robert, at Tinchebrai and subjected Normandy to the English Crown

1155   Papal Bull of Laudabiliter, supposedly authorising the invasion of Ireland by Henry II of England

1157   Invasion of Wales by Henry II

1163   Henry II received the homage of the major princes of Wales at Woodstock

1169   Start of the Anglo-Norman invasion of Ireland

1171   Henry II invaded Ireland

1172   Synod of Cashel recognised Henry II as Lord of Ireland

1175   Treaty of Windsor by which the High King of Ireland agreed to become a liegeman of the King of England

1177   Council of Oxford at which Henry II granted Ireland to his son, John, as Lord of Ireland

1204   Normandy surrendered to Philippe II of France

1217   Following the defeat of a French invasion of England, the Treaty of Lambeth recognised Henry III as sovereign of the Channel Islands

1266   Treaty of Perth by which Alexander III of Scotland purchased the Hebrides and the Isle of Man from Norway

1283   Completion of the conquest of Wales by Edward I of England

1290   Death of the Maid of Norway, giving rise to thirteen claims to the throne of Scotland

1292   Edward I upheld the claim of Sir John de Balliol to the Scottish throne and accepted the submission of Scotland to English sovereignty

1297 ● First Anglo-Norman Parliament in Ireland

1333 ● Edward III announced that he had legitimately taken the Isle of Man into his hands and granted it to Sir William de Montacute

1402 ● In an attempt to suppress Owain Glyn Dŵr's rebellion, punitive laws were imposed on the Welsh by the English Parliament

1406 ● Isle of Man granted by Henry IV of England to Sir John de Stanley

1468/69 ● Orkney and Shetland pledged to secure the dowry of Margaret of Norway on her betrothal to James III of Scotland, subsequently taken on default

1482 ● Berwick-upon-Tweed was surrendered to the Duke of Gloucester (the future Richard III) and became part of England

1494 ● Poynings' Law subjecting the powers of the Irish Parliament to those of the English Parliament

1536 ● Act of Union between England and Wales

1537 ● Irish Act declaring Henry VIII to be the supreme head of the Church in Ireland

1541 ● Irish Act declaring Henry VIII to be King of Ireland

1557 ● Start of the English Plantation of Ireland

1688 ● William of Orange invaded England

1689 ● English Bill of Rights and Scottish Claim of Right

1691 ● Final defeat of the Jacobites in Ireland at Aughrim followed by the Treaty of Limerick

1707 ● Union of England and Scotland to form Great Britain

1746 ● Final defeat of the Jacobites in Scotland at Culloden, following which the Scots were disarmed

1765 ● Isle of Man purchased by the Crown from the Duke and Duchess of Atholl, making the Crown Lord of Man

1801 ● Union of Great Britain and Ireland

1829 ● British Government purchased all of the remaining rights of the Duke and Duchess of Atholl over the Isle of Man

1866 ● Isle of Man permitted to keep the revenue of the island, subject to an annual payment to the British Government

1914 ● Irish Home Rule Act passed, but immediately suspended for the duration of the First World War

1920 ● Government of Ireland Act dividing Ireland between six of the nine counties of Ulster and Southern Ireland, both with their own Parliament, but leaving the British Parliament at Westminster supreme

1921 ● Peace treaty between the United Kingdom and representatives of the Dáil Eireann followed by the constitution of the Irish Free State

1937 ● The Irish Free State became a republic

1940/45 ● German occupation of the Channel Islands

1998 ● Scotland Act devolved powers to a new Scottish Parliament

1998 ● Following a second referendum in Wales, the National Assembly for Wales was established

1998 ● Good Friday Agreement between the British Government, the Government of the Irish Republic and the various political factions which had been involved in the Troubles, providing for the constitutional status of Northern Ireland to be determined by plebiscite

Introduction

In the summer of 1174, King William I of Scotland invaded the north of England, knowing that the English King, Henry II, was fully occupied elsewhere in suppressing a rebellion by three of his sons. In the course of that summer, the Scots laid siege to Alnwick Castle in Northumberland. On 13 July, in his camp outside the walls of Alnwick, William was having dinner when he was surprised by an English attack. During the fighting that ensued, his horse was killed, William was thrown to the ground and, disastrously for Scotland, was captured. He was taken to Normandy, where he was held as a prisoner in Henry's castle at Falaise. There, in December, he agreed to the terms of a treaty by which Scotland was made subject to the Crown of England. In York the following summer effect was given to the treaty by the homage which William and his nobles then did, and the oaths of fealty they swore, to King Henry of England.

In the bitter struggle for domination between England and Scotland, William was not the only Scottish monarch to have been a prisoner of the English: John de Balliol was captured in 1296 and forced not only to abdicate but also once again to surrender Scotland to an English King, Edward I; David II was held for eleven years following the rout of the Scots and his capture at the Battle of Neville's Cross in 1346; James I was held for eighteen years following his initial capture by pirates at sea in 1406 while attempting to escape to France from the clutches of his uncle, the Duke of Albany; and Mary Queen of Scots, having sought refuge in England in 1568, was held by her cousin, Queen Elizabeth, for nineteen years ending with her execution.

The struggle was not one between the English and the Scots alone. Nor was it confined to military conquest. It included the ruthless colonisation by the English of Wales and Ireland and, importantly, the imposition of the English language. In 1536 Henry VIII required the administration of justice and government in Wales to be conducted in English, not Welsh; and that remained the position until 1993. In 1537 he made English the official language of Ireland and made the teaching of English compulsory. Even James VI of Scotland (by then also James I of England) in 1609 required the chiefs of Highland clans to send their eldest sons, or failing sons their eldest daughters, to Lowland schools where they would be taught to speak, read and write in English.

Yet England itself was once part of the Danish empire; it was then conquered by the Duke of Normandy, whose duchy included the Channel Islands; it was briefly a vassal of the Holy Roman Empire and then for over a hundred years a vassal of the Holy See. Ireland, once ruled by native Irish chiefs, was a vassal of the Holy See until Henry VIII's break with Rome. Wales, once a principality, was swallowed whole by England. The Hebrides, Orkney and Shetland, originally part of the kingdom of Norway, became part of the kingdom of Scotland. The Isle of Man too was once part of the kingdom of Norway, later becoming part of the kingdom of Scotland, then a possession of the English Crown and even for a while an independent sovereign state.

How was it that all of these parts now comprised in the United Kingdom, the Channel Islands and the Isle of Man and – known formally as the British Islands,[1] but more commonly, if less precisely, as the British Isles – became subject to the sovereignty of the British Crown? How were they united under one Crown and why are the Isle of Man and the Channel Islands not part of the United Kingdom?

It is frustration at the absence of any comprehensive answer to these questions that has driven me to write this book. It is a book that attempts to cut a slice through British history, to tell the story of the acquisition of that sovereignty. It is an attempt to fill the gaping holes left by schools and to fit together the pieces of the jigsaw, many of which may be familiar, but their place in history all too often forgotten, overlooked or even unknown. It is not its purpose to pass judgment on the events, but simply to tell the story of them. Nor does it pretend to be a work of original scholarship: instead it seeks to draw together the threads that tell the story of conquest, colonisation and loss, leaving the territory of the British Isles as it is today.

A clue is perhaps to be found in the commonplace confusion of England with the kingdom of which it forms but one part. Since England emerged as a kingdom in its own right, it has been an aggressive predator against its neighbours. In 1850 Viscount Palmerston, curiously an hereditary Irish peer with a seat in the House of Commons at Westminster, in trying to justify his gunboat diplomacy[2] to the House, referred to the Government of England and the strong arm of England, confusing England, like so many before and since, with the United Kingdom of which he was then the Secretary of State for Foreign Affairs and which, at the time, consisted not only of England but also of Wales, Scotland and the whole of Ireland.

The book is inevitably selective, not because some parts of the story might be thought today to be unpalatable, but in an attempt to keep it within relatively manageable bounds. It attempts to identify some at least of the principal landmarks on the way. There are not only the battles for territory, some well known, others less so, but also the treaties which were agreed and the laws which were made, many of which have their own story to tell.

On the marriage of Mary Queen of Scots with François, the Dauphin of France, in 1558, a treaty was concluded between the kingdom of Scotland and the kingdom of France by which not only did François become the King of Scotland, but on the accession of François to the throne of France, the two countries were united under one crown. There was even a secret agreement concluded at the same time as the marriage whereby, if Mary died without children, her rights to the English throne were to pass to the King of France.

Among the statutes, many of which were devoted to the colonisation by England of other parts of the British Isles, one was designed to segregate the colonists in Ireland completely from the native population, forbidding them, among many other things, from wearing native Irish dress.[3] Another prohibited the importation of victuals or armour into Wales other than to provision English castles or towns or by special licence from the King or his council.[4] Yet another prohibited the wearing of Highland dress in Scotland.[5]

So how was it, then, that this sovereignty was acquired? While today nations are more sensitive to calls for self-determination and to international recognition than to the brute force of conquest, unsurprisingly the rules of the game have changed over the centuries: the answer in the past for the most part was by force of arms, by treaty (often at the point of a sword) or by ruthless colonisation.

Before embarking on the story, there are some common threads which it may be helpful to explain at the outset.

Succession to the throne

At the heart of much of the story is the king or queen and the territory which they controlled. Just as the rules relating to the acquisition of sovereignty have changed, so too have the rules relating to succession to the throne. Until the coronation of Edward II in 1307, English kings did not succeed to the throne by inheritance, but by election, as in all old Teutonic kingdoms. The election was by the supreme council of the kingdom, the Witenagemot or Witan. Its members were the king (once elected) and the principal people of his kingdom, such as the ealdormen (the governors of the shires), the bishops and the king's principal servants. The candidates for election were generally restricted to the royal family, and the choice depended on suitability, particularly military prowess. A preference was given to sons born after the father had come to the throne (the *porphyrogeniti* – sons born in the purple), particularly those recommended by the last king. In practice and over time the eldest son was preferred, unless he suffered from some obvious shortcoming.

The Witan also had the power to depose a king, although that was very rarely exercised, one of the notable casualties being Æthelred the Unready who was deposed for a time in favour of the Danish King, Sweyn Forkbeard, in 1013. Two hundred years later, in the prelude to Magna Carta and notwithstanding the Pope's disagreement, the English barons offered the crown of England to the future King Louis VIII of France. The question of deposition also vexed the English Parliament on three subsequent occasions, but they ducked it by procuring the abdication of the king (Edward II in 1327 – followed by his death or disappearance in mysterious circumstances; and Richard II in 1399 – who also then died in mysterious circumstances) or by declaring his abdication (James II in 1689 following his flight to France).

After the conquest of Normandy by Henry I, succession to the Channel Islands followed that of England. With the conquest of Wales by Edward I, there was (at least in the eyes of the English) no separate kingdom in Wales. Until the time of Henry VIII there was no crown of Ireland and from his time succession to the kingdom of Ireland was not distinct from succession to the kingdom of England. In Scotland succession by primogeniture did not become a clearly accepted custom until the eleven-year-old Malcolm IV succeeded his grandfather, David I, in 1153. Before that, support of the

Scottish magnates or even, on some occasions, of the English was necessary. And the Isle of Man was a law unto itself.

Homage and the oath of fealty

Throughout much of the story with which this book is concerned, the acceptance of the sovereign power of the king or queen over the magnates of their kingdom was demonstrated by the ceremony of homage – an arcane ritual by modern lights, but of great significance at the time. So far as the British Isles are concerned, the ceremony was instituted by William the Conqueror and was an aspect of the feudalism that he brought with him from Normandy. (Although it tends to some extent to give a false impression of the history, and particularly the culture, of those who played a part in the story, I have generally adopted the Anglicised form of names, being more familiar and therefore more readily recognisable: William the Conqueror or William I of England is perhaps more familiar than Guillaume le Bâtard or Guillaume II de Normandie.)

There were two principal elements to homage. One was the obligation of fidelity (*fealty*), the personal relationship of lord and tenant (*vassal*) founded on agreement between them, the lord owing protection and the vassal service. The other was the holding of land (a *fief*) by the vassal on condition of rendering a service, originally and typically military service, a superior proprietary right being retained by the lord, the grantor. In some circumstances the vassal could make a payment to the lord in lieu of providing the service, known as a quit-rent (*quietus redditus*). It was of the essence of feudalism that the vassal owed fealty to his immediate lord. However, unlike in France, William also required an oath of fealty from all tenants, not just the tenants-in-chief, with a view to depriving any rebellious tenant-in-chief of the support of his vassals.

On the grant of a fief, the vassal was publicly invested with the land by some symbol of delivery, called 'livery of seisin'. For the land which had been granted, he then did homage, so called from the word used in the ceremony 'Je deveigne votre homme' – I become your man. The ceremony consisted of the vassal kneeling before his lord with sword ungirt and head uncovered, placing his hands between those of his lord and saying (originally in Norman French) 'I become your man from this day forward, of life and limb, and of earthly worship; and unto you shall be true and faithful, and bear to you faith for the tenements I claim to hold of you.'[6] The lord then kissed his vassal on the cheek and received the oath of fealty. In the case of a sub-tenant (*vavasour*), his oath of fealty was guarded by a reservation of the faith due to his sovereign lord the king or queen.

To this day, the coronation of the British monarch entails a ceremony of homage and an oath of fealty in return for which the monarch swears to govern the people in accordance with the laws and customs of the realm.[7]

Crown lands

Following his initial invasion and victory over King Harold at Senlac Hill in 1066, William the Conqueror subjugated much of England by seizing the lands of those who had taken up arms against him, such as those of Harold and his family, and, subsequently, of those who were perceived not to support him. As time went by, even those who had managed to hang on to their land were expected to surrender it to the King and receive it back from him by way of re-grant. Of the lands which he had seized, William kept large tracts for himself, including the 'forests' reserved for the royal hunt – so named not because they were forests in the modern sense of wooded areas, but because they were outside (Latin *foris*) the common law and subject to the peculiar laws of the forest. The rest he granted to his loyal supporters, who in turn parcelled it out to sub-tenants. Importantly, however, every grant, or re-grant, was accompanied by an oath of fealty to the king.

As the feudal system of tenure spread, not only did the king receive oaths of fealty from more and more of his subjects but, importantly, he also acquired paramount title to more and more of the land. The paramount title was a source of great power to the king because a tenant who fell from favour might find that his land was forfeited to the king; indeed forfeiture was the automatic consequence of a tenant's conviction for treason. One example of land to which the king did not originally acquire paramount title was in Orkney and Shetland, formerly part of the kingdom of Norway, where there was a different form of land tenure: this came to a head when King Christian I of Norway defaulted on the dowry of his daughter, Margaret, which had been promised to King James III of Scotland on their betrothal in 1468 and secured on King Christian's stake in the islands.

The lands that William the Conqueror and his successors acquired and kept for themselves (known as Crown lands) were one of the principal sources of revenue needed to fund the government of the kingdom. Although the source was supplemented from time to time by (among other things) forfeitures or expropriations, such as the vast increase arising from the dissolution of the monasteries between 1536 and 1541, more often it dwindled as a result of sales to raise urgently needed funds, particularly in time of war, and as a result of improvident grants made to royal favourites and followers; it all but dried up as a result of the reckless disposals by the Stuart kings and even William III in the seventeenth century, necessitating an ever-increasing burden of taxes. A statute of Queen Anne in 1702[8] put a stop to the outright disposal of land by the monarch. Finally, in 1760 George III surrendered all that remained of the Crown lands, except (wisely as matters turned out) for the Duchy of Lancaster and the Duchy of Cornwall, in return for an annual allowance known as the Civil List; instead he and his successors were granted the right by Parliament to acquire and dispose of land like any other private individual, such as the acquisition by Queen Victoria of the Sandringham Estate for the future King Edward VII in 1862.

Although there were occasions when a 'fine' was paid by a vassal to the king in return for some indulgence, the fine in that context was a price or tribute, rather than a penalty.

Local government of the kingdom was progressively divided between shires. A shire (*scir*) means simply a share or subdivision of a larger whole. The system had originated in the kingdom of Wessex and had spread as that kingdom expanded. The *scir-gerefa* or sheriff was the king's steward and judicial president of the shire. The shire was ruled by an ealdorman who was generally a member of the king's Witan. The shire system was adopted by the Normans and continues vestigially even today. 'Shiring' refers simply to the imposition of the shire system.

Chronology, dates and changes to the calendar

In the hope of making it easier to follow, the book has been divided up broadly following the chronological sequence of consolidation between England, the Channel Islands, Scotland, the Isle of Man, Wales, and what was to end up as Northern Ireland. To tell the entire story in chronological order was too indigestible. There is however a short timeline of the principal events on pp. 8-9.

The chronology is not, of course, helped by the change from the Julian to the Gregorian calendar, which is a colourful story in itself. In 1582 Pope Gregory XIII issued a bull – simply a document under seal – to abandon the Julian calendar then in use, the better to reflect the cycles of the sun and moon and thus, importantly from the perspective of the Roman Catholic Church, to determine the date of Easter. As a result, in most Roman Catholic countries the beginning of the new year was changed from 25 March to 1 January and a much-needed adjustment was made which entailed skipping ten days. This had no direct impact on Protestant England or Presbyterian Scotland (or indeed on the Eastern Orthodox Churches[9]). However, under a decree of James VI,[10] Scotland adopted 1 January as the start of the new year with effect from 1600, but did not make any other adjustment at that stage, so 1 January 1600 in Scotland was 1 January 1599 in England.

Finally, after more than one and a half centuries, what was now the British Government decided to follow its Western European neighbours. By the Calendar (New Style) Act 1750 (which applied to Great Britain, the Isle of Man and the Channel Islands and purportedly to Ireland), the start of the new year was officially changed from 25 March (Lady Day) to 1 January, beginning on 1 January 1752; and the Gregorian calendar was to be substituted for the Julian calendar such that 3 September 1752 was to be 14 September 1752 (giving rise to the complaint that people had lost eleven days of their lives) with a leap year every four years except in each centennial year.[11] (There is still today one curious vestige of the Julian calendar to be found in the British tax year. In order to avoid losing eleven days of revenue, in 1752 the Government adopted a tax year which ended on 4 April, i.e. eleven days after what would have been the end of the Julian year on 24 March. Then, because 1800 was not a leap year in the Gregorian calendar, the tax year was extended by a further day to end on 5 April, as it still does today.)

In Ireland the position is more complicated for two reasons. First, whereas the British colonists were generally Protestant, the vast majority of the native Irish were Catholics and, given the opportunity, would have followed Pope Gregory's lead. The Gregorian calendar was therefore adopted in the territories controlled by Hugh O'Donnell and Hugh O'Neill in the Nine Years' War (1593–1603). It was also adopted to a limited extent in the territory controlled by the Catholic Confederation of Kilkenny from 1642 until the Confederation was crushed by Cromwell eight years later. Even then it was problematic, particularly in Ulster, because the Catholics stood out by the celebration of holy days eleven days apart from their Protestant neighbours. Secondly, the British Act of 1750, without any constitutional justification, purported to apply to Ireland and was adopted in practice there. That constitutional anomaly was rectified by an Irish Act in 1782 which brought the Irish calendar into line with the British.[12]

Generally the references to years here are to those of the Gregorian calendar.

There is one further complication relating to dates which arises in the context of the initial numbers identifying statutes. Until 1896, apart from Scottish statutes, these do not refer to a date at all but only to the number of the session of Parliament in the reign of the particular monarch.[13]

Currency

There are various references to amounts of money which were to be paid, not least as a king's ransom. More often than not, they were expressed in 'marks' or, where Scotland was concerned, 'merks'. The mark or merk was a measure of weight of silver or (more rarely) gold. As a measure of silver, it was two thirds of a pound weight (Latin *libra* – hence the ornate £ sign), originally worth two thirds of a pound sterling. It was not necessarily in the form of coin, and in England it never was; it could, for example, be in ingots (a commonplace in Viking hoards). I have not indicated present values of the sums mentioned because their economic value depends critically on what could have been purchased with them at the time: a simple adjustment for inflation is not really a sufficient measure.

England

✠

The conquest of Britain by the Romans began in earnest in AD 43. In AD 142, on the orders of the Emperor Antoninus Pius, the Romans began to build a wall between the Firth of Clyde and the Firth of Forth, where the separation between the west coast and the east coast of Britain is at its thinnest. Although the Romans ventured further north, the land to the south of the wall was the greatest extent of the province known by the Romans as Britannia and its Celtic inhabitants as Britons.

With the pressure to defend their territory nearer home against the likes of Alaric the Goth (or sometimes Visigoth) and, later, Attila the Hun, the Romans withdrew their forces from Britain around the beginning of the fifth century. With their departure, eastern England was colonised progressively by Germanic tribes from Continental Europe, known commonly as the Anglo-Saxons: the Angles came from Angeln, a district north of the River Eider in Lower Schleswig; the Saxons from Lower Saxony; the Jutes from Jutland; and the Frisians (albeit more often as traders than as colonists) from Friesland in the north-west of what is now the Netherlands. The initial wave of colonisation, in Kent at least, was by Angles led by two brothers, Hengest and Horsa, who landed at Ebbsfleet at the northern end of Sandwich Bay in 449, reportedly at the invitation of a particularly dissolute king, known as Vortigern. Importantly the colonists brought with them the seeds of the language which is the everyday English of today, displacing the Celtic language spoken by the indigenous Britons, known as Brythonic (P-Celtic) which survives in various forms as Welsh, Cornish and Breton.[14]

Three centuries after the departure of the Romans, the Vikings began to arrive. They were 'men of the fjords' (*viken* in Old Norse), characteristically

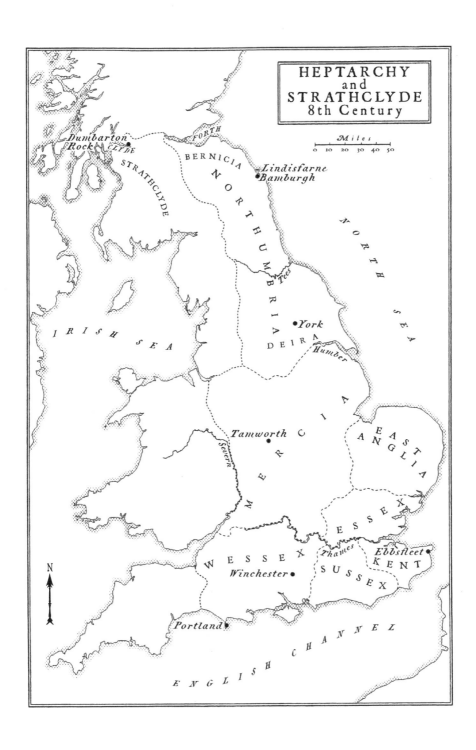

HEPTARCHY
and
STRATHCLYDE
8th Century

Miles
0 10 20 30 40 50

STRATHCLYDE

Dumbarton
Rock
CLYDE

FORTH

BERNICIA

Lindisfarne
Bamburgh

NORTHUMBRIA

NORTH SEA

Tees

IRISH SEA

York

DEIRA

Humber

Tamworth

MERCIA

EAST
ANGLIA

Severn

ESSEX

WESSEX

Thames

Ebbsfleet

Winchester

SUSSEX

KENT

N

Portland

ENGLISH CHANNEL

sea rovers. They came initially from the fjords of the south-west coast of
Norway, but the name in time came to refer to any raiders from northern
Continental Europe. Their first recorded raid took place in 786, when
Norsemen arrived at Portland in three ships from Hordaland in west
Norway and killed the local reeve by whom they had been confronted.[15]
That was followed in 793 by the devastation of the Holy Island of Lindisfarne
and surrounding countryside, presaged, we are told, by immense flashes of
lightening and fiery dragons seen flying in the air.[16]

The rise of the kingdom of Wessex and the birth of the kingdom of England

By the time of the early Viking raids there were broadly seven recognisably
distinct areas which had been colonised by the Anglo-Saxons, the seven
sometimes known as the 'heptarchy' (the seven kingdoms), consisting
of Northumbria, Mercia, Wessex, Sussex, Kent, Essex and East Anglia.
Northumbria[17] stretched from the Firth of Forth to the Humber (hence
Northumbria) and from the east coast to the Pennines in the west; Mercia
(the marchlands) encompassed much of the Midlands; Wessex (the land
of the West Saxons) to the south of Mercia, stretched from Sussex (the
land of the South Saxons) somewhat to the east of what is now Devon; and
Sussex, Kent, Essex (the land of the East Saxons) and East Anglia (the land
of the Angles) were much as they are today. What is now Cumbria was not
colonised by the Anglo-Saxons to the same extent: it formed part of the
kingdom of Strathclyde, centred on the great natural fortress of Dumbarton
Rock on the north shore of the Firth of Clyde.

Of those seven kingdoms, there were three which came to dominate
the building of the kingdom of England. They were Wessex, Mercia and
Northumbria, with their capitals, at least for most of the time, at Winchester,
Tamworth and York.

Before the rise of the kingdom of Wessex to dominance in the ninth
century, there were brief intervals when one ruler was acknowledged as the
ruler of much of what was to become England. With the death of Wihtred
of Kent in 725 and of Ine of Wessex the following year, Æthelbald, who had
been King of Mercia since 716, had no serious rival in southern England
and, by 731, all of England south of the Humber accepted him as their lord.
In a charter of 736 he even described himself as *rex Britanniae* (king of

Britain). His long reign came to an end in 757 when he was assassinated by his bodyguard at Seckington, near Tamworth. After a brief interregnum, Æthelbald was succeeded as King of Mercia by Offa, famous for his dyke forming a boundary between his kingdom of Mercia and the Welsh. Initially Offa's rule extended little, if at all, beyond the Mercians. However, by 774 he styled himself as *rex Anglorum* (king of the Angles – or English) and in one instance at least as *rex totius Anglorum patriae* (king of the whole of the land of the Angles). Although there is nothing to suggest that before that date he had any authority north of the Humber, it is possible that Æthelred, on becoming King of Northumbria that year, had submitted to him with a view to strengthening his own position.

The rise to power of the kingdom of Wessex began in 825 in the reign of King Egbert (r. 802–839) and, although there were setbacks at the hands of the Danes in the next generation, it continued under his grandson, Alfred the Great (r. 871–899), his great-grandson, Edward the Elder (r. 899–924), and his great-great-grandson, Æthelstan (r. 924–939), culminating in Æthelstan's overwhelming victory at Brunanburh in 937.

In 825 there was one of the most decisive battles in the history of Anglo-Saxon England. It was fought between King Egbert of Wessex and King Beornwulf of Mercia at Ellendun. The site of the battle is not known for sure but was probably a depression between two ridges, inaptly named Windmill Hill, just to the south of the park where Lydiard House now stands near Swindon. It was a hot summer's day such that 'more soldiers were suffocated with sweat than with blood',[18] the slaughter on both sides being prodigious. Although the Wessex army was greatly outnumbered, the Mercians were totally defeated.

Egbert's victory brought to an end the Mercian domination of southern England. Following an invasion of Kent and Sussex by Egbert's son, Æthelwulf, by the end of the following year all areas south of the Thames had submitted to Egbert. Then in 829 Egbert subdued the Mercians themselves and, when confronted by his army at Dore south of Sheffield, the Northumbrians submitted to him too. However, his success was short-lived, because by the end of the following year Wiglaf, the Mercian king whom he had deposed, had regained his throne. Finally, in 838, a year before his own death, Egbert defeated the Cornish and their Viking allies at the Battle of Hingston Down (just to the west of the River Tamar), thus bringing Cornwall within his realm.

Although Viking raids by Danes had begun in 835, there was a sea change in 865. Hitherto the raids had been isolated hit and run enterprises. In 865 however, the Danes arrived in force in East Anglia with a great army organised and equipped for conquest. Over the next thirteen years there were numerous battles from which, after various setbacks, the Danes emerged largely victorious, King Osberht and King Ælla of Northumbria and King Edmund of East Anglia being killed and King Burhed of Mercia being driven to flee abroad in the process. Among the kings, there were only two survivors: one was Æthelred, King of Wessex, who died of natural causes in 870, and the other was his brother and successor, King Alfred, both grandsons of Egbert. It was Alfred who earned the sobriquet 'the Great', the only English monarch ever to do so.

At Easter 878 Alfred had withdrawn with forty men to Athelney, then an island in the swampy land on what is now the Somerset Levels, between Burrowbridge and Lyng. There he built a fortification from which, with the aid of the men of Somerset, he made sorties against the Danes. Seven weeks later he moved first to Egbert's Stone to the east of Selwood (a possible site for which on Kingsettle Hill was marked in the eighteenth century by a splendid tower), where he was joined by the men of Somerset, Wiltshire and Hampshire west of the Solent, and proceeded from there to Island Wood in west Wiltshire.

The following day he moved with his army towards Edington, just to the east of Westbury. It seems likely that the Danes had taken up a defensive position along the ridge about 3½ miles south of Edington, on the south side of which there is still today an 'ancient ditch', and possibly that Alfred took up a position at what is now Battlesbury Camp facing the ditch. Wherever precisely it took place, battle was joined and the Danes were put to flight, pursued by Alfred's forces all the way to their fortified encampment at Chippenham. There, having been besieged for three weeks, their King, Guthrum, sued for peace – peace to which Alfred agreed on terms that Guthrum be baptised and withdraw his army from Wessex. A few weeks later, Guthrum was royally entertained by Alfred at Wedmore in Somerset, where he was baptised. True to his word, by the following year he had withdrawn his forces to East Anglia.

The Danes then settled in East Anglia and the eastern part of Mercia under King Guthrum. The area which they had colonised became known as the Danelaw, reflecting the adoption of the laws and customs of the Danes.

Alfred had two children by whom his mission was carried on: one was his daughter Æthelflaed and the other was his son, Edward, known as Edward the Elder. Alfred died in 899 and was succeeded by Edward as King of Wessex. In the meantime, Æthelflaed had married Æthelred, King of Mercia, and when her husband died in 911 she succeeded him as Queen – becoming known as 'the Lady of Mercia'. By the time of her death in 918, Æthelflaed and Edward had between them subdued most of England south of the Humber. The first significant victory came in 910, when a combined force of Mercians and West Saxons defeated a raiding army of Northumbrian Danes at Wednesfield near Tettenhall. It was followed by relentless fortress building as one area after another was subdued. The year 917 was a year of victories: Æthelflaed captured the strategic stronghold of Derby; a great English host defeated the East Anglian Danes at Tempsford, to the east of Bedford, killing the last of their kings; and Edward captured Colchester. The following year the Danish army surrendered to Æthelflaed at Leicester.

Æthelflaed died shortly after her victory at Leicester. Before he learnt of his sister's death, Edward had taken Stamford, but with the news of her death he lost no time in securing his position by occupying the Mercian capital at Tamworth, a fortified settlement where the River Anker joins the River Tame (but before the days of the magnificent motte and tower which the Normans were to build there later). By the end of 918 the remaining strategic northern strongholds of Nottingham and Lincoln had surrendered. Edward then removed any final threat to his claim to be King of the Mercians by procuring the abduction of Æthelflaed's daughter, Ælfwynn, and carrying her off to Wessex.

While all of this was going on, Vikings from Dublin had established a colony on the Wirral in the west and a Viking named Raegnald had invaded Northumbria in the east and taken York. In an attempt to protect his kingdom from invasion via the Mersey from the west, Edward built a new fortress at Thelwall, repaired the old Roman fortifications at Manchester and added to those which his sister had built at Runcorn, Chester and Eddisbury. Nevertheless, these new defences were not enough to deter Sihtric, Raegnald's cousin, from invading north-west Mercia with an army from Dublin and sacking Davenport in Cheshire. It was probably as a result of this attack that in 920 Edward moved north. He built a new fortress at Nottingham on the south bank of the Trent opposite the existing fortress and linked the two with a bridge. From there he proceeded to Bakewell in the Peak District and built another fortress nearby. It is not known where he went from Bakewell nor are the circumstances of the crowning event of his reign known, but that same year, 920, as the *Anglo-Saxon Chronicles* record: 'the king of Scots and all the nation of Scots chose him as father and lord; and [so also did] Raegnald and Eadwulf's sons and all those who live in Northumbria, both English and Danish and Norwegians and others; and also the king of the Strathclyde Britons and all the Strathclyde Britons.'[19]

What prompted this submission by the northern kingdoms is not recorded, but it may have been their own desire for mutual recognition and protection. The King of Scots in question was Constantine II; Raegnald was by this time King of southern Northumbria (known as Deira) at York; Eadwulf was King of northern Northumbria (known as Bernicia) at Bamburgh; and the King of Strathclyde was probably Owain ap Dyfnwal.

Edward died in 924. By the time of his death he controlled all of England south of the Humber and even parts of Wales. Although he had received the submission of the four kings in 920, his reach did not in reality extend to their kingdoms. That was left to Æthelstan, his son, by whom he was succeeded.

Æthelstan was the son by Edward's first wife, Ecgwynn, and a grandson of Alfred the Great. Of Æthelstan William of Malmesbury recounts:

> For even his grandfather Alfred, seeing and embracing him affectionately when he was a boy of astonishing beauty and graceful manners, had most devoutly prayed that his government might be prosperous indeed, he made him a knight unusually early, giving him a scarlet cloak, a belt studded with diamonds, and a Saxon sword with a golden scabbard. Next he had provided that he should be educated in the court of Æthelflaed his daughter, and of his son-in-law Æthelred; so that, having been brought up in expectation of succeeding to the kingdom, by the tender care of his aunt and of this celebrated prince, he repressed and destroyed all envy by the lustre of his good qualities; and after the death of his father, and decease of his brother, he was crowned at Kingston.[20]

Both the cloak and the belt were symbolic: the belt was a *cingulum*, a symbol of rank of a Roman military officer; and the cloak was a vestment of the consulate, a symbol of the pre-eminent magistracy of Rome.

At the time of Edward's death Æthelstan had a half-brother, Ælfweard. Whereas Æthelstan had been brought up at the Mercian court, Ælfweard had been brought up at the court of the kingdom of Wessex in Winchester, making him more likely than Æthelstan to be chosen by the Witan of Wessex as their next king. Fortuitously, the death of Ælfweard within days of his father solved that problem and Æthelstan was elected as King of both Mercia and Wessex.

The following year Æthelstan was not just consecrated as king, but crowned with a crown, rather than the traditional helmet, at Kingston-upon-Thames in 925. Kingston was chosen for the ceremony not only as the traditional site for the coronation of the West Saxon kings and a strategic point where there was a bridge across the river, but importantly because the Thames marked the border between the two kingdoms.

At the time of his coronation Æthelstan's kingdom embraced the whole of England south of the Humber. By the time of his death fourteen years later he was the king of the whole of England and more.

In 927 Æthelstan seized the opportunity to conquer Northumbria, the last Viking kingdom. Raegnald, the King of the southern Northumbrians, who had submitted to King Edward in 920, had died the following year. He had been succeeded by his cousin, Sihtric, who had made peace with Æthelstan and married Æthelstan's daughter into the bargain. But in 927 Sihtric too had died. His son, Olaf, was chosen to succeed him, supported by his uncle, Guthfrith, King of the Dublin Vikings. Before Guthfrith could reach its capital, York, to lend his support to Olaf, Æthelstan invaded Northumbria and captured York, Olaf taking refuge in Dublin and Guthfrith in Scotland.

Following his victory, Æthelstan sought recognition of his supremacy by the submission of the other kings of mainland Britain. On 12 July 927 Constantine II of Scotland, Hywel Dda of Deheubarth (south-west Wales), Ealdred I of Bamburgh (northern Northumbria) and Owain I of Strathclyde (or possibly Morgan ap Owain of Gwent) made peace with Æthelstan and submitted to him. The submission appears to have taken place near what is now Eamont Bridge, at the confluence of the River Lowther and the River Eamont south-east of Penrith (although there is also some suggestion that it was at Dacre[21] about 6 miles to the west). With the benefit of the submission, Æthelstan styled himself not just as King of England but also as King of the whole of Britain (*rex totius Britanniae*).

As for Guthfrith, whom Constantine had promised to hand over to Æthelstan, he escaped and, having gathered support, laid siege to York. In the event the siege was a failure and was abandoned. Guthfrith, after a period on the run, then gave himself up to Æthelstan. In the meantime Æthelstan razed York to the ground to prevent any further insurrection and distributed the considerable booty found there among his army.

In 934 Æthelstan invaded Scotland. Why he did so is unclear. Possibly it was to redress a breach by Constantine of the terms of the peace agreed at Eamont Bridge. More probably it was opportunism on the part of Æthelstan, encouraged by the deaths of three potential opponents: his half-brother and rival, Edwin, had been drowned in the English Channel in 933, supposedly on the orders of Æthelstan himself; earlier in 934, Guthfrith had died; and a King of Northumbria, whose identity is unclear, had also died that year. Indeed, it may have been Constantine's support for a successor to the King of Northumbria, whom Æthelstan opposed, that provoked the invasion. Æthelstan's army marched deep into the Highlands, burning and looting as they went, and a fleet of his ships ravaged the Scottish coast as far north as Caithness. Fresh terms were offered to Constantine, which, in the face of such an onslaught, he had little alternative but to accept.

Three years later, in 937, an alliance was formed between Olaf Guthfrithson, who had succeeded Guthfrith as King of Dublin in 934 and had subsequently subdued all the Viking settlements in Ireland, Constantine II, King of Scotland, Owain MacDomhnuil, King of Strathclyde, probably Aralt, King of Man and the Isles, and possibly other Celtic chieftains. Driving the alliance were the loss of York in 927, the desire of Constantine to redeem his subjugation in 934 and the threat to Strathclyde posed by the growing power of Æthelstan.

In the autumn of 937 at a place referred to in the *Anglo-Saxon Chronicles* as Brunanburh, the army of Æthelstan totally defeated the vast armies of the alliance. Æthelstan's victory reinforced the submission which he had received from the Kings at Eamont Bridge ten years earlier and left him to reign over a territory recognisable as the England of today. From almost nothing sixty years earlier, the kingdom of Wessex had become the kingdom of England. Starting with the defeat of the Danes by his grandfather, Alfred, at Edington in 878, followed by the conquests of his aunt, Æthelflaed, and his father, Edward the Elder, which had culminated in the submission of the four Kings in 920, Æthelstan had established his sovereignty over England.

Surprisingly for a battle of such importance, the site of the Battle of Brunanburh is as yet unknown and has been the subject of much scholarly debate. A *burh*, to which the name Brunanburh refers, is a fortified settlement: that much is clear. The ancient chronicles give the site a variety of names, most beginning with Brun, save (principally) for the Icelandic saga known as *Egil's Saga* which refers to Vin-heath by Vin-wood.[22] Between them they refer to Constantine's son-in-law, Olaf Sihtricson, arriving with a large fleet in the mouth of the Humber, to the advance of the allied army far into England, to Æthelstan's army coming north to meet them, to a battle among the hills, and to the fleeing Norsemen of Olaf Guthfrithson (ruler of the Dublin Vikings – not to be confused with Olaf Sihtricson) taking to their ships at Dingesmere to sail back to Dublin.

Among the many theories, there are two which are perhaps more plausible than others, one that the battle was fought on the Wirral and the other that it was fought some way north of Derby. The site on the Wirral is now in the parish of Bromborough, close to the shore of the Mersey, with the main part of the fighting at Bebington Heath or possibly Wargraves. Dingesmere, from where Olaf Guthfrithson is reported to have escaped by boat, is either Meols or more likely Heswall Point in the shelter of the Dee.

There are two sites some miles north of Derby, both founded on the theory that Æthelstan passed through Derby on his way north based on the coins minted there. One is to the west of Brough in the Peak District where there is a tumulus just to the south-west of the River Noe and the village of Hope where swords, spears, spurs and bridle bits have been found near the Bradwell Brook. The other, founded on military probabilities, is on the old Roman road known as Ryknild Street between Brinsworth and the River Rother. Both at a pinch would have been within striking distance of the Humber by river.

Albeit written down three centuries after the event, *Egil's Saga* tells a story of what happened not just in the battle but, importantly, in the lead up to it.[23] Egil knew about it because he and his brother Thorolf with 300 of their Norse followers had joined Æthelstan as mercenaries. Olaf Sihtricson (Constantine's son-in-law, referred to confusingly as King of Scotland) was in command of Constantine's army of Scots. He had marched south and defeated the Northumbrians in a great battle. Alfgeir, one of the two earls appointed by Æthelstan to rule Northumberland, managed to escape from the battlefield and to warn Æthelstan of the invasion. Realising the danger

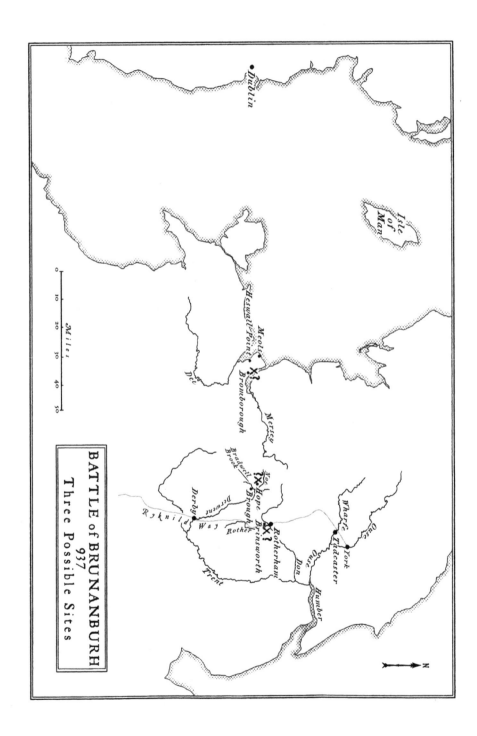

BATTLE of BRUNANBURH
937
Three Possible Sites

to his kingdom, Æthelstan went south to gather a great army, including Egil, Thorolf and their men, and then marched north, levying troops on the way. Having encountered Olaf, Æthelstan pitched camp at Vin-heath at the narrowest point between a wood, Vin-wood, and a river and there offered battle a week thence. In the meantime, Æthelstan tried to buy off Olaf, but to no avail. There followed an initial and indecisive engagement in which Æthelstan's main army was not involved but in which Thorolf managed to run one of his opponents through with his halberd and then plant the halberd in the ground with his hapless victim impaled upon it.

The decisive battle was fought the following day. It lasted all day, indeed it may have begun long before dawn when Olaf mounted a surprise attack in which a bishop was killed, having been mistaken for Æthelstan. The loss of life on both sides was prodigious, the battle becoming known as the Great War. Among the allies of Olaf, five kings and several earls died. Æthelstan, however, survived and by his victory 'became the father of medieval and modern England'.[24]

Nevertheless, the fruits of his victory were precarious, for Æthelstan died in 939, precipitating a prolonged power struggle for control of Northumbria which culminated in the murder of its King, the splendidly named Eric Bloodaxe, and the submission of his kingdom in 954. Five years later, Edgar, a grandson of Edward the Elder and half-nephew of Æthelstan, was elected as King of the West Saxons, the Mercians and the Northumbrians, thus once more uniting the sovereignty of all three kingdoms under one crown. Edgar was crowned at Bath in 973 and later that year he sailed round the coast with a huge fleet and landed at Chester. There eight kings submitted to him, rowing him a in a boat which he steered up and down a stretch of the Dee followed by his nobles in a procession of boats. England was united once more, but it was soon to be lost to the Danes by Edgar's son, Æthelred the Unready ('unready' meaning ill-advised – from Old English *unræd* – rather than ill-prepared).

The Danish empire

Æthelred had come to the throne in 978 following the murder of his half-brother Edward the Martyr at Corfe Castle. By that time the flow of silver from the Muslim world to Scandinavia in return for Scandinavian goods such as furs and walrus ivory was drying up, partly as a result of the exhaustion of the silver mines and partly as a result of the closing by the princes of Kiev of the trade route from the Volga which stretched between the Gulf of Finland and the Volga delta in the Caspian Sea, giving access to the great trade routes to the south of the Caspian via Gorgan. The Danes, therefore, started to look elsewhere and, beginning in 980, they returned to raid the coast of England to extort money, which became known as danegeld. Provoked by this new wave of extortion and fearing for the safety of his own life and kingdom, Æthelred ordered that all of the Danes living among the English should be massacred on St Brice's day, 13 November 1002. Unlike the Sicilian Vespers two centuries later, Æthelred's order badly backfired.

One of the victims of the massacre was Gunhilde, sister of Sweyn Forkbeard, King of Denmark. She was beheaded on the orders of an ealdorman, Eadric Streona[25] (Eadric the Grasper), aptly described in the *Chronicle of John of Worcester* (as will be seen) as 'a man of low birth but his tongue had won for him riches and rank; ready of wit, smooth of speech, he surpassed all men of that time, both in malice and treachery and in arrogance and cruelty".[26] Eadric was married to Æthelred's daughter, Edith, making his betrayal of his father-in-law in what was to follow even more despicable.

Of Gunhilde, William of Malmesbury records that she possessed considerable beauty and had come to England with her husband, a powerful nobleman, and, having embraced Christianity, had made herself a pledge of Danish peace. 'She bore her death with fortitude, and she neither turned pale at the moment, nor, when dead, and her blood exhausted, did she lose her beauty; her husband was murdered before her face, and her son, a youth of amiable disposition, was transfixed with four spears.'[27]

Driven principally by revenge for his sister's death, the following year Sweyn mounted a series of raids, landing initially at Sandwich, by which over the next decade he wrested control of most of England, driving Æthelred in 1013 to take refuge first on the Isle of Wight and then in Normandy with his brother-in-law, Richard II, Duke of Normandy.[28] It was on this occasion that the Witan deposed Æthelred in favour of Sweyn.

Sweyn died at Candlemas, 2 February, 1014 and was succeeded in England by his son, Cnut. On receiving news of the death, all of Æthelred's councillors who had remained in England called on him to return. Initially Æthelred sent his son, Edward – the son by his second wife, Emma – (the future Edward the Confessor), with the message that the grievances of the

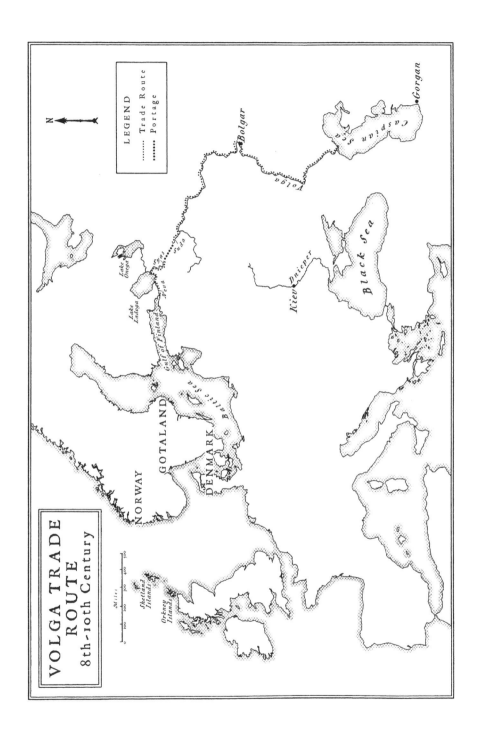

VOLGA TRADE
ROUTE
8th-10th Century

LEGEND
...... Trade Route
•••••• Portage

people would be redressed and that every Danish king would be declared to be an outlaw. Æthelred himself followed shortly afterwards. However, his aspirations were short-lived. Boosted by the defection of Eadric Streona to Cnut with 40 ships in 1015, the following year Cnut together with Eadric invaded England, arriving with 160 ships and ravaging the country as he moved inland.

Æthelred died on St George's day, 23 April, 1016, and was succeeded by Edmund (Ironside) – his son by his first wife, Ælfgifu. Edmund managed to defeat Cnut in a number of skirmishes which forced the Danes to retreat to the Isle of Sheppey, where they established their base, safe from Edmund who had no fleet. At that stage the duplicitous Eadric and his men re-joined Edmund. As succinctly put in the *Peterborough Manuscript*, 'There was no more unwise decision [by Edmund] than this was.'[29] From Sheppey, Cnut advanced into Essex and from there raided Mercia. Learning of the raid, Edmund assembled an army 'from the entire English nation'[30] and at Ashingdon in south-east Essex caught up with the Danes as they returned laden with booty. Ashingdon stands at one end of a low hill, the only hill on the otherwise flat ground between the River Crouch and the Thames. It is less than 2 miles from Burnham Roads on the Crouch where it is likely that Cnut had left his ships, being largely unaffected by the tide. Caught before he had had a chance to re-embark, Cnut had no choice but to stand and fight. It seems likely that he took up position at the far end of the low hill where Canewdon now stands. At all events, on 18 October 1016 they joined battle, in the course of which, and with disastrous consequences for Edmund, Eadric defected once more, taking others with him. Edmund was totally defeated, many of his nobles being killed.

Edmund himself survived and fled west to Gloucestershire, pursued by Cnut. However, after Cnut had refused an offer from Edmund to resolve their differences by single combat (Cnut appreciating that Edmund was very much bigger than him) and on the advice of Eadric and others, peace was agreed between them. The agreement was reached by the two Kings on Ola's Island in the River Severn near Deerhurst (probably what was then an eyot formed between the Naight Brook and the river). There they agreed to divide England between them, north of the Thames to Cnut and south of the Thames to Edmund.

Suspiciously shortly afterwards, on 30 November 1016, Edmund died and Cnut succeeded to the whole kingdom. Whether the succession had been agreed on Ola's Island, thus raising the possibility that Edmund had been murdered, or was simply the result of popular support, is unclear. However, William of Malmesbury tells us that Edmund was indeed murdered at the behest of none other than Eadric, having prevailed on two of Edmund's attendants to drive 'an iron hook into his posteriors, as he was sitting down for a necessary purpose'.[31]

One way or another, Cnut was now King of England.

The consolidation of Cnut's power then proceeded apace. In the spring of 1017 he was acclaimed as King of England at an assembly in Oxford and that summer, to neutralise any interference from abroad, he married Æthelred's widow, Emma. The following year he succeeded to the throne of Denmark on the death of his elder brother, Harald II, and finally, on 29 July 1030, he conquered the kingdom of Norway at the Battle of Stiklestad during which the Norwegian King, Olaf II, was killed. Thus it was that England became part of the Danish empire, albeit briefly.

The Norman Conquest

The Norman Conquest was not some opportunistic and unprovoked attack on England, but rather the vindication of a justifiable claim among others to the English throne following the death of Edward the Confessor in 1066. However, William the Conqueror's claim was not the only one.

Cnut had died in 1035, whereupon his empire had been divided: Harthacnut, his son by his second wife, Emma (Æthelred's widow), succeeded to the throne of Denmark; Magnus, whose father, King Olaf, had been defeated by Cnut at Stiklestad, was acclaimed by the Norwegians as Magnus I; and England was ruled by Harald, Cnut's son by his first wife, Ælfgifu of Northampton, initially as regent and then by election as king from 1037, ruling as Harald I. When Harald died without heirs in 1040, Harthacnut (the King of Denmark and, incidentally, a grandson of the Duke of Normandy) succeeded to the English throne too. Then, when Harthacnut died without heirs in 1042, he was succeeded in Denmark and Norway by Magnus and in England by Edward (the Confessor), the elder son of Æthelred the Unready by his second wife Emma (and so a half-brother of Harthacnut).

The succession of Magnus was founded on an agreement which he had made with Harthacnut in 1038 or 1039 to the effect that the survivor between the two of them should inherit both of the kingdoms of Norway and

Denmark. Magnus died young in 1047 and his heir was his uncle, Harald Hardrada. Harald Hardrada was ultimately forced to yield Denmark to Cnut's nephew, Sweyn (who became Sweyn II of Denmark), but he remained as King of Norway. Founded on his lingering claim to be King of Denmark, Harald also had a claim to be King of England. It was that claim which drove him to invade England in 1066 following the death of Edward the Confessor.

In order to understand the justification for William the Conqueror's claim to succeed Edward, it is necessary to wind the clock back. Edward was the son of Æthelred the Unready by his second marriage and Emma by her first marriage; he was therefore a half-brother of Edmund Ironside (a son of Æthelred by his first marriage). It so happened that he was also a stepson of Cnut following Cnut's marriage to Emma after Æthelred's death. Importantly so far as the Norman Conquest is concerned, Emma was the daughter of Richard I, Count of Rouen (subsequently styled Duke of Normandy).

The forebears of the dukes of Normandy were Norse immigrants in the kingdom of the Western Franks: they were not Franks, nor were they French. Edward's great-great-grandfather through Emma was Göngu Hrólfr. He was born in the second half of the ninth century in the west of Norway and nicknamed Göngu – Walker – Hrólfr because he was so big that no horse could carry him.[32] In the early part of the tenth century he led, or was among the leaders of, a Viking raid and subsequent colonisation of the land around the mouth of the Seine, later moving up river and seizing the settlement, where ultimately he and his Vikings settled too; it became the city of Rouen. Göngu Hrólfr (sometimes Latinised as Rollo) was the first recognisable ruler of what became Normandy – the land of the Norsemen.

On 20 July 911 the Seine Vikings had been defeated after a great battle at Chartres by the forces of Charles III (the Simple), King of the Western Franks. Following the battle, in the autumn of 911 agreement was reached between King Charles and the Vikings (sometimes referred to as the Treaty of St-Clair-sur-Epte) by which Charles agreed to grant to the Vikings the fiefdom of Rouen together with several districts on the coast which were dependent on Rouen, essentially upper Normandy between the Epte and the Risle. In return the Vikings agreed to call a halt to their depredations and to be baptised as Christians, Göngu Hrólfr himself being baptised shortly afterwards. The fiefdom was expanded in 924 to include the area between the Risle and the Vire (principally the Bessin region) as a reward for Viking support the previous year of King Rudolf, Charles's next successor but one. It was expanded once more in 933 to include the Côtentin peninsula and the Avranchin region between the Vire and the coast following the support given by Göngu Hrólfr's son and successor, William Longsword, to King Rudolf in suppressing a revolt by the Bretons. William Longsword's son and successor was Richard I, Count of Rouen (d. 996). It was Richard who adopted the title of 'marquis' and his son, Richard II (d. 1026), the title of 'duke', from which the 'duchy' of Normandy derived its name.

When Sweyn Forkbeard seized the throne of England from Æthelred the Unready in 1013, Æthelred's wife, Emma, had fled with her children to Normandy and the protection of her brother, Richard II, the then Duke. Emma's son, Edward, spent most of the following years in exile, for much of the time in Normandy (where presumably he would have encountered Richard's grandson, the future William the Conqueror). He returned finally to England in 1041 at the invitation of his half-brother, Harthacnut, by whom he was adopted as a member of the royal court and almost certainly as his heir. When Harthacnut died 'as he stood at his drink' in 1042,[33] Edward was elected king by popular acclamation and was crowned at Winchester with much pomp on Easter Day 1043.

During Edward's reign, Godwin, Earl of Wessex, rose to great power in England, Edward having married Godwin's daughter, Edith, in 1042. However, between 1051 and 1052 he fell badly out of favour. During that period, Edward's first cousin once removed, William II, Duke of Normandy (the future William the Conqueror), sailed to England with a large retinue and was well received by Edward. At some stage, and it was probably during this visit, Edward promised that on his death the throne of England would pass to William.

Godwin had died in 1053 and was succeeded as Earl of Wessex by his eldest surviving son, Harold Godwinson. In 1062 Harold reached the apogee of his power by defeating an uprising by Gruffudd ap Llywelyn, the powerful ruler of the Welsh, which had been supported by Harold's younger brother, Tostig, Earl of Northumbria. Two years later, Harold swore an oath of fealty to William and to support William's claim to the English throne. Indeed, he may at one stage have been betrothed to Adeliza, one of William's daughters. The following year there was a rebellion by the Northumbrians and, with Edward's approval, Tostig was ousted. Then Edward fell ill and, anticipating his end, the leading members of his council met in London and agreed that he should be succeeded by Harold, a decision which appears to have been endorsed by Edward on his deathbed.

Edward died childless on 5 January 1066, leaving therefore five potential claimants to his throne: Harold Godwinson (who happened to be Edward's nephew by marriage), by virtue of Edward's deathbed promise; William II, Duke of Normandy and Edward's first cousin once removed, by virtue of William's earlier promise; Sweyn II as King of Denmark; Harald Hardrada as claimant to the throne of Denmark; and Edgar, the young grandson of Edward's half-brother, Edmund Ironside.

Harold Godwinson wasted no time. He procured his election by the Witan and was crowned King of England (probably in Westminster Abbey) the very next day. Edgar, being only a youth in exile and without resources, did not get a look in; and Sweyn does not appear to have made a move. Harald Hardrada, on the other hand, arrived later that summer with 300 ships, joined forces with Tostig in the Humber, sailed up the Ouse and took York. Hearing of what had happened, Harold Godwinson, who was then in the south of England, mustered a great army, marched north and on 25 September took his enemies by surprise at Stamford Bridge on the River Derwent and routed them.

The site of the bridge appears to have been about 400 yards upstream from the modern bridge by which the A166 crosses the river. Harold Godwinson approached from the west. Initially the Norwegians took up positions on both sides of the river, but those on the west bank were soon driven back across the bridge to the east, save for one brave defender of immense size who (like Horatius on the bridge over the Tiber) held off the attack until (according to one version) an ingenious Englishman managed to get under the bridge and spear him (presumably in the groin) from beneath.[34] With the death of the defender, the English swept over the bridge and put the Norwegians to flight, killing their King and Tostig in the process. Harold Godwinson then chivalrously allowed the survivors among the Norwegians to sail away, having exacted a promise from Olaf, the King's son, that they would never return – a promise which, in the event, was kept.

In the meantime, William, although not disputing Edward's deathbed promise, contended that Edward's prior promise to him and Harold's oath of fealty took precedence, for which he won the support of the Pope, presumably at least in part on that basis. In September he assembled a fleet and, having sheltered from storms at St-Valéry in the mouth of the Somme, waited for a fair wind; on 27 September, two days after Harold's victory at Stamford Bridge, he sailed. Initially he landed at Pevensey on an undefended shore, but later moved east along the coast to Hastings where he fortified his camp. Hearing of William's invasion, Harold marched his army all 250 miles south within little more than a fortnight and took up a position on Senlac Hill, about 6 miles north-west of Hastings.

It is reported by William of Malmesbury that at this stage William sent a message to Harold proposing that Harold should relinquish his kingdom in accordance with his oath or hold England as William's vassal or decide the matter by single combat in sight of the whole army, but that, if the proposals were rejected, the matter should be decided by battle.[35] Harold simply dismissed the messenger without even listening to the message, thus sealing his fate.

At dawn on 14 October 1066, St Calixtus's Day, the Normans began to advance along the road from Hastings towards London. Either then or earlier, they had been alerted to the presence of the English army on the hill and, having reached the crest, deployed for battle. Harold in the meantime drew up his forces in a defensive line along a ridge, near the centre of which Battle Abbey now stands: facing the Normans downhill, he waited for their assault. The battle began with a barrage of arrows from the Norman bowmen, which had little impact on the wall of shields presented by the English. It was followed by the Norman infantry: they were not only successfully repelled, but the Bretons on their left wing fled, prompting the English right to break ranks and pursue them down the hill where they were overrun by the Norman cavalry. A similar fate met those of the English left who repelled and pursued a contingent of Norman cavalry. The Normans then changed their tactics by loosing a high-angled creeping barrage of arrows that enabled their troops to envelope the English line. It was during this barrage that Harold was shot in the eye, at least according to the Bayeux Tapestry. Although he was bravely defended by his house-carls, they were no match for the Norman knights who broke through to where he stood and hacked him to death.

On the news of Harold's death, the magnates in London immediately chose Edgar (Edmund's grandson and a great-grandson of Æthelred the Unready) as king, but to no avail. With reinforcements from Normandy, William proceeded north-west to Berkhamsted, raiding the surrounding country as he went. Although he had conquered but a small part of England, the panic-stricken Witan elected him as king and he was crowned in Westminster Abbey by Aldred, the Archbishop of York, on Christmas Day 1066.

William only remained in England for a few months before returning to Normandy. He had at that stage adopted much of the machinery of government which he had found, albeit replacing some of those in high office with his own supporters. To secure his hold on the crown, he also embarked on 'the most extensive and concentrated programme of castle-building in the whole history of medieval Europe',[36] which included by the time of his death the White Tower of the Tower of London, using the distinctive stone imported from Caen to the extent that suitable stone had not been available locally. He returned in December 1067, followed by his wife, Mathilde, who was acclaimed and crowned as queen in May 1068. However, his conquest was not destined to be so easy. The next two years were marked by widespread insurrection, destruction and bloodshed, from which William emerged as a brutal victor. Then, starting in 1070, he began systematically to destroy the existing power structures and to subjugate the people by dispossessing them of their lands and excluding almost all of them from any form of public office.

Within a few years pre-conquest England was completely submerged, with the entire ruling class of Church and State speaking Norman French. Normandy was not a dependency of an English king, rather it was a feudal duchy of France, of which England was no more than an offshoot.

Prompted by the threat of invasion by King Cnut, the great-nephew of the King Cnut who had died in 1035, William returned to England not only to secure support but also to take stock of his resources. He obtained support by summoning all of the most powerful men to Old Sarum, near Salisbury, and on 1 August 1086 received oaths of fealty from all of them. His resources were assessed by two great surveys, one directed to the military service he might expect from his feudal tenants and the other to the pattern of landowning and taxes. Although the threat went away when Cnut was murdered the following year, the latter survey culminated in the production (albeit after William's own death) of what became known as the Domesday Book.

Having left England for the last time in the autumn of 1086, in July of the following year William died on campaign in France. He was succeeded in Normandy by his eldest son, Robert Courteheuse, and in England by his second son, William Rufus.

During the first few years of his reign, William Rufus devoted much of his time to undermining the power of his brother Robert in Normandy. However, in August 1091 he returned to England and together with Robert invaded what is now Lothian to put a stop to the depredations of King Malcolm of Scotland in territory to which both Malcolm and William Rufus laid claim. Although the campaign started well, the Norman fleet was wrecked off the coast of Northumberland, forcing Rufus to compromise. Through the good offices of Edgar, who had been chosen as King of England immediately after the death of Harold on Senlac Hill and who had in the face of William the Conqueror's onslaught taken refuge with Malcolm over twenty years earlier, Rufus relinquished his claim to Lothian in return for a formal act of submission by Malcolm.

Over the next two years, save for a period when he was struck down by an illness from which he nearly died, William Rufus directed his energies to the subjugation of the Marches with Wales and Scotland – the word 'march' being derived (most immediately) from the Old English word *mearc* meaning boundary. It was in the course of the latter campaign that on 13 November 1093 King Malcolm was killed and his invading army defeated by the Normans following a surprise attack at the foot of Alnwick Castle in Northumberland.

Following the departure of his brother Robert on the First Crusade in 1096, William Rufus spent much of his time in Normandy, the governance of which had been left to him during his brother's absence and the right to which had been pledged to him as security for the enormous loan of 10,000 silver marks which he had provided to finance the crusade. However, before Robert had returned from the Holy Land and had had a chance to redeem the pledge, William Rufus was killed.

On 2 August 1100, on one of his occasional visits to England, William Rufus was out hunting in the forest known as the New Forest (so called having been newly protected in his father's reign for the pleasures of the royal chase). There he was struck by an arrow – shot, apparently accidentally, by one of his close companions called Walter Tirel. He died almost immediately, prompting Walter Tirel to take flight. William's younger brother, Henry, who was also in the hunting party, then made his move. He galloped immediately to Winchester to take control of the royal treasury and, having procured his election by the Witan, seized the throne of England, being crowned in Westminster Abbey only three days later, inevitably raising the question whether William's death had been an accident at all.

The conquest of Normandy

At the time of William Rufus's death, Robert was away on the First Crusade. He returned to Normandy later that year. The following year (1101) he gathered his forces and on 20 July he landed at Portsmouth to claim the throne of England for himself. His army marched up the Meon Valley to Warnford and from there to Alton where it was confronted by King Henry's army. Although preparations were made for battle, the leading men on both sides were unwilling to engage. Instead a compromise was reached and confirmed by the oaths of twelve nobles from each side: Robert agreed to forego his claim to the throne in return for an annual payment of 3,000 silver marks, and that if either of them should die without an heir, the survivor should succeed to the other's dominions. Having settled matters and after staying in England for a few months longer, Robert returned to Normandy.

However, the peace did not last long. By 1103 Henry had begun successfully to destabilise Robert's dominion over Normandy, one way or another disaffecting many of the Norman magnates. Matters came to a head in the spring of 1106 when Henry crossed over the Channel to Normandy ostensibly to avenge the arrest of one of his principal supporters, Robert FitzHamo. Although there was a meeting between Henry and his brother in May, it achieved nothing.

It was on 28 September that year in south-west Normandy that the decisive battle was fought. Henry had laid siege to the castle of Tinchebrai (of which not a trace remains today) which was held at the time by the comte de Mortain, one of the remaining nobles still loyal to Robert. Robert, accompanied by de Mortain, had approached with his forces with a view to raising the siege. Although Henry then offered a compromise by which he would govern Normandy leaving Robert with half of the duchy and compensation for the loss of the other half, Robert rejected the offer out of hand. Henry therefore deployed his huge and well prepared army, said in one account to number more than 40,000 men, ready for battle.[37] Initially, gallant charges led by de Mortain gained ground, but Henry's army was too numerous and, within an hour, Robert's army had been put to flight, their line having been broken by Breton cavalry led by William d'Aubeny. Both Robert and de Mortain were captured. Robert remained a prisoner in England for the rest of his life, albeit in some comfort, being held initially at Devizes Castle and then at Cardiff Castle, where he died in 1134.

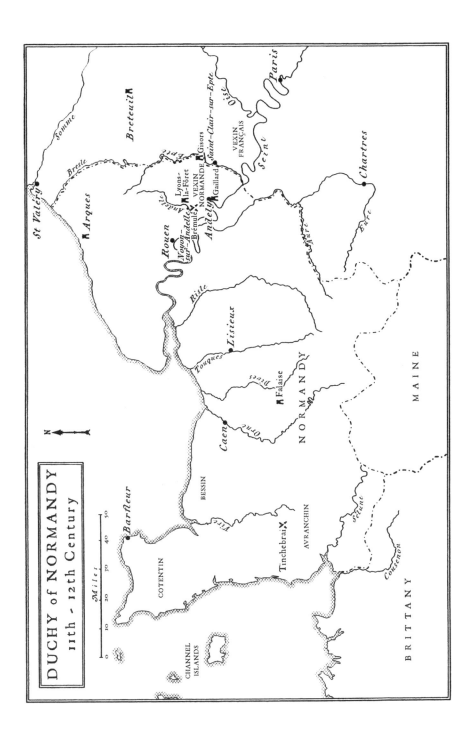

DUCHY of NORMANDY
11th - 12th Century

N

Miles
0 10 20 30 40 50

CHANNEL
ISLANDS

COTENTIN

Barfleur

BESSIN

AVRANCHIN

Tinchebrai✕

BRITTANY

Caen

Falaise✕

NORMANDY

MAINE

Lisieux

St Valéry

↑ Arques

Breteuil↑

Somme

Bresle

Epte

Lyons-
la-Forêt↑

Rouen
Noyon-
sur-Andelle
Brémule✕
Andely

VEXIN
NORMANDE↑Gisors

Saint-Clair-sur-Epte

VEXIN
FRANÇAIS

Gaillard↑

Oise

Paris

Seine

Chartres

Eure

Eure

Risle

Touques

Touques

Dives

Orne

Vire

Sélune

Couesnon

On the strength of Henry's victory at Tinchebrai and the capture of Robert, there was no longer any question of England being a dominion of the Duke of Normandy. Rather, the boot was on the other foot and Normandy was subjugated to the English Crown: while remaining a fiefdom of the King of France, it became, not part of the realm of England, but a dominion of the English Crown.[38]

The surrender of the kingdom

Although England had thrown off the Norman yoke in 1106, within little more than a century it had been surrendered first to the Holy Roman Empire and then to the Holy See.

In 1192, whilst returning from the Third Crusade, King Richard (the Lionheart – one of Henry I's great grandsons) was captured near Vienna while crossing the territory of Leopold V, Duke of Austria. Initially he was held in secret by the Duke at (what was then) his remote castle at Dürnstein, set on a rocky outcrop above the River Danube about 50 miles west of Vienna. It was here that Richard was reputed to have been found by his minstrel, Blondel, by answering to Blondel's song beneath the castle walls. Although the Duke was subsequently excommunicated by the Pope for having failed to protect a returning crusader, after weeks of negotiation he struck a bargain with Heinrich VI, the Holy Roman Emperor, and handed Richard over to him as a prisoner.

Richard was held first at Speyer, then at Trifels (in the mountains to the west of Speyer) and finally at court in the imperial palace at Hagenau in what is now Alsace. To win his freedom he agreed initially to pay a huge ransom of 100,000 marks (about 30 tons of silver) and to supply 50 galleys, 200 knights and 100 crossbowmen to support the Emperor's invasion of Sicily. Subsequently, however, the ransom was renegotiated. In order to gain the support of the Emperor in recovering what he had lost to his younger brother, John, and to King Philippe II of France while he had been on crusade (and which was the subject of a separate humiliating agreement with Philippe[39]), not only did Richard agree to pay 100,000 marks to the Emperor and a further contingent sum of 50,000 marks but also, on the advice of his mother, Eleanor of Aquitaine, to surrender his kingdom to the Emperor and to receive it back as an imperial fief for which he was to pay an annual tribute of 5,000 marks. Having paid the 100,000 marks, provided hostages as security for the payment of the contingent sum and surrendered his kingdom, on 4 February 1194 Richard was released after more than a year in captivity. His surrender of the kingdom was hushed up at the time in England and the circumstances in which it was formally restored (if ever) are obscure, although Roger of Howden's *Chronica* says that it was restored by Heinrich on his deathbed three years later.[40]

It was Richard's younger brother and successor, John, who surrendered his kingdom to the Holy See in 1213 in order to win the Pope's protection against Philippe II. But that is another story, better told in the context of the Channel Islands, the loss of Continental Normandy and the invasion of England by Philippe's son, Louis.

The final piece of the English jigsaw

Although Cornwall had been part of the kingdom of Wessex since the Battle of Hingston Down in 838 and thus had become subject to the Crown of England, there remained one piece missing from England. In the wake of Henry VIII's break with Rome, he dissolved the monasteries, seizing their wealth. Tavistock was one of those seized and with it the priory on Tresco, bringing with it much of the Scilly Isles. The priory lands were then annexed to the Duchy of Cornwall and by 1550 all of the Scilly Isles were under the direct rule of the Tudors.

The Channel Islands

With the conquest of Normandy by Henry I in 1106, the Channel Islands were subjugated to the English Crown. Lying only a short distance to the west of the Côtentin peninsula of Normandy, very much closer to France than to England, they have been a bone of contention between the English and the French for centuries, initially as part of the duchy of Normandy and, following their separation from the duchy, in their own right.

The four main islands are Jersey, Guernsey, Alderney and Sark. But there are in addition Herm, Jethou, Lihou and Brecquou together with a number of rocky islets, the Casquets, the Ecréhous and the Minquiers. (Jersey, Guernsey and Alderney end in 'ey', the Old Norse and hence Norman word for an island.)

Duke William I (Longsword) of Normandy (r. 933–942) –whose granddaughter, Emma, many years later married Æthelred the Unready – added the Channel Islands to his duchy in about 933. Thus, when William the Conqueror, a great-great-grandson of William Longsword, succeeded to the duchy in 1035, it included the Channel Islands and, after 1066, he was King of England too. When the tables were turned at Tinchebrai, Henry I had not only won Normandy for the English Crown, but as part of it he had won the Channel Islands too.

Nevertheless, Henry's coup in Normandy did not go uncontested by the French. For the next century and more it was the battle for the duchy with France which would determine the question of sovereignty over the islands.

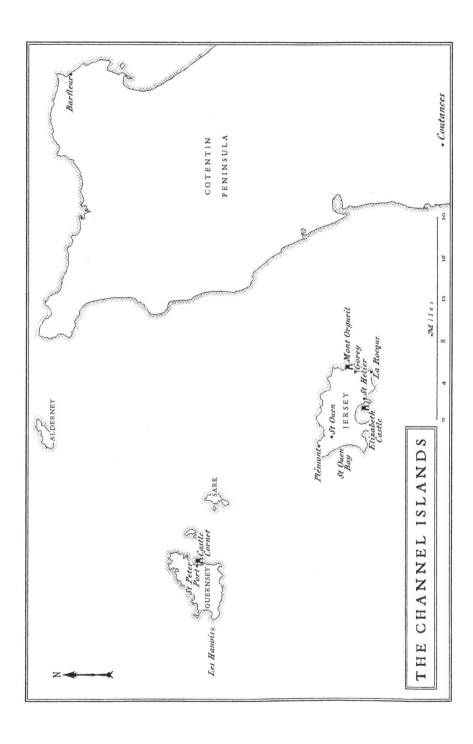

THE CHANNEL ISLANDS

The battle for the duchy

In 1109 Henry and Louis VI met at the border fortress of Gisors, which stands above the River Epte, halfway between Paris and Rouen, the Norman capital. There Louis challenged Henry to fight for Gisors in single combat, a challenge which Henry, no doubt wisely, declined. Over the next decade, Louis furthered his cause by championing the claim to Normandy of William (known as William Clito – the prince), the young son and heir of the imprisoned Duke Robert of Normandy, Henry's nephew. Although peace was agreed at a meeting between Louis and Henry at Gisors in 1113 in confirmation of which Louis granted the whole of Brittany to Henry, by the autumn of 1118 Henry's hold on Normandy was beginning to crumble, partly as a result of defections and partly as a result of William Clito's growing popularity. Taking advantage of Henry's weakness, forces loyal to Louis invaded Normandy. In August 1119 Louis accompanied by his army crossed the River Epte into Normandy.

Fortuitously, in furtherance of a dispute with the Archbishop of Rouen, the Archbishop's opponent betrayed the fortified manor and township of Andely to Louis, which Louis then took. Andely lies on one of the great bends of the River Seine about 15 miles south-east of Rouen and consisted in those days of one of the two villages (Le Grand Andely) which today make up Les Andelys. Meanwhile, Henry, although only about 7 miles to the north of Andely at his fortress at Noyon-sur-Andelle (now known as Charleval), was unaware of how close the French were.

On 20 August, Henry, having heard mass at Noyon-sur-Andelle, accompanied his troops on a foraging expedition. Unknown to him, the French, equally unaware of his presence, were themselves proceeding towards Noyon-sur-Andelle in the expectation that they would capture the castle there through treachery. It was at that stage that Henry's pickets spotted the standards and glinting helmets of the French army on the move. Guided by smoke from a barn to which the French had set fire, Henry deployed his forces in battle order on the plain of Brémule (now in the commune of Gaillardbois), just to the south of Noyon-sur-Andelle. When Louis saw that at last he had the opportunity to engage Henry, he brought up his army for battle. A fierce, but disorderly, attack by the French was repulsed and, although the attack was renewed, many of the French knights were unhorsed and captured. With the battle going against him,

Louis followed the advice of his companions and fled. During his flight, he lost his horse and ultimately found his way back to Andely on foot, as did his protégé, William Clito.

Notwithstanding his victory, Henry was himself badly injured during the battle when William Crispin, the dispossessed comte d'Evreux, caught sight of him, rushed through the ranks and struck him on the helmet with two mighty sword-blows. Whether it was an enraged Henry or one of his knights who struck the assailant down, the assailant was captured and Henry survived. Such was chivalry that the next day Henry returned the horse with its saddle, bridle and regal trappings to Louis and Henry's son and heir, William, sent back to his cousin, William Clito, the palfrey which he had lost in the battle.

Following the disaster at Brémule, Louis momentarily abandoned his invasion and returned to Paris. However, the following month he was encouraged by those still eager to settle old scores with Henry to invade once more with a view on this occasion to recovering the castle at Breteuil and restoring it to Eustace (the son of Henry's future successor, Stephen), by whom it had been forfeited for supporting William Clito the previous year. The French advance on Breteuil was blocked by the stout defence mounted by its new owner, Ralph the Gael, to whom Henry had recently granted it. Hearing of the French attack, Henry despatched reinforcements which he then himself followed with a huge force. On catching sight of Henry's approach, the French and their allies turned tail and fled.

Peace was finally agreed between Henry and Louis under pressure from Pope Calixtus II. During October the Pope was presiding over the Council of Reims, when Louis appeared before him to complain of the fate of Duke Robert, still a prisoner in Henry's hands, and to seek the Pope's assistance. In Henry's absence, the Archbishop of Rouen then spoke in his defence. The following month the Pope visited Henry at Gisors and appears to have been persuaded by Henry's defence, because he subsequently sent envoys to Louis informing him that there was no cause for further hostility, a judgment to which Louis submitted for the time being. Importantly, the peace was confirmed the following year when Louis accepted the homage of Henry's only legitimate son, William, as lawful heir to the duchy of Normandy, thus recognising the legitimacy of Henry's rule over Normandy.

However, Henry's triumph in Normandy was soon eclipsed by his son's death. On the evening of 25 November 1120 Henry embarked at Barfleur on the north-eastern tip of the Côtentin peninsula on a ship bound for England. William and his immediate entourage were to follow in another ship, named the *White Ship*. Unfortunately the crew of the *White Ship* had been plied with drink and encouraged by their drunken passengers to try and overtake the King's ship. Although the sea was calm, in the gathering darkness the *White Ship* struck a rock on leaving the harbour, capsized and sank. Everyone on board was drowned except for one man, a butcher, who managed to cling to a spar and was rescued by fishermen the following morning. Roger of Wendover tells us that the fate of those who perished was said to have been divine retribution for sodomy.[41]

Henry had had two legitimate children, both by his first wife, Edith-Matilda, daughter of King Malcolm III of Scotland: one was William and the other was a girl, Matilda. Edith-Matilda had died in 1118 and, following William's death on the *White Ship*, Henry lost no time in marrying again in the hope of fathering a legitimate male heir. His second wife was Adeliza, the daughter of the comte de Louvain and duc de Brabant, but sadly for Henry she bore him no children at all.

As to Matilda, she was married first in 1114 to Heinrich V of Germany, who died without any legitimate children in 1125, and secondly, in 1128, to Geoffrey, Count of Anjou, Maine and Touraine, known as Geoffrey Plantagenet reputedly because he sported a sprig of broom (*plante genest* or *planta genista*) in his hat.[42] Ultimately, through their son, the future Henry II, Geoffrey became the father of the Plantagenet dynasty. Although succession to the throne of England or to the duchy of Normandy by a woman would have been unprecedented and indeed contrary to the pervasive principles of the Salic laws of the Franks, Henry I ensured on two occasions that Matilda was acknowledged by his prelates and nobles to be his heir in default of a legitimate son. The first occasion was in 1126, when Matilda had returned to England following the death of Heinrich, and the second at Northampton in 1131.

In the event, Matilda was to be disappointed. Having gone to his castle at Lyons-la-Forêt in Normandy in the expectation of hunting, her father fell ill and on 1 December 1135 he died. Rather than proceeding immediately to England to stake her claim to the throne, Matilda was sent by her husband to Argentan where she had loyal support. In the meantime, her first cousin, Stephen, another grandchild of William the

Conqueror, raced from Boulogne to England and seized the throne, and with it, nominally at least, seized Normandy too.

Although Stephen spent time in Normandy in 1137, he never returned, being distracted for most of his reign by civil war in England against Matilda and later her son, Henry II, in his struggle to hold on to the crown. During his time in Normandy Stephen was recognised as lawful successor to Henry I when Louis VI accepted the homage of his son and heir, Eustace, and again in 1140 when Louis VII accepted the homage of Eustace on the occasion of Eustace's betrothal to Louis' sister, Constance. But Stephen never held sway over the whole of the duchy and he had lost it completely by 1145.

Starting in 1136, Matilda's husband, Geoffrey, progressively subdued the duchy in Henry's name, greatly assisted by the defection of Matilda's illegitimate half-brother, Robert, Earl of Gloucester, to her camp the following year bringing with him his territory around Caen and Bayeux. In 1141 Geoffrey won Lisieux, Falaise and the country to the south and west of the Seine. In January 1144 he crossed the Seine and secured the submission of Rouen. That summer in Rouen Cathedral he was formally invested with the title of Duke of Normandy. By the end of the year not only did he have control of every castle in the duchy except for Arques, but he was also recognised as Duke by Louis VII. A few months later, Arques (now Arques-la-Bataille) too fell. Then in 1149, much to the annoyance of Louis VII, Geoffrey and Matilda together ceded the duchy to Henry, and thereafter ruled the duchy in his name.

Nevertheless, the battle for the English crown, and with it the battle for the duchy, continued. Pitted against each other were Eustace, asserting his claim through his father, King Stephen, and Henry claiming through his mother, Matilda. Henry had made abortive attempts to raise his standard in England in 1147 and again in 1149. Two years later Eustace took up arms in Normandy, but was forced to withdraw when his ally, his brother-in-law Louis VII, fell ill and recalled his forces, leading to the acceptance by Louis of the homage of Henry for the duchy. The following year Eustace was thwarted again, this time by a truce struck between Louis and Henry. Then, in 1153, Henry sailed to England and raised an army among his supporters. Matters came to a head in August when Stephen cornered Henry at Wallingford Castle, only to find that his own army would not continue the fight. Robbed of armed support and much to his chagrin, Stephen was driven to negotiate for peace. To make matters worse, that same month Eustace died childless, leaving Stephen without an heir. The peace negotiations culminated in the Treaty of Wallingford in November that year, by which Stephen agreed to recognise Henry as his heir in return for Henry's agreement to defer his claim to the throne until Stephen's death.[43] So it was that the civil war, which had tainted the whole of Stephen's reign, was finally ended. Within a year, Stephen too had died,[44] leaving the field clear for Henry. Shortly before Christmas 1154, Henry was crowned as Henry II in Westminster Abbey,[45] uniting Normandy with the English Crown once more.

The loss of Normandy by King John

In 1152 the failing marriage between Louis VII and Eleanor, Duchess of Aquitaine, was annulled by the Pope on the convenient ground that they were cousins within the prohibited degrees of consanguinity. To the consternation of Louis, Eleanor then married Henry, bringing with her the vast duchy of Aquitaine in south-west France, radically altering the balance of power between Louis and Henry. By Henry she bore five sons, William, the young Henry, Richard, Geoffrey and John. Three of them died before their father: William in infancy; Henry from dysentery and childless, but whose wife had brought the eastern part of the Vexin between the Epte and the Oise as part of her dowry; and Geoffrey in a jousting tournament. However, before he died, Geoffrey had married Constance, the only child of Duke Conan IV of Brittany and heiress to the duchy; it had been agreed that Geoffrey would rule Brittany in Constance's name and do homage for Brittany to his father; by him she bore a posthumous child, Arthur. Henry himself died in 1189 and was succeeded by Richard (Coeur de Lion – the Lionheart), leaving his youngest son, John, with no territorial prospects (hence his nickname, Jean sans Terre – John Lackland) other than the lordship of Ireland with which he had been invested by his father in 1177.

Then on 6 April 1199 Richard died without any legitimate children, having been wounded in the shoulder by a bolt from a crossbow during the siege of the castle at Châlus near Limoges. Although Geoffrey's posthumous son, Arthur, had on the face of it a better claim to the throne, John wasted no time and was crowned in Westminster Abbey on 27 May that year.

Notwithstanding that he had originally had four elder brothers, on his coronation John succeeded to one of the greatest empires in Europe, as King of England, Lord of Ireland, Duke of Normandy, Count of Anjou, Maine and Touraine, Duke of Aquitaine and potentially also as Duke of Brittany. The fly in the ointment of his succession was Arthur. While Arthur was still a boy, as yet without a son, his heir was unquestionably John. But there was no knowing how long that would last.

Not only was there Arthur to contend with, but there had also been persistent attempts by King Philippe II of France with varying degrees of success to conquer the English King's possessions in France. The hostilities had started six years earlier in the reign of King Richard and there had been no obvious end to them in sight. However, a treaty of peace was finally concluded between Philippe and John on the island of Le Goulet in the Seine on 22 May 1200, the terms of which had been agreed in principle at the beginning of that year. Under the treaty Philippe recognised John as the rightful heir to Normandy, Anjou, Maine and Touraine as fiefs of France for which John agreed to do homage and to pay a relief of 20,000 marks, and John also agreed to cede the whole of the Vexin (i.e. the area bounded by the Seine, the Andelle and the Oise) together with the castles and towns which Philippe had seized in south-east Normandy following Richard's death.

The peace did not last. In 1202 John married Isabelle d'Angoulême, who had been abducted by her father to prevent her from marrying her fiancé, Hugh de Lusignan. Provoked by John's monstrous treatment of the de Lusignan family, Philippe, as their sovereign, moved to protect them. Not only did he launch an attack on Normandy but he granted Anjou, Maine, Touraine and Aquitaine to Arthur. In the course of the hostilities that ensued, Arthur laid siege to the castle at Mirebeau where John's mother, Eleanor of Aquitaine, had taken refuge. There, on 1 August 1202, he was surprised by John's men and, together with Hugh de Lusignan, was captured. Initially Arthur was held in the castle at Falaise but in January 1203 he was moved to Rouen. Nothing more is heard of him after that; rumour had it that he was killed by John's own hand, although Shakespeare tells a different story, with Arthur leaping to his death when trying to escape from his captors.[46]

In the spring of 1203 Philippe began what turned out to be his final assault on John's Continental empire. While he seized the castle at Saumur, one of John's strongholds on the Loire, John's disaffected subjects allied themselves with Philippe, successfully besieged several other castles and occupied the city of Le Mans, the capital of Maine. In this way John's enemies sliced his empire in two, cutting off Normandy from the provinces further south.

Having failed to persuade Philippe to call off his offensive in return for payment, John managed to recapture some of his castles. Then in August 1203 Philippe resumed the offensive, marching his army down the Seine to assault the greatest of John's castles, the supposedly impregnable Château Gaillard which had only recently been built. The castle stands on a steep hill commanding a great bend in the river about 15 miles south-east of Rouen near Andely,[47] the village of which Louis VI had briefly taken possession before his defeat at Brémule by Henry I nearly a century earlier. Its keep and inner curtain wall were constructed with elegantly tapered, but nonetheless formidable, machicolations which are still visible today. Initially John remained in Rouen, leaving the defence of the castle to William Marshal, the future Regent of England. However, following one of the longest sieges in European history and the flight of John from Rouen to England in December 1203, the castle fell on 6 March 1204 as a result of some of Philippe's men gaining access to the middle ward by an unguarded window of the chapel high up against the south-west wall. Having taken that prize, Philippe then picked off other castles in Normandy, many surrendering with a view to achieving favourable peace terms.

On 1 June 1204 the military commander of Rouen, Pierre de Préaux, struck a temporary truce with Philippe, agreeing to surrender if no help arrived from England in thirty days. Desperate messages were sent to John telling him that, if he did not come at once, he would lose everything. John immediately ordered his army to assemble at Portsmouth, but was thwarted by lack of support from his barons; indeed there were no signs at all of any serious military preparations. Word must have been carried back to Rouen that no help was to be expected and that the citizens would have to fend for themselves, for on 24 June, a week before the truce was due to expire, Pierre de Préaux surrendered his command and Philippe rode in triumph through the gates of the city. With the fall of the duchy's capital, the remaining towns and castles of Normandy submitted to Philippe.

Not only had John lost the duchy, including therefore the Channel Islands, to the French, but he had also been confronted with a rebellion within the islands themselves. The rebels, consisting of several of those with fiefs in the islands, had been led by Reginald de Carteret. Unable to crush them, towards the end of 1203 John seized members of their families, including de Carteret's nephew, and imprisoned them in various fortresses in England.

Following his conquest of Normandy, Philippe II sent emissaries to negotiate with the islanders with a view to obtaining the peaceful return of the islands to him. However the islanders would have none of it and the negotiations ran aground. Nevertheless, by 1205 it appears that Philippe had made himself master of the islands. The circumstances in which he did so are unclear but it is unlikely that there had been any serious, or at least armed, contest.

The Channel Islands had by this stage become essential to King John as a staging post to recapture his territories in France. He therefore engaged a colourful brigand, named in Norman French Wistace le Moine or in English Eustace the Monk, to re-take the islands for him. Although Eustace was hostile to Philippe because he had had a long-running feud with one of Philippe's allies, the Count of Boulogne, John took the precaution of securing the success of this venture by taking Eustace's wife, daughter and uncle as hostages. In the event Eustace fulfilled his mission by re-taking the islands with a naval assault in 1206. To ensure their continued loyalty to him, John took hostages from among the islanders, only releasing them in 1214. As for Eustace, he was well rewarded for his work, apparently being granted the fief of the islands themselves and subsequently building a palace for himself in London.

Although John had recovered the islands, the next blow was a summons to appear before the Court of the Twelve Peers of France to answer for the murder of Arthur. Without the benefit of a safe-conduct for his attendance and return, John refused to attend the court. An *arrêt* of disinheritance (a judgment depriving him of his property) was accordingly pronounced against him as a contumacious vassal. In October 1206, urged on by his indignant barons, John landed with an army at La Rochelle but achieved nothing more than a two year truce on terms recognising much of the judgment against him.

In 1213, in an attempt to secure the co-operation of his vassals in an invasion of England, Philippe denounced John as an enemy of the Church and proclaimed a holy war against him. To that end he called together an assembly of French barons at Soissons and, having secured their support (other than that of John's son-in-law, Ferrand, Count of Flanders – then part of France), assembled one of the largest armies that France had ever seen. However, the Papal Legate to England, Pandolfo Verraccio, while ostensibly supporting Philippe, embarked on secret correspondence with John in which he persuaded John of the tenuousness of his position. The upshot was that John agreed not only to restore to their benefices and compensate the clergy whom he happened to have banished, but, of rather greater moment, to surrender the kingdom of England and lordship of Ireland[48] to the Holy See and to receive them back as a vassal of the Pope on condition of doing homage and making an annual payment of 1,000 marks sterling.[49] Thus it was that the kingdom of England and the lordship of Ireland became vassal states of the Holy See,[50] an arrangement which the English Parliament repudiated in 1366 when it concluded that the original surrender had been invalid for want of agreement by Parliament and because it had been contrary to John's coronation oath, the payments, notwithstanding demands by the Pope, having stopped in 1333.[51]

On the back of John's submission to Rome, Pandolfo persuaded Philippe to abandon his invasion of England on the ground that it would be a mortal sin to attack a faithful vassal of St Peter. Having assembled a vast army for the invasion, Philippe was not easily dissuaded. Undeterred, Pandolfo suggested to Philippe that he attack Flanders instead, on the basis that Count Ferrand had denied Philippe's right to make war on John at a time when John had been excommunicated. The French fleet, reported to have amounted to 1,700 sail, proceeded first to Gravelines (between Calais and Dunkirk) and then to the Flemish port of Damme (now swallowed by Zeebrugge). In the meantime, Philippe's army marched by Cassel, Ypres and Bruges and laid siege to Ghent.

On 25 May 1213, John received messengers from Count Ferrand asking urgently for help. In response John mustered his forces and on 28 May 1213 they set sail for Flanders under the command of John's half-brother, the Earl of Salisbury, and Renaud, Count of Boulogne. To their surprise, the English found the entire French fleet at anchor at Damme only lightly guarded. They fell on it, captured part, set fire to part and set the rest adrift. The remnants of the French fleet were then blockaded such that Philippe preferred to set fire to them rather than to let them be captured too. For the time being this put an end to any French threat of invasion of England.

Encouraged by this success, John prepared to attack France in an attempt to recover the territory that he had lost. Having overcome the resistance of some of his barons, he marshalled his forces at Portsmouth and in February 2014 disembarked with them at La Rochelle. The plan was for John to advance from the Loire while Salisbury, Ferrand and John's nephew, Otto IV,[52] the Holy Roman Emperor, attacked from the north. While waiting for the arrival of Otto, Salisbury began to ravage the north of France. Philippe

Sandwich
Dover Bay Damme
Ghent
Flanders
Bouvines Tournai
Valenciennes

ENGLISH CHANNEL

Vermandois

Rouen
Channel Le Goulet
Islands DUCHY Seine Paris
OF
NORMANDY Champagne

DUCHY Royal
OF Rennes Le Mans Domain
BRITTANY of
Maine France

Roche-au-Moine
Mirebeau Angers Blois Burgundy
Saumur
Anjou Tours Nevers
Touraine

BAY Poitou
Poitiers Bourbon
of DUCHY
La Rochelle La Marche
OF
BISCAY Châlus
Limoges
AQUITAINE Auvergne
Périgord

Aquitaine
Toulouse

N

Gascony

MEDITERRANEAN SEA

THE LOST
ANGEVIN EMPIRE
13th Century

Miles
0 20 40 60 80 100

therefore decided to split his army, leading part northwards and leaving the remainder under the command of his son, Louis (later Louis VIII). After being repulsed by Louis at Roche-au-Moine, the English forces in the west retreated to their transports at La Rochelle, giving up everything which they had recently gained.

Otto, having finally readied his army in the Rhineland, linked up with Salisbury at Valenciennes, 30 miles south-east of Lille, on 23 July. Three days later, Philippe, concerned that his army was insufficient to meet the enemy and that the enemy were too close for comfort, set out from Tournai for Lille. On 27 July the forces of Otto and Ferrand encountered the French unexpectedly on the banks of a little tributary of the River Lys near the bridge of Bouvines. Warned that his enemies were pursuing him and about to attack (notwithstanding that it was Sunday), Philippe halted his army and, having crossed the river, moved from column to battle array. His enemy was then faced by the difficulty of deploying their own column rapidly into battle lines. Mayhem ensued: Philippe was unhorsed, the Duke of Brabant fled, Otto was carried from the field by his wounded and terrified horse, Ferrand was badly wounded and, together with the Count of Boulogne and the Earl of Salisbury, was captured. This catastrophic defeat marked the end of the road for John and, although he concluded a truce with Philippe for five years, he lost almost all of his Continental possessions once and for all.

The defeat of the French and their recognition of English sovereignty over the Channel Islands

The scale of the defeat at Bouvines was such that John was driven by his barons the following year to agree to the terms of Magna Carta. Antagonised by the King's treatment of them and particularly by the scutage (payment in lieu of military service) which he had exacted to fund his disastrous war with France, many of the barons rebelled. Initially they demanded that the King should reissue Henry I's coronation charter of liberties, the terms of which were then progressively expanded to become the Articles of the Barons. After months of negotiation and prevarication and the fall of London to the rebels, on 10 June 1215 the King's great seal was fixed to the Articles of the Barons at Runnymede. Five days later, after negotiation of further concessions to the rebels, the King returned to Runnymede and sealed the document which came to be known as Magna Carta (the Great Charter).

The King returned to Runnymede once more on 19 June, where the rebels renewed their homage and oath of fealty to him.

Article 61 of Magna Carta provided for the enforcement of its terms by twenty-five barons (in the event all opponents of the King) with power to seize the King's possessions until satisfied that sufficient amends for any breach had been made. Almost immediately and almost inevitably the King transgressed. Infuriated by its terms, he even persuaded Pope Innocent III to issue a Bull on 24 August 1215 purporting to annul the charter. By September that year, he and his supporters were at war with the rebel barons. But it was a war with a twist, for it culminated in the formal recognition by France that King John's successor, Henry III, was the sovereign of the Channel Islands.

Having suffered a number of setbacks in the war, the barons had turned to Philippe's son, Louis, asking him for help and offering him the English crown. The offer of the crown was justified by the barons on the grounds that John had already abandoned the throne to the Holy See without their consent and Louis was the rightful heir in right of his wife, Blanche of Castile, a granddaughter of Henry II and the daughter of John's only surviving sibling, Eleanor of Castile. More importantly in the short term, however, many of John's army were mercenaries who owed allegiance to Philippe and might readily defect.

Against the wishes of his father and of the Pope, Louis agreed to the proposal. Having turned his coat to support Louis, Eustace the Monk assembled a fleet of ships at Calais, where Louis and his knights embarked. They landed at Stonar near Sandwich on 21 May 1216. John was at Dover at the time but, whether through cowardice or fear of his mercenaries defecting, he did not try to stop Louis' advance. On 2 June Louis entered London and the following day received the homage of the rebel barons.

Over the next few months, he seized control of much of eastern England, save for the critical stronghold of Dover Castle, to which in due course he laid siege. While Louis was engaged in the siege, John marched north through the east of England ravaging the country as he went. On crossing the sands of the Wash at the estuary of the River Wellstream, he lost many of his men and horses and much of his baggage train in the quicksands, including to his great grief his holy relics and, it seems likely, his regalia too. Although John himself survived, it was not for long. Having reached Newark, he died of dysentery (or – as rumour had it – poison) on 18 October.

John was succeeded by his nine-year-old son, Henry III, for whom the elderly William Marshal (the hereditary marshal of the royal household and Earl of Pembroke in right of his wife) acted as guardian and principal regent until the Marshal's own death three years later. With London in the grip of the French, Henry underwent a ceremony of coronation, albeit without a crown, in Gloucester Cathedral on 28 October 1216, during the course of which he did homage to the Pope for his kingdom of England and lordship of Ireland, recognising their surrender by his father to the Holy See three years earlier.

With William Marshal at the helm, the tide of war was finally turned. Louis had returned from France with reinforcements in April and divided his forces, one half being despatched to Lincoln to join the siege of the castle there and the other half renewing the siege of Dover Castle. Although the town of Lincoln had fallen to the rebels in the summer of 1215, the garrison of the castle had remained loyal to John and held out against the siege which followed. The castle, standing on the crest of a steep hill, was a critical stronghold, commanding not only the intersection of Ermine Street and the Fosse Way but also the River Trent at its foot, giving access to the Humber and, via the Ouse, to York. To relieve the siege, William Marshal mustered a large army at Newark, including barons who foresaw the danger of continuing to support the rebel cause. From there he marched towards Lincoln, arriving on 20 May 1217.

The French and those rebels who were still with them misjudged the size of the King's army and, rather than engaging on open ground, made the fatal mistake of remaining within the town walls. The castle garrison opened a postern gate giving access to the castle from outside the town walls, enabling part of the King's army to enter and attack the French from the ramparts of the castle while the remainder forced two of the town gates. With mayhem in the narrow congested streets followed by a sortie from the castle, the French were routed.

In the aftermath of the battle the victors found the baggage wagons of the French and their supporters and an orgy of looting began – an orgy which did not end before the treasures not only of the churches but also of the cathedral itself had been ransacked, giving rise to the battle being dubbed the Lincoln Fair. It was to avoid 'insult' by the victors that many of the women of the town together with their household property, children and female servants took to small boats on the river; but, the boats being overladen, the women were unable to manage them and all of those on board were drowned.[53]

Louis himself was engaged in the siege of Dover when, on 25 May, he received news of the defeat at Lincoln. Realising the danger he was now in, he abandoned the siege, moved to London and sent both to his father and to his wife for help. His father had been reconciled with the new Pope, Honorius III, and could not be seen to be helping his son in a venture of which the Pope and his predecessor so strongly disapproved. However, the Lady Blanche immediately sent reinforcements to her husband and began to assemble a fleet at Calais. Learning of the preparations which were being made by the French, William Marshal proceeded to the coast to take counter-measures. There were a number of skirmishes both off Dover and off Calais during the ensuing weeks, including one off Dover on 29 May when the English fleet made a successful feint at fleeing up wind only to return downwind to attack.

Matters finally came to a head in an engagement off Sandwich on 24 August 1217. The French fleet was heading from the Channel towards the Thames when the English fleet under the command of the castellan of Dover Castle, Hubert de Burgh, was sighted. Seeing what appeared to be a few small ships coming from the English coast, the French commander, Robert de Courtenay (uncle of the French Queen), gave what turned out to be the fatal order to attack. The English, making a similar feint to the one which they had made so successfully on 29 May, gained the wind and rushed eagerly upon their enemy. The leading French ship, then under the command of the renegade Eustace the Monk, veering, struck one of the English ships. Three English ships then turned to attack her, later joined by a fourth much taller ship (known as a 'cog') from which pulverised lime was thrown, so blinding the French sailors as they looked up wind. The English then boarded and captured Eustace's ship. After a search, they found Eustace in her hold where he was captured by Richard, an illegitimate son of King John. Although Eustace offered a large sum of money to save his life, Richard would have none of it and without more ado drew his sword and cut off Eustace's head. The capture of the leading French ship marked the turning point of the battle and those few ships of the French fleet which were not then captured or destroyed escaped to Calais.

With victory at sea, William Marshal was able to blockade the French garrison in London and to force Louis to surrender. The terms of the surrender were recorded in a peace treaty which was concluded at Lambeth on 20 September 1217 between Louis and Henry III.[54] Under the treaty Louis not only abandoned his claim to the English throne but also acknowledged that Henry was entitled to possession of the Channel Islands (Article 9). Specifically, Louis undertook to order the brothers of Eustace the Monk to surrender the islands, of which Eustace had been the tenant-in-chief since 1206, to Henry, an undertaking which was in due course fulfilled.

By virtue of the treaty, the Channel Islands were formally separated from the duchy and ceased to be a fief of the kingdom of France. As a result, they became potential enemies of France, amply justifying the building of two castles, one at Gorey in Jersey (Mont Orgueil) and the other on an islet to the east of St Peter Port on Guernsey (Castle Cornet), which had been begun following the loss of continental Normandy in 1204.

The Treaty of Lambeth was followed in 1259 by the Treaty of Paris[55] under which Henry agreed to resign forever the family claims to Normandy, Anjou, Maine, Touraine and Poitou and to do homage for Aquitaine. The treaty is ambiguous as to the fate of the Channel Islands, but the International Court of Justice concluded in 1953 that any feudal title of the kings of France to them must have lapsed as a consequence of the events of 1204 and the years immediately following.[56]

In 1328, Charles IV of France died without a male heir. He was succeeded by Philippe VI de Valois. At Philippe's coronation in Amiens Cathedral on 6 June 1329 Edward III of England, as Duke of Aquitaine and a peer of France, did homage to him as King of France.[57] This was the last occasion when an English king was willing to accept the status of a feudal inferior of the king of France. Thus it was that in 1340 Edward III proclaimed at an early stage of the Hundred Years' War that England never was or ought to be in obedience to France nor should the people of England ever be put in subjection to the kings of France.[58]

The Hundred Years' War

Notwithstanding the homage done at his coronation, the succession of Philippe VI did not go unchallenged by England. The late King Charles had a sister, Isabella, widow of the late King Edward II. As a woman she had no right to the throne of France. Notwithstanding her own ineligibility, she claimed it on behalf of her son, Edward III, leading in 1337 to the outbreak of the Hundred Years' War. During the war the Channel Islands were attacked on a number of occasions. Guernsey and some of the smaller islands were in French hands between 1338 and 1340, indeed Castle Cornet remained in French hands until 1345.

The first phase of the war was brought to an end by the Treaty of Bretigny (as subsequently corrected at Calais) in 1360, following Edward's victory over the French at Poitiers in 1356 and the capture of the French King, Jean II.[59] Jean was ransomed for the colossal sum of 3 million gold crowns and, in return for Edward renouncing his claim to the throne of France, Jean recognised Edward's sovereignty over Aquitaine, Calais and the Channel Islands. However, the treaty did not put an end to further French assaults on the islands, Guernsey being attacked in 1372 and Jersey the following year and again in 1380.

In furtherance of a truce which had been agreed in 1396, Edward's widowed successor, Richard II, married as his second wife Isabelle de Valois, the daughter of the French King, Charles IV. In the negotiations for the marriage, the French pressed, but pressed in vain, for the surrender of the Channel Islands as an integral part of Normandy.

In 1413, Henry V, young and ambitious, succeeded to the English throne. His brief reign saw the resumption of hostilities against France and his resounding victory at Agincourt in 1415. In support of the war effort, he seized the substantial lands of the French abbeys on the islands (except for that at Marmoutiers) and, importantly, stemmed the flow of revenue from them to France, diverting it to his own treasury. Indeed, so successful was he that by the Treaty of Troyes in 1420 the mad French King, Charles VI, recognised Henry as the lawful heir to the throne of France and agreed to Henry's marriage with his daughter, Catherine.[60] However, with the death of both Henry and then Charles in 1422 and the succession of Henry's infant son, Henry VI, the tide of war turned against the English, a turn which was marked by the French victory at Orléans under the banner of Jeanne d'Arc (Joan of Arc).

In the final phase (1449–53) of the war, the French confidently launched a powerful two-pronged attack on the English positions in Normandy and Gascony. In 1450 at Formigny near Bayeux they annihilated the English army. In July 1453 at Castillon, 25 miles east of Bordeaux, the English made their final stand and were utterly defeated, Bordeaux falling three months later. The pale of Calais and the Channel Islands alone remained in English hands.

The Wars of the Roses

Whether it was the defeat at Castillon that finally tipped King Henry VI over the edge, his already fragile mind went to pieces that same year, leading to the contest for the English throne between his Lancastrian faction, led initially by his indomitable wife, Margaret of Anjou, on the one hand and Henry's third cousin, Richard, Duke of York, on the other (both being great-great-grandsons of Edward III). Thus it was that the Wars of the Roses between the Houses of Lancaster (with its symbolic red rose) and York (with its white) began in earnest.

Following Richard's defeat and death at the Battle of Wakefield on 30 December 1460, which had then been avenged at the bloody Battle of Towton on 29 March 1461, his son proclaimed himself King of England and was crowned as Edward IV in Westminster Abbey on 28 June that year. Margaret therefore sought help on three fronts: from her cousin, Pierre de Brézé, comte de Maulévrier and grand sénéschal of Normandy; from her uncle, Charles VII of France; and from France's allies, the Scots, with whom she and her family had in the meantime taken refuge.

To Pierre de Brézé Margaret promised the Channel Islands free from the sovereignty of England so that they would be held as a French fief in the Lancastrian cause. King Charles had then allowed de Brézé to assemble a fleet to seize the islands. In May 1461 Jean de Carbonnel captured Jersey on behalf of de Brézé, succeeding partly due to the incompetence of the Warden, John Nanfan, and partly due to the treachery of the de St Martin family.

Unfortunately, on 22 July 1461, the day on which Margaret had written to him directly for help, her uncle Charles died. He was succeeded by his son, Louis XI, who had previously supported the Yorkist cause. Undaunted, Margaret visited the French court in the spring and summer of 1462 and on 28 June concluded a treaty with Louis at Tours by which, notwithstanding her prior arrangement with de Brézé, she agreed to hand over the Channel Islands and Calais to Louis as security for a loan.

In the meantime, based at Mont Orgueil, de Carbonnel held the island in the name of the duchy of Normandy and the Lancastrian cause, albeit not without resistance. Among those who resisted was Philippe de Carteret, the seigneur of St Ouen in the west of Jersey, who was reputed to have escaped arrest by the French when his horse jumped a sunken lane 18 feet deep and 22 feet wide.

Above: King Alfred's Tower, Kingsettle Hill in Somerset. The tower was built in the eighteenth century and marks a possible site of King Alfred's rallying point in 878 before defeating the Danes at Edington.

Right: Two of the Lewis Chessmen, carved from walrus ivory in the twelfth century, probably in Norway, and found on the Isle of Lewis in 1831. By the twelfth century Lewis was part of the kingdom of Norway. There had once been a thriving trade in arctic products, such as walrus ivory and furs, between Scandinavia and the Middle East via the Volga and the Caspian Sea, but that had dried up by the twelfth century.

Opposite, above: A scene in the eleventh century Bayeux Tapestry of the battle on Senlac Hill (the 'Battle of Hastings'), depicting Norman cavalry attacking the English infantry following a barrage of arrows.

Opposite, below: A scene in the Bayeux Tapestry depicting King Harold being hit by an arrow in the eye and then being hacked to death by a Norman knight.

Above: Château Gaillard with Le Petit Andely and the River Seine in the background. The supposedly impregnable castle fell to Philippe II on 6 March 1204, spelling the end of King John's continental empire.

Above: The poisoning of King John and the Coronation of Henry III. John died at Newark in October 1216 having contracted dysentery while fleeing from the invading forces of Prince Louis (the future Louis VIII) of France. Rumour had it that he had been poisoned by a monk at Swineshead Abbey in Lincolnshire, illustrated in this late thirteenth century manuscript above. He was succeeded by his young son, Henry III, whose coronation is shown on the next page.

Opposite, above: The Battle of Sandwich 24 August 1217. By the Treaty of Lambeth, which followed the English victory later that year, the French recognised the sovereignty of Henry III over the Channel Islands and their separation from the continental duchy of Normandy. (From James Grant *British Battles on Land and Sea*, 1873.))

Opposite, below: Mont Orgueil (or Gorey) Castle stands on a peninsula at the head of Gorey Bay on the east coast of Jersey. It was built to defend the island against the French following the separation of the Channel Islands from the duchy of Normandy at the beginning of the thirteenth century.

Above: Elizabeth Castle, built on a tidal islet off St Helier on the south coast of Jersey. It was named after Queen Elizabeth I by Sir Walter Raleigh who was its Governor between 1600 and 1603. The construction of the castle began in 1594 as part of the reinforcement of the island against the threat of invasion by Catholic forces, particularly from Spain following hard on the heels of the Spanish Armada in 1588. Following a mortar bombardment, it was surrendered to Parliamentary forces on 12 December 1651 at the end of the Civil War.

Below: *Castle Cornet, Guernsey* by Jacob Knyff, c.1650 . Castle Cornet stands on a rocky islet off St Peter Port on the east coast of Guernsey. Originally fortified in the thirteenth century when the Channel Islands were separated from the duchy of Normandy and the Norman French became enemies. It was reinforced in 1597 against the threat of invasion by Catholic forces. It was the only Royalist stronghold on Guernsey during the Civil War and was surrendered to Parliamentary forces in December 1651 a few months after the defeat of Charles II at Worcester.

Above: *The Death of Major Peirson, 6 January 1781* by John Singleton Copley, 1783. In January 1781 the French invaded Jersey. Major Peirson, the Lieutenant Governor's second in command, refused to obey an order to surrender. With the aid of the local militia, he cornered the French in the Market Square of St Helier (now Royal Square). Although in the battle that followed he was killed by a French sniper (who was immediately shot by Peirson's black servant, Pompey), the French were defeated.

Below: Dunadd near Lochgilphead, the probable citadel of the kingdom of Dalriada.

Below: A set of British postage stamps overprinted by the Nazis for use in German occupied Jersey (auctioned in 2006).

Above: Bamburgh Castle, although Norman and
later, stands on the site of the citadel of the kingdom
of Bernicia on the coast of Northumberland.

Right: 'Rhynie Man'. A Pictish stone found close to
the Craw Stane near Rhynie, Aberdeenshire, now
in Woodhill House, Aberdeen. The site of the stones
may have been the centre of the Picts, before they
were conquered first by the Vikings and then in 843
by the King of Scots, Kenneth MacAlpin.

Below: *Dumbarton Castle from the West* by John
Clerk of Eldin (1728–1812). Dumbarton Rock was
the citadel of the Kingdom of Strathclyde. It is on the
north bank of the Firth of Clyde, at the confluence
with the River Leven. The picture shows the
remarkable defensive position of the rock, with the
rivers almost completely surrounding it.

The end of the Lancastrian coup came in the summer of 1468 when Sir Richard Harliston, a Yorkist vice-admiral, sailed with his fleet to Guernsey. From there he made contact with de Carteret's local forces on Jersey and landed men secretly at Plémont on the north-west tip of the island. Together they moved stealthily round the coast and by dawn had surrounded Mont Orgueil Castle where de Carbonnel's troops were garrisoned. Aided by a naval blockade, the castle fell after a siege of nineteen weeks and de Carbonnel surrendered. As a reward for his efforts, Harliston was then appointed Governor of the Islands by Edward IV.

It was during the reign of Edward IV that some further protection of the islands from the French was achieved. Ever since their separation from Normandy at the beginning of the thirteenth century, the Channel Islands and the ships of the islanders had been the targets of French raids. Although letters of protection issued to individual islanders by the French had alleviated the problem to some extent, they were not enough. In 1480 during a lull in the perennial warfare between England and France and as a means of protecting the ships of their respective nations from capture as prize in any future conflict, Edward IV and Louis XI agreed that Guernsey should enjoy the privilege of neutrality so that ships could take refuge in Guernsey waters unmolested, a privilege which was subsequently extended to include Jersey. Then, on the petition of Edward and the islanders to the Pope, not only was the privilege confirmed but it was also extended by a Papal Monition of 1481 and a Papal Bull of 1483 to outlaw the French raids under threat of excommunication.

The Tudors

Edward died in 1483 and, following the disappearance of the princes in the Tower, was succeeded by his brother as Richard III. With the death of Richard on Bosworth Field in 1485, the Plantagenet dynasty and the rule of the House of York came to an end. Richard was succeeded by the victor, Henry Tudor, as Henry VII. In an attempt to sever the remaining links between the Channel Islands and France, Henry procured a Papal Bull which purported to transfer the Channel Islands from the see of Coutances in Normandy to Winchester, but which in the event went largely unheeded.

Although the Papal Bull may have had little impact, Henry VIII's break with Rome and the Protestant Reformation in Continental Europe undoubtedly did. At the instigation of the Pope, they precipitated an outbreak of war with France, starting with the Battle of the Solent in 1545 in which Henry's flagship, the *Mary Rose*, was lost, and ending, after intermittent lulls, with the fall of Calais in 1558 – ironically during the reign of his ardently Catholic daughter, Mary. It was during those hostilities that the French captured the then uninhabited island of Sark in 1549, fortified it and used it as a staging post for raids on the other islands, leading the English to make a huge investment in the fortification of Alderney. It was not until 1554 that Sark was finally recovered and subsequently colonised by islanders.

Mary died in 1558 not long after the loss of Calais, leaving Philip II of Spain as her widower. She was succeeded by her Protestant half-sister, Elizabeth, who, having rebuffed Philip's marital advances, in 1572 concluded the Treaty of Blois with the Regent of France, Catherine de Médicis, allying England and France against Spain. Ever concerned by the threat of invasion by Catholic forces, particularly from Spain following the English intervention in the Protestant Netherlands against Spanish rule, the provocative execution of the Catholic Mary Queen of Scots in 1587 and the attempted invasion by the Spanish Armada in 1588, like her father before her Elizabeth continued to strengthen the fortification of the Channel Islands. The fortification culminated in the building of Elizabeth Castle on a tidal islet off St Helier on the south coast of Jersey, where work began in 1594, and the extensive strengthening of Castle Cornet at St Peter Port on the east coast of Guernsey, where work was completed in 1597.

The Reformation in Continental Europe also brought with it the spread of Calvinism from Normandy and Brittany to the islands and a flood of Calvinist Huguenots fleeing from Catholic persecution in France. The final ecclesiastical break from Rome had been made in 1569 when Elizabeth by Order in Council transferred the Channel Islands from the see of Coutances to the see of Winchester. It was Elizabeth's intention that uniformity with the Church of England should be established, but it ran into difficulties because of the difference in language: for the most part the islanders spoke only Norman-French. The following year Elizabeth was excommunicated by the Pope.

Significantly for what was to come, in the reign of her successor, James I, Episcopalian Anglicanism was introduced successfully in Jersey, but was stoutly resisted in Guernsey.

Rebellion and the Civil War

With the outbreak of the Civil War in England in 1642, it transpired that the sympathies of Jersey were predominantly Royalist (being largely Episcopalian) whereas those of Guernsey (largely Calvinist with many Huguenots) were with the English Parliament, albeit that both Deputy Governors were staunchly Royalist. The Royalist sympathies of Guernsey's Deputy Governor, Sir Peter Osborne, led to a coup in 1643, the States of Guernsey (the Parliament of Guernsey) declaring Guernsey, Alderney and Sark to be a republic. Sir Peter retreated to Castle Cornet where he held out until 1651, surviving on exiguous supplies from Jersey. Although there was trouble on Jersey in 1643, it was short-lived and the island remained loyal to the Crown; so much so, indeed, that within nineteen days of the execution of King Charles I in 1649, the Deputy Governor, Sir George Carteret, had proclaimed Charles II as king.

Following the defeat of Charles II at Worcester in September 1651, the Commander-in-Chief of the victorious Parliamentary Army, Oliver Cromwell, turned his attention to the Channel Islands. On 20 October a fleet of 12 warships and 70 supply ships and transports under the command of General-at-Sea Blake arrived off St Ouen's Bay in Jersey. Having been delayed by rough seas, the troops (2,200 in all) under Colonel Heane landed in the bay two days later. Although the island militia under the command of Sir George Carteret managed to repel the first onslaught, they were quickly defeated. Sir George himself together with the remnants of his force took refuge in Elizabeth Castle, but his refuge did not last long. Following a mortar bombardment and an unsuccessful attempt to obtain help from the King, who was by then in France, Elizabeth Castle surrendered on 12 December. Three days later, Castle Cornet, the only Royalist stronghold on Guernsey, surrendered too. In a laudable and perhaps uncharacteristic display of chivalry by the Commonwealth commanders, both Sir George Carteret and Sir Peter Osborne together with their followers were allowed free passage abroad.

With the restoration of Charles II as King of England in 1660, the governance of the Channel Islands reverted to Royalist hands, even Guernsey retaining its ancient privileges notwithstanding its brief republican adventure.

The not so Glorious Revolution and the French

In the event, the restoration of the Stuarts to the English throne was short-lived, coming to an end with the flight of James II and his entourage to France in December 1688 and the accession of his daughter, Mary, and her husband, William of Orange, early the following year (a story told more fully in the context of Scotland to which it is central). Although the accession of William and Mary to the English throne was conditioned on their acceptance of parliamentary sovereignty as enshrined in the English Bill of Rights, the Bill did not extend to the Channel Islands: rather the medieval relationship between the islands and the English Crown remained as it always had been.

At the time of his accession, William, as Stadholder of the Dutch Republic, was engaged in a war against Louis XIV of France. On becoming king, he dragged England into the war too. To protect Dutch shipping from attacks by the French, William revoked the privilege of neutrality which the Channel Islands had enjoyed for more than two centuries.

The war with France was brought to an end in 1697 by the Treaties of Ryswick (by one of which, incidentally, Louis recognised William as King of Great Britain).[61] Notwithstanding that the war had ended, that did not prevent the islanders from exploiting the revocation of the privilege of neutrality and seizing French ships as prize. This came to a head during the American War of Independence (1775–83) in which the American colonists were supported by the French. Long irritated by attacks on their shipping and possibly to cause a diversion, in 1779 the French attacked Jersey, but on that occasion were beaten back. However, in 1781 matters took a more dramatic course.

A somewhat disreputable soldier of fortune, calling himself baron de Rullecourt, secretly reconnoitred Jersey and, with the blessing of the French King, Louis XVI, raised a small army to invade the Channel Islands. On 5 January 1781 about 2,000 troops embarked at Granville and set sail for Jersey. Hampered by weather and difficulties of navigation, only about half of the troops managed to get ashore. Ill-assorted and poorly armed, they landed at La Rocque on the south-east tip of Jersey, some during the night and others early the next morning, believing that the island was at that time well defended by upwards of 4,000 men, although, in the event, it was 'Old Christmas Night' and many of the garrison's officers were on leave and some of the men had been out drinking. Having taken the garrison of the small fort at La Rocque by surprise and disarmed them, de Rullecourt marched to St Helier. Having surprised the garrison there too, he captured the Lieutenant Governor, Moyse Corbet, and duped him into believing that the French force was far more numerous than in fact it was. Thinking that it would be futile to resist, Corbet was persuaded to sign letters of capitulation. However, Corbet's second in command, Major Francis Peirson, was better informed and, on receiving orders from Corbet to surrender, boldly refused to obey. With the aid of the local militia, Peirson cornered the French in the marketplace of St Helier (today's Royal Square). Although he died in the battle that ensued, the French were defeated, de Rullecourt dying of his wounds shortly afterwards – an event which became known as the Battle of Jersey. As for Corbet, he was sent to London and court-martialled, never to return.

Twelve years later, following the execution of Louis XVI in the turmoil of the French revolution, Great Britain was again at war with France. Although the war continued sporadically until the defeat of Napoleon at Waterloo in 1815, the Channel Islands were not directly affected. However, the war prompted a review of offshore security and in 1801 the Channel Islands were formally recognised by the British Government as Crown dependencies (as opposed to colonies), the British Crown being responsible for their defence and foreign affairs, a status which they continue to enjoy to this day.

The German occupation

Just as the islands had not been directly affected by the Napoleonic wars, they were not affected by the First World War other than the service of islanders in the armed forces, the establishment of a base for French seaplanes on Guernsey and the establishment of a camp for German prisoners-of-war on Jersey. Things were very different when it came to the Second World War.

On the afternoon of 30 June 1940, Hauptmann Liebe-Pieteritz on a routine reconnaissance flight, seeing that the airfield on Guernsey was completely deserted, took it upon himself to test the island's defences and landed, in the event unchallenged. Fortified by this discovery, four German transport planes, having scared away the cows from the runway, landed there later that evening. On board was a platoon of Luftwaffe troops under the command of Major Lanz. On arrival, Lanz was handed a letter by Inspector Sculpher, the head of the island police force. The letter, in English, had been prepared in the light of the earlier landing by Liebe-Pieteritz. It had been signed by the Bailiff (the presiding officer of the civil administration of the island) and declared not only that the island was open but also that there were no armed forces to resist invasion. Lanz spoke little English and Sculpher no German. Having managed to explain that he wanted to be taken to the chief man of the island, Lanz was taken to the Attorney-General of Guernsey, Ambrose Sherwill. There, with the aid of an interpreter, he announced that the island was under German occupation. The next day, following signals of willingness to surrender Jersey in response to a German message dropped there by air, German troops landed on Jersey too. The unopposed occupation of the other islands then followed, being completed by 4 July.

There was no defence against the German invasion for the simple reason that a fortnight earlier the War Cabinet had decided that the Channel Islands were to be completely demilitarised. So it was that British territory was surrendered to enemy occupation.

In the event, the demilitarisation of the islands worked generally to the advantage both of the islands and of Britain. Other than a bombing raid on 28 June 1940 before Liebe-Pieteritz had landed and the Germans had discovered that the islands were undefended, the islanders were spared what would inevitably have been a bloody defence following the defeat of the British Expeditionary Force and the evacuation from Dunkirk earlier that summer. On the whole the occupying forces treated the islanders well. Until he was replaced by the dyed-in-the-wool Nazi Vice-Admiral Hüffmeier, Colonel Graf von Schmettow was from September 1940 the benign military commander-in-chief of the islands. However, following a long-running stand-off between the two of them, in February 1945 von Schmettow was recalled at Hüffmeier's instigation on the grounds that he was too magnanimous. The generally benign treatment under von Schmettow had no doubt been enjoyed by the islanders because, unlike any other German-occupied territory, there was no organised resistance movement, most men of fighting age having been evacuated before the invasion – although the latter gave rise to its own problems. Nevertheless, the rules of war were such that the Germans were entitled to impose the cost of the occupation on the islanders.[62]

Throughout the occupation, the courts and legislatures were allowed to continue, albeit that all legislation was subject to the prior approval of the German commandant. Church services were allowed, including (surreally) prayers for the Royal Family and for the welfare of the British Empire. The

British Post Offices in the Channel Islands continued to operate. Originally, the Germans had intended overprinting the stocks of British stamps with a swastika and the words 'Jersey 1940'. However, as a result of protests that the overprinting defaced the head of the sovereign (George VI), the overprinted stamps were destroyed except for a small number – now highly collectable. By December 1940 Guernsey had run out of penny stamps and diagonally printed twopenny stamps were used instead.

Militarily the islands were useful to the Germans during the early stages of the occupation, with the airfields on Jersey and Guernsey used extensively by aircraft during the Battle of Britain between July and October 1940. However, following the loss of air supremacy in 1940 and the invasion of Russia in June 1941, Hitler became obsessed by the need to defend the islands against an Allied invasion. The fortification of the islands began before the construction of any other part of the Atlantic Wall and by 1944 they had become the most impregnable part of it. From the Allied perspective this was distinctly useful because it tied up equipment and a huge number of troops, as it turned out to no purpose.

The fortifications were built by foreign prisoners – prisoners of war, political prisoners, criminals and even those simply seized on the streets of other occupied territories. Their brutal treatment at the hands of the Germans contrasted markedly with the treatment of the majority of the islanders themselves.

With the liberation of France in the summer of 1944, Churchill planned not only to trap the German forces of occupation on the islands but to starve them there. As a result, the Germans struggled to supply the islands and by the end of the year many of the islanders themselves were starving. Finally some relief for the islanders was provided by the Red Cross, starting with the arrival of their ship the *Vega* in Guernsey on 27 December.

Notwithstanding the Allied advances in Europe, on 25 March Vice-Admiral Hüffmeier told his troops that he intended to hold out with them until the Fatherland had regained its lost territory and had won the final victory. So fanatical had Hüffmeier become that a month later two of his officers, Baron von Helldorf and Baron von Aufsess, were plotting to assassinate him.

In the event no such drastic course was needed because on 7 May 1945 the German High Command agreed to an unconditional surrender, which was to take effect at 00.01 on 9 May. Nevertheless, there was concern that

Hüffmeier might decide to fight on alone, so a signal was sent to him saying that he must be aware of the German surrender and proposing that his representative should rendezvous 4 miles off Les Hanois light to the west of Guernsey to sign an instrument of surrender, an operation which the British codenamed Nestegg. Hüffmeier replied that his representative would be at the rendezvous at noon the following day. At 10 am on Tuesday 8 May 1945, the destroyer HMS *Bulldog* escorted by the destroyer HMS *Beagle* sailed from Plymouth for the rendezvous.

The Germans arrived at the appointed hour in a rusty minesweeper flying a swastika. A young German naval officer, Kapitänleutnant Zimmerman, went aboard the *Bulldog* with authority to do no more than receive armistice terms to convey to Hüffmeier. Brigadier Snow, in command of Operation Nestegg, gave him an instrument providing for immediate surrender and a letter informing Hüffmeier not only that there was no question of an armistice but also requiring that either he or a properly accredited representative attend a further rendezvous at midnight. Zimmerman told Snow that Hüffmeier had ordered him to say that if the British ships did not move away from the island Hüffmeier would consider their continued presence as an act of provocation. Nevertheless, at midnight Major-General Heine, Hüffmeier's military adviser, arrived at the appointed rendezvous aboard an armed trawler with authority to sign an unconditional surrender. Early on 9 May (a day later than VE day) Heine signed. Shortly after, British troops landed in Guernsey and the German occupation was ended.

Hüffmeier was captured at St Peter Port that same day. Three days later he was taken as a prisoner on board HMS *Beagle*. After his release he returned to Germany and died in obscurity in Münster in 1972. The islands have enjoyed their peaceful existence as dependencies of the British Crown ever since.

Scotland

The land to the north of Hadrian's Wall, which runs between Newcastle and Bowness on Solway, and subsequently that part north of the Antonine Wall between the Forth and the Clyde, was known by the Romans as Caledonia and by the Celts from Ireland as Alba.

At the time of the departure of the Romans in the fifth century, Caledonia north of Hadrian's Wall was occupied by four different groups of people. In the south-east, the area south of the Forth and stretching as far south as the Tees, known as Bernicia,[63] were the Anglo-Saxons who had emigrated from the lands between the mouth of the Rhine and the Baltic, driving the native Britons westwards into Wales and Cornwall and northwards into Cumbria and Strathclyde. In the north and east between the Forth and Caithness were the Picts, who were of Celtic stock and had come from Continental Europe long before. To the west, embracing Argyll, Kintyre and the neighbouring islands, lay the kingdom of Dalriada (Dál Riata) occupied by Celts from the north of Ireland. And in an area in the south-west stretching from the Clyde to south of the Solway in Cumbria were the Britons of Strathclyde, also of Celtic stock. It was the people of Dalriada whom the Romans called the Scoti or Scotti.

Bernicia was ruled from a fortress at Bamburgh, built on a great rock on the Northumbrian coast looking out to the Farne Islands, topped to this day by a magnificent castle, albeit now of Norman and later periods. The stronghold of the Picts is uncertain, but may have been near Rhynie, a few miles south of Huntly in Aberdeenshire, where the Craw Stane, inscribed with Pictish symbols, still stands. Dalriada was ruled (or at least probably ruled) from a fortress at Dunadd. The fortress was built on a rocky outcrop

THE FOUR KINGDOMS
OF NORTH BRITAIN
AFTER THE DEPARTURE
OF THE ROMANS

N

a few miles north of Lochgilphead, which stands today like an island in a sea of fields, bounded on two sides by the River Add and with a view of the sea at Crinan to the west. The citadel of the kingdom of Strathclyde stood on Dumbarton Rock on the north shore of the Firth of Clyde where the River Leven joins the Clyde. It was a natural fortress which was almost impregnable until its well dried up when besieged by the Vikings from Dublin in 870. It was re-fortified by General Wade following the Jacobite risings in 1715 and 1719 and it is his elegant buildings that can be seen there today.

The origins of the inhabitants of the far north-west, Skye, the Outer Hebrides and Shetland are unclear, all of them having suffered thorough ethnic cleansing at the hands of the Vikings. However, there is some indication that the inhabitants of Orkney were Picts.

By the eighth century, Vikings from the fjords of Vestland in what is now south-west Norway had begun to raid the islands of Orkney and Shetland and, further to the west and south, the Hebrides. By the middle of the ninth century, they had begun to settle there. They had been encouraged in this direction in part because the trade between Scandinavia and the Middle East in furs, walrus ivory and other arctic commodities in return for silver did not extend to Vestland: the inhabitants of Vestland, deprived of the luxuries that could be bought with Middle Eastern silver, had begun to look elsewhere.

The consolidation of mainland Scotland

In 839 Viking raiders defeated the Picts, killing their King, Ewen. Four years later Kenneth MacAlpin, King of the Scots of Dalriada, took advantage of the Viking victory and conquered the Picts once and for all. Having disposed of all rival claimants, Kenneth made himself king of the whole of the mainland north of the Forth, after which little more is heard of the Picts. 'And so he was the first of the Scots to obtain the monarchy of the whole of Albania, which is now called Scotia.'[64]

Kenneth moved his capital from Dunadd to Forteviot, south-west of Perth, he transferred St Columba's remains from the monastery on Iona, which St Columba had founded, to Dunkeld and he took the coronation stone – the Stone of Destiny – to Moot Hill at Old Scone, just north-east of Perth. It was on the Stone of Destiny at Scone that all Scottish kings were crowned thereafter until the stone was taken to England as part of the spoils of war by Edward I, the Hammer of the Scots, in 1296.

There were then no significant territorial gains by the Scottish kingdom until the eleventh century, although in the meantime there were assertions of sovereignty on the part of the English king over the Scottish kingdom; some justified, others less so. It was King Constantine II, a grandson of Kenneth MacAlpin, who submitted to King Æthelstan at Eamont Bridge in 927, whose territory as far north as Caithness was ravaged by Æthelstan in 934 and whose invasion of England was utterly defeated by Æthelstan at Brunanburh in 937.

Two generations later, King Kenneth II (Constantine's second cousin twice removed) did homage for his kingdom to the English King, Edgar. The occasion on which he did so was Edgar's coronation in Bath in 973 when Edgar was crowned ostensibly as King of 'Britain'. After the coronation, Edgar sailed round the coast and proceeded to Chester, which stands on the River Dee. There, he embarked from his palace on the river and, taking the rudder of the boat, was rowed upstream by eight kings to the monastery of John the Baptist and back again. Among those eight kings, all signalling their submission to Edgar, was Kenneth.

The precise circumstances in which the Scots acquired sovereignty over Lothian, the area between the Forth and the Tweed to the east of the kingdom of Strathclyde, are unclear, save that they had done so by 1018. In 1005 Malcolm II had succeeded his father, Kenneth II, as King of Scots and had immediately set about ravaging Northumbria, investing Durham the following year. Uhtred the Bold, a son of the ruler of Northumbria, then retaliated and 'slew nearly the whole of the Scots'. Uhtred himself was later killed and his brother, Eadwulf Cuttlefish, fearful of retribution for the devastation, ceded to the Scots 'the whole of Lothian, for amends and steadfast peace. In this way was Lothian added to the kingdom of the Scots.'[65]

Although it is obscure, the slaying of the Scots by Uhtred may refer to a great battle at Carham which lies to the south of the River Tweed, 3 miles west of Coldstream. The battle was said to have been fought following the appearance of a great comet for thirty nights, which would have been in the late summer of 1018. It was between the Northumbrians and the allied forces of Malcolm and Owain the Bald, King of Strathclyde. Nearly all of the population between the Tweed and the Tees were said to have perished.[66]

To the west of Lothian lay the kingdom of Strathclyde, which by the beginning of the eleventh century stretched from the Firth of Clyde to the southern Lake District, with its citadel still on Dumbarton Rock on the north bank of the Clyde. As with Lothian, the circumstances in which Strathclyde became part of the Scottish kingdom are also unclear. In 1031, a year after his conquest of the kingdom of Norway at Stiklestad, the Danish King, Cnut, was under pressure to defend his Norwegian territory, which at that time included Orkney, Shetland and the Hebrides; all were restive and giving some support to Tryggvi, a pretender to the Norwegian throne. Cnut therefore invaded Scotland and procured the submission of three kings – Malcolm II, King of Scots; MacBeth, Mormaer of Moray and future King of Scots of Shakespearian fame; and Iemarc or Echmarcach, who was probably Lord of the Rhinns of Galloway. There is, however, no reference in the chronicles to any submission by a king of Strathclyde, suggesting that there was no separate kingdom of Strathclyde at that stage.

Owain the Bald is the last King of Strathclyde to have been named. He died in 1018. There is no record that he had any sons. It appears likely, therefore, that Owain died without issue and was succeeded by Malcolm II's grandson and heir, Duncan, who had somehow managed to establish a claim to the throne of Strathclyde through the female line. Thus, when Duncan succeeded his grandfather as Duncan I in 1034, the frontiers of Scotland were extended to include Strathclyde. Part of the territory south of the Solway was then lost by the Scots when Siward, a Northumbrian earl, at the command of the English King, Edward the Confessor, defeated Duncan's successor, MacBeth, in 1054. However, it was taken once more by Duncan's son, Malcolm III, at some stage between 1066 and 1070.

The Norman influence

Initially the Normans did not appear to regard Strathclyde, even that part south of the Solway, as part of the England which they had first conquered in 1066: Carlisle and the surrounding area were omitted from the Domesday Book of 1086. However, in 1092 William Rufus, who had succeeded to the English throne on the death of his father, William the Conqueror, in 1087, invaded the region and incorporated what became the county of Cumberland[67] into his kingdom, colonising it with churls (yeoman farmers) to till the land, thus establishing a border in the west with Scotland at the Solway Firth.

Further east, matters took a different turn. In 1068 Edgar the Ætheling, grandson of the English King Edmund Ironside, and a potential claimant to the English throne, had, together with his sisters, Margaret and Christina, taken refuge from the Norman invasion with Malcolm III in Scotland. Two years later, having married (or possibly at that stage still aspiring to marry) Margaret and in league with Edgar, Malcolm proceeded with a host of Scots through Cumbria (then under his sway) and harried the whole of Teesdale and the surrounding country, Edgar even going as far as York where many of the Normans were killed. Learning that Earl Gospatrick of Northumbria had in the meantime invaded Cumbria, Malcolm took his revenge on the Northumbrians, sparing no-one, capturing many and carrying them off to Scotland as slaves. Inevitably William the Conqueror reacted and in August 1072 he arrived with his army by sea, disembarking in the Firth of Forth. Malcolm met him further north at Abernethy and, apparently without a fight, submitted to him, doing him homage and giving him hostages, including his son Duncan (the future Duncan II), to secure his submission.

On his accession in 1087, William Rufus released Duncan. With Duncan no longer held hostage, the Scots invaded Northumbria again in 1091. At that stage they were driven back, peace then being agreed through the intervention of Malcolm's brother-in-law, Edgar. Two years later, Malcolm attempted to meet William Rufus in Gloucester, but was rebuffed. He therefore returned to Scotland, marshalled his forces and invaded England once more, devastating the country as he went. Unfortunately for him, on his way back to Scotland he was trapped by some of the Earl of Northumbria's knights and killed by the Earl's steward. He was succeeded in turn by four of his surviving sons (Duncan, Edgar, Alexander and David) with his brother, Donald, usurping the throne initially and then again after Duncan had been murdered at Donald's instigation.

Although after the foray in 1072 the Normans (as distinct from the Plantagenets) did not themselves invade Scotland again with a view to conquest, they did lend armed support first to Duncan and, after Duncan was murdered, to his brother, Edgar, to wrest the throne from their usurping uncle, Donald, who first was blinded and then died as Edgar's prisoner. Nevertheless, the Normans did progressively colonise Scotland, initially exerting their influence indirectly through Malcolm's sons. They did not become directly involved, however, until the reign of the youngest son, David I (r. 1124–53), who had been educated and knighted at the court of the English King, Henry I.

David encouraged Normans to settle both north and south of the Forth and under his grandson, William the Lion (r. 1165–1214), the process was taken further. In effect a Norman settlement took place under the auspices of the Scottish Crown. Lothian and Strathclyde were particularly affected, but there was also Norman penetration further north in Fife and Moray. Thus it was that Norman families such as Fraser (Fraise or Fraisier), Sinclair (St-Clair), Bruce (de Brus), Balliol (de Bailleul) and Wishart (Guiscard) were established in Scotland.

It was Norman influence that led to the adoption of the feudal system of land tenure and the shiring of much of Scotland, other than the remoter parts of the Highlands, by the end of David I's reign. (The shiring of the Highlands was not completed until the seventeenth century.)

It was David who granted the vast border estate of Annandale to the Norman family of de Brus in 1124 and it was a direct descendant of that family who was to become one of Scotland's greatest kings, best known as Robert the Bruce, and forebear of the Stewart dynasty (later spelled Stuart by Mary Queen of Scots and her descendants).

The early conflict over the border with England

Although by the end of the eleventh century a boundary between Scotland and England could be discerned stretching between the Solway Firth in the west and and the River Tweed in the east, not only was the territory on both sides of that boundary destined to be the subject of centuries of warfare but so too was the very sovereignty over Scotland itself.

The seeds of much of the hostility were sown as a result of the marriage between Henry I of England and Edith-Matilda, daughter of Malcolm III of Scotland and, as it turned out, sister of four Scottish kings.

Following the drowning of their son, William, when the *White Ship* capsized off the coast of Normandy in 1120, Henry I and Edith-Matilda had only one surviving child, Matilda.[68] On two occasions Henry had prevailed on his prelates and nobles to swear that they would accept Matilda as his rightful heir, the first in 1126 and the second in 1131. Nevertheless, when Henry died in 1135, his nephew, Stephen, riding roughshod over any rights which Matilda might have had, seized the English throne, leading inexorably to civil war.

Among those who had sworn to support Matilda was her uncle David, then King of Scotland. She therefore wrote to him, reminding him of his oath to her father and asking for his help. True to his word, David gathered an army and, together with other nobles who had sworn to support Matilda, overran much of Cumbria and Northumbria. Stephen reacted quickly, moving north with a great army. The two kings met at Durham in February 1136 and there they agreed to terms for peace, Stephen taking Northumbria, David keeping Cumbria and David's son, Henry, being granted the earldom of Huntingdon for which he then did homage to Stephen.

Despite this agreement, two years later, while Stephen was preoccupied with crushing Matilda's allies in the south of England, David saw another opportunity to vindicate Matilda's claim to the English throne. He started by invading Northumbria, devastating the country as far south as the Tyne. He then moved west, his army routing a force of English knights as far south as Clitheroe on 10 June 1138. In July he returned to the east with an army said to number 26,000 and, having passed Durham, crossed the River Tees. The atrocities committed by the Scots at every stage of their campaign were unspeakable and undoubtedly deserving of divine retribution.

In Stephen's absence, Thurstan, the Archbishop of York and Stephen's deputy in the north, rose to the occasion. His envoys with an offer of peace having been dismissed with derision by David, he issued an edict summoning every able-bodied man in his diocese to arms. His army gathered on what was then part of Cowton Moor about 3 miles north of Northallerton (now on the Great North Road). Their rallying point was a ship's mast which had been erected on a wagon, from the top of which hung a silver pyx containing consecrated bread ('the body of Christ') together with banners of the saints, known ever since as the Standard. The Archbishop is also reported to have had passages dug beneath part of the moor in which noisome instruments (*petronces* – presumably some kind of horn) were concealed with which to terrorise the animals that the Scots would drive before them as their vanguard into the attack.[69]

Early in the morning of 22 August 1138, the Scots sought to take the Archbishop's army by surprise by approaching under cover of a mist, but to no avail. The animals, terrified by the noise, turned tail and fled straight into the ranks of the advancing Scots. The Scots were then overwhelmed both by the religious fervour of their opponents and by an almost continuous barrage of arrows, to which the Galwegians (the men of Galloway) in the front rank were particularly vulnerable, being without armour and for the most part naked. Then, with the loss of several of their leaders, those Scots who had survived the onslaught fled, leaving so much equipment behind on the moor that the place became known as Bagmoor. The thousands of Scots dead were buried at a place named Scotspit, a name echoed today in Scotspit Lane.

In September, Alberic, Bishop of Ostia, a legate sent by the Pope, sought to broke a truce between the two Kings. Although no agreement had been reached before he returned home, negotiations continued into the new year. Stephen was under growing pressure to conclude an agreement in order to free up resources to meet an imminent threat of invasion by Matilda from Normandy. Whether by virtue of an invasion of Scotland by Stephen or from political necessity, an agreement was finally reached at Durham on 9 April 1139 in the presence of Matilda by which Stephen granted the earldoms of Cumbria and Northumbria (except for Newcastle and Bamburgh) to David's son, Henry, but taking Henry as a hostage to secure the peace. Henry then travelled south and joined Stephen's court at Nottingham. Sure enough, in September that year, Matilda did invade and the civil war in England reached a new pitch.

A decade later, Matilda's young son, confusingly also called Henry, had been knighted at Carlisle by his great-uncle, King David. On the occasion of receiving his knighthood Henry had promised that, if he ever became king of England, he would give Northumbria to David, including Newcastle and all of the land between the Tweed and the Tyne. David died in 1153; his own son Henry having predeceased him, he was succeeded by his grandson, Malcolm IV. A year later, on Stephen's death, Matilda's son Henry succeeded to the English throne as Henry II. When in 1157 Malcolm claimed that he was entitled to the whole of Northumbria and Cumbria, Henry responded saying that he was not to be defrauded of so large a part of his kingdom.[70] Being still young, Malcolm was all too easily overawed and agreed to abandon his claim, receiving nothing more than confirmation of his earldom of Huntingdon.

In 1165 Malcolm IV died and was succeeded by his brother, William. At some stage shortly afterwards, William fell out with the English King and agreed to provide Louis VII of France with military support against him. This was the first of many alliances between Scotland and France against England which came to be known as the Auld Alliance, commonly renewed on the accession of each Scottish king, the last occasion being in 1745.

The perennial hostility between England and France had at that stage been exacerbated by the marriage between Henry II and Eleanor of

Aquitaine. Eleanor had been married to Louis until their marriage was annulled in 1152 on the specious pretext of kinship, but in reality because Eleanor had failed to produce a son. No sooner was she free than Eleanor had married Henry. At a stroke, she had not only deprived Louis of the enormous duchy of Aquitaine but she had then transferred it to his rival, Henry.

As if his troubles with Louis in France were not enough, in 1173 Henry was confronted by a rebellion in England by his three eldest surviving sons, all (be it noted) by Eleanor, namely the young Henry, Geoffrey and Richard, seeking to depose their father in favour of the young Henry. Seeing the opportunity to make good the claim to Cumbria and Northumbria which Malcolm had abandoned, William collected an army and proceeded to Wark Castle on the south bank of the Tweed between Carham and Coldstream (little of which remains today), to which he laid an inconclusive siege. From there he proceeded to invade Northumbria and then Cumbria finally reaching Carlisle. Although he had retreated to Roxburgh when duped into believing that there was a large English army approaching, he moved south once more, but this time with disastrous consequences.

On 13 July 1174, the Scots were laying siege to Alnwick Castle. Although much of his army was engaged in plundering the surrounding country, William was confident that there was no threat of attack and was enjoying dinner with some of his entourage in the open fields before the castle. In the meantime a troop of English cavalry which had set out from Newcastle early that morning in search of the Scottish King had been lost in the mist. When the mist suddenly cleared they saw Alnwick Castle and, much to their surprise, the Scottish King in the open before them. At first William thought that the troop was part of his own army returning with their spoils. Then, realising that the standards were those of the English knights, he mounted his horse and led those who were with him into the attack. In the fierce engagement that followed, his horse was killed and fell on top of him and, together with almost all of his men who had not been killed, he was captured.

Miraculously, or so it seemed to him, Henry received the news of William's capture on the morning after he had kept a night vigil and done penance at the tomb of Thomas à Becket for whose murder four years earlier he held himself to blame.

William was held first at Richmond (in Yorkshire) and then taken via Southampton to Normandy where he was imprisoned in Henry's castle at Falaise. While still imprisoned there, on 8 December 1174 he agreed to a treaty for peace and his ransom on terms over which he had little choice.[71] They were Draconian. The opening paragraph recited without colour of diplomacy the complete subjugation of Scotland: 'William king of Scots, has become the liegeman of the lord king [Henry] against every man in respect of Scotland and in respect of all his other lands; and he has done fealty to him as his liege lord, as all the other men of the lord king are wont to do.'

Under the treaty, William agreed that the Scottish Church should submit to the English Church and that representative liegemen of William should do homage to Henry not only on their own behalf but also on behalf of William's heirs. The treaty recorded that William had delivered to Henry the castles of Roxburgh, Berwick, Jedburgh, Edinburgh and Stirling and it obliged William to pay for the garrison of each of them at Henry's pleasure. It also recorded that William had delivered his brother David and twenty other hostages as security, it being agreed that William and David would be released when the castles had been handed over and that each of the other hostages would be released when his heir had been delivered as a hostage in his stead.

The treaty concluded and the castles having been handed over, William was allowed to return to Scotland, where he arrived in February the following year. True to his word, on 10 August 1175, together with his brother David and other Scottish nobles, he did homage and swore fealty to Henry at York Minster. As a token of his subjection to Henry, William placed his cap, lance and saddle upon the altar. Following this humiliating ceremony, William and his household were allowed to return to Scotland.

Although the Treaty of Falaise may have represented the greatest and most humiliating extent to which the Scottish Crown had been subjected to the Crown of England, its effect was short-lived. In 1186 William married Ermengarde de Beaumont, a cousin of Henry, and received Edinburgh Castle back from Henry by way of dowry, subject to payment of 100 marks annually and the service of 40 knights. Three years later Henry died and was succeeded by his son, Richard I, the Lionheart. Richard, keen to raise funds for a crusade, agreed to accept 10,000 marks of silver in return for rescinding the terms of the treaty and explicitly restoring to William the castles at Berwick and Roxburgh, the marchlands of Scotland and the earldom of Huntingdon.[72] However, Richard refused to throw Cumbria or Northumbria into the bargain.

Richard was killed at Châlus in 1199 and was succeeded by his brother,

John. The following year William met John on a hill outside Lincoln and on 22 November did homage to John, presumably for his English lands alone. Although William then claimed Northumbria, Cumberland and Westmoreland as his heritage and there was much wrangling over it, John prevaricated and no agreement was reached.

Nine years later, John summoned William to meet him at Newcastle. Although the two Kings met, again no agreement was reached between them. Something then followed which provoked John to despatch a large army to the border. What it was is not clear. It may have been his discovery that William had made an alliance with one of John's enemies by marrying one of his daughters to the Count of Boulogne; or had made, or had at least sought to make, an alliance with another of John's enemies, King Philippe II of France. William had also on two occasions torn down a castle that John had been building at Tweedmouth on the north (at that time the Scottish) bank of the Tweed, killing or capturing all those who had been engaged on the work.

In the event John, accompanied by an overawing army, met William at Norham Castle on the south bank of the Tweed, the picturesque ruins of which still stand above a great bend in the river – much painted by Turner. There on 7 August 1209 they agreed to make peace.[73] William agreed to pay £13,000[74] for the liberty of the harbour of Berwick and for permission to tear down the castle at Tweedmouth. He also agreed to quitclaim (surrender) all of the lands which he held of John in England in return for John re-granting them to William's son and heir, Alexander, for which Alexander would then do homage and swear fealty. Although William refused to surrender Alexander as a hostage, he did surrender his two elder daughters, Margaret and Isabella, to John's custody, one to be married to one or other of John's sons, Henry or Richard, and the other possibly therefore being prevented at least from marrying one of John's enemies. Fifteen hostages were also given by William to secure peace. Later that year Alexander did homage and swore fealty to John at Alnwick.

William died in 1214 and was succeeded by Alexander, as Alexander II. John died two years later and was succeeded by his elder son, Henry, as Henry III. In 1221 some rapprochement between the two was achieved when Alexander married Henry's sister, Joan. The following year attempts were made to delineate the border between Scotland and England, but the representatives of the two Kings fell out on each occasion. Nevertheless, on 25 September 1237 a compromise was reached in a treaty between Alexander and Henry, known as the Treaty of York.[75] The agreement which had been made by their respective fathers at Norham in 1209 was effectively torn up. Alexander quitclaimed to Henry any hereditary rights which he had to Northumberland, Cumberland and Westmoreland and abandoned his claim for repayment of the 15,000 silver marks[76] which had been paid by his father to King John. In return, Henry agreed to grant the fiefdom of 200 librates of land (i.e. having a value of £200 per annum – a very large sum) in the counties of Northumberland and Cumberland on condition of homage and an oath of fealty in respect of them and the annual rendering of one red falcon. The treaty also provided for the release of Alexander's sisters, Margaret and Isabella, and the other hostages who had been taken by King John (although it is conceivable that the sisters and other hostages had already been released by virtue of an obscure provision of Magna Carta).[77]

It was during Alexander's reign that the first steps were taken to win the Hebrides for the Kingdom of Scotland.

The Hebrides

Latin authors referred to the islands off the west coast of Scotland as the Hebudes. It is ironic that the name of the islands today may have originated from nothing more than a mistake in transcription which turned the 'u' in Hebudes into the 'ri' in Hebrides.

In 874 or thereabouts, Haraldur Hárfagri (Harald Fairhair), who had as a child inherited the small kingdom of Vestfold, won a great naval battle at Hafrsfjord, near Stavanger in south-west Norway, thereby establishing himself effectively as king of most of coastal Norway as far north as the border with Tröndelag. Many of those whom Harald had defeated then fled west, settled in Shetland, Orkney and the Hebrides and started to raid the coast of Norway during the summer months. Harald therefore assembled a great fleet and invaded the islands, killing all of the Vikings who had not fled to sea. Although Scots and Irish opportunists took advantage of Harald's subsequent departure to invade and plunder the Hebrides, the islands were reconquered by Ketil Flatnose ostensibly at Harald's behest, although Ketil appears then to have refused to acknowledge Harald's sovereignty.

A century later and twenty-seven years after Harald Hardrada had lost his life and kingdom at the Battle of Stamford Bridge, his grandson succeeded to the throne of Norway as Magnus III, known as Magnus Barefoot or Bareleg. In 1098, Magnus turned his attention to the islands to the north and west of mainland Britain. He assembled his fleet and a great host and set sail from Norway. He proceeded first to Orkney and thence to the Hebrides, the Isle of Man and Anglesey, burning and plundering as he went, and took possession of the islands. From Anglesey he went to Kintyre and from there to the Scottish mainland, where at some stage he made a pact with the Scottish King, Malcolm III, by which he agreed to peace in return for recognition of his right to possess the islands to the west of the mainland. Having wintered in the Hebrides he returned to Norway the following summer with the remainder of his men and much booty via Orkney.

One and a half centuries later, the Scottish king, Alexander II, resenting the way in which the Hebrides had been captured by the Norwegians, set his mind to acquiring them from the Norwegian King, Haakon IV. Starting in 1244, he sent emissaries to Haakon to enquire whether he would be willing to give up the Hebrides, or even to sell them for refined silver. But the emissaries were rebuffed by Haakon saying that he had no need of refined silver. Although Alexander importuned him constantly, Haakon remained obdurate. In 1249 Alexander saw a new opportunity. Harald, Haakon's vassal King of the Hebrides and the Isle of Man, had been lost at sea the previous autumn and had been succeeded by another of Haakon's vassals, named John. So Alexander, having mustered men and ships to take the Hebrides by force, sent word to John tempting him with the offer of a large dominion on the mainland in return for his kingdom, an offer which John, not wishing to break his oath of fealty to Haakon, refused. During Alexander's lifetime nothing more came of this venture: while his fleet lay in the Sound of Kerrera off Oban in the Firth of Lorn, he had a dream in which he was told to turn back; then, as ill luck would have it, he caught a fever and died.

Where Alexander had failed, his son and heir, Alexander III, in due course succeeded. Alexander the son was only seven when his father died. He was crowned at Scone and two years later, on Christmas Day, he was knighted at York by the English King, Henry III. The following day he was married to Henry's infant daughter, Margaret, thus cementing the peace which had prevailed between the kingdoms of Scotland and England since the Treaty of York.

The wresting of the Hebrides from the King of Norway began in 1262, when Alexander announced that he intended to seize the islands and the Earl of Ross and his followers laid waste to Skye, burning churches, killing women and children, even impaling little children on their spears which they shook until the bodies reached their hands. Hearing of Alexander's intentions and to avenge the depredations in Skye, in May the following year Haakon began to gather his forces at Bergen and two months later set sail for Shetland. Haakon's own ship was large and new, its prow fitted with a gilded dragon's head and neck; the gilding on the ships and the shields of the men glittered in the sunlight as they left.

From Shetland the fleet proceeded south via Orkney through the Inner Hebrides terrorising the inhabitants into submission. Haakon put in to Kerrera to marshal his fleet which by then numbered somewhere between 100 and 200 well-equipped ships. He then divided his forces, sending some ships to subdue Kintyre, some to Islay, some to Gigha and others to Bute. Finally, he put in to land in Arran Sound. From there he sent messengers to Alexander with a list of the islands to the west of Scotland to which he laid claim and seeking peace. In the event there was little difference between them, but Alexander refused to cede Bute, Arran or the Cumbraes (the name of the latter islands referring to the Cymric people of Strathclyde). However, because the summer was nearly over and the weather was likely to deteriorate, Alexander believed that it was in his interest to prolong the negotiations. In response Haakon announced either that peace should be agreed or that the two armies should fight, but Alexander refused to engage.

Being desperately short of supplies, Haakon sent forty ships up Loch Long which were then carried overland to Loch Lomond (presumably over the narrow saddle to where the village of Tarbet stands today – a 'tarbert' or 'tarbet', from Gaelic *tairbeart*, being a place where a ship can readily be drawn overland from one stretch of open water to another). The Norwegians then ravaged the islands in the loch and the surrounding shores, plundering whatever was there. However, having returned to Loch Long at the end of September, several of the ships were wrecked in a great storm.

That same storm also drove many of the other Norwegian ships from their anchorage off Great Cumbrae onto the coast near Largs, the imposing dragon on the prow of the King's ship losing its nostrils as a result of a collision. The Scots then seized the opportunity to attack the Norwegians who had been driven ashore, initially with success, many of the Norwegians escaping to sea in their ships. Late on in the day, however, the Norwegians re-grouped and mounted a bold assault on the Scots. Notwithstanding their far superior numbers and the higher ground which they held, the Scots were put to flight, enabling the Norwegians to bury their dead, retire to their ships and to sail away.

On the voyage home, Haakon put in to Orkney. While at Kirkwall he fell ill and died there on 16 December. He was succeeded by his son, Magnus IV (later styled Magnus VI).

The following year, 1264, messengers were sent from Orkney to Alexander seeking peace. On the first occasion they were rebuffed with threats of violence; Alexander even sent an army to plunder Caithness, which was then in Norwegian hands. A second embassy, this time from Norway, was treated more favourably, but nevertheless returned to Norway with nothing more than an invitation, should Magnus so wish, to send messengers again in the summer.

No doubt fortified by the events of the past two years, in 1265 Alexander despatched an eloquent monk from Melrose to Magnus with an offer to buy the Hebrides and the Isle of Man. After some debate among the Norwegian nobles, this proposal was accepted by Magnus, culminating in a treaty which was executed in Perth 'on the Friday next after the festival of the apostles Peter and Paul' – 2 July 1266. By this treaty Magnus resigned all claim to the Hebrides and the Isle of Man (as opposed to the islands of Orkney and Shetland which were explicitly excepted) agreeing that they should become subject to the laws and customs of Scotland (in contrast to what happened with Orkney and Shetland two centuries later). In return Alexander and his successors were to pay 100 merks (equivalent to English marks) of sterling silver annually in perpetuity together with a payment of 4,000 merks spread over the next four years.[78] There is some indication that Alexander did homage to Magnus for the islands,[79] suggesting that Magnus retained some vestigial sovereignty over them, but that was not the way things turned out in the end.

The Scots were slow to pay up, with the last instalment of the 4,000 merks not reaching Norway until 1282. It is not known when the annual payments dried up, but the Norwegians are known to have had difficulties in collecting the money owed during the fourteenth and fifteenth centuries. The debts were eventually written off as part of the marriage settlement between King James III and Princess Margaret of Denmark, Norway and Sweden in 1468, finally vesting any want of sovereignty over the islands in

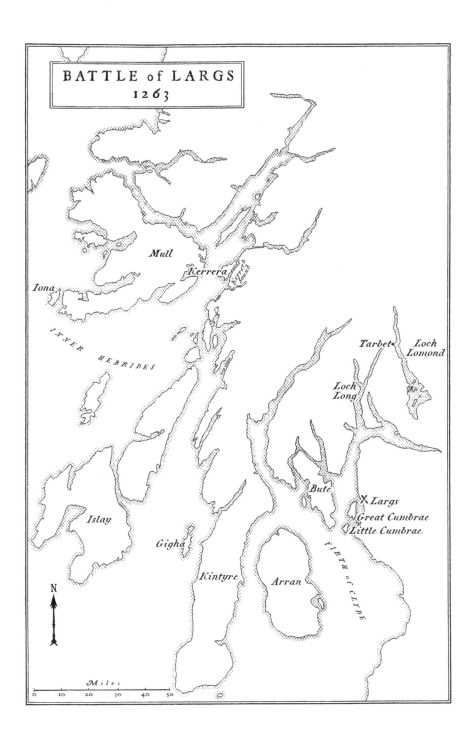

BATTLE of LARGS
1263

Mull

Kerrera

Kerrera Sound

Iona

INNER HEBRIDES

Tarbet

Loch
Lomond

Loch
Long

Bute

X Largs
Great Cumbrae
Little Cumbrae

Islay

Gigha

Kintyre

Arran

FIRTH of CLYDE

N

Miles

0   10   20   30   40   50

the King of Scotland.

Although possession of the Hebrides had been ceded to Alexander in 1266, it would take more than three hundred years for the king of Scotland to gain effective control of them from the clan chiefs in whose grip they were held. It was finally achieved by the Band and Statutes of Iona between 1609 and 1616. Traditionally the clan chiefs had been a law unto themselves, administering their own, often questionable, justice, exploiting their tenants, feuding with each other and failing to pay their dues to the king. Importantly, they spoke Gaelic, maintained Gaelic culture and were in large part Catholics. To bring them to heel, in 1608 King James VI (by then also James I of England) appointed Andrew Knox, the Bishop of the Isles based on Iona, to negotiate what turned out to be a distinctly one-sided compromise. Although threatened with military force, initially the chiefs were reluctant to come to terms. Nine of them, however, accepted an invitation the following year to visit the King's military commander, Lord Ochiltree, on board his ship off the coast of Mull ostensibly to hear a sermon from the Bishop.[80] Once on board, they were kidnapped and held until the principal terms had been agreed.

It took seven more years, punctuated by insurrections, for all of the terms to be hammered out, but the principal terms were those to which the chiefs had agreed in 1609. Under the Band (Scots for an agreement), the nine captive chiefs promised both to obey, and importantly to enforce, the laws of the land, thus bringing to an end their own, often quixotic, jurisdiction. Together with other chiefs, they also subscribed the Statutes, which included the gist of the Band. One, to break the distinctly Gaelic way of life, obliged the chiefs to send their eldest son, or failing sons their eldest daughter, to Lowland schools where they would be taught to speak, read and write in English. By another, Presbyterian ministers were to be appointed to the parishes and dissent suppressed. Another restricted traditional Gaelic hospitality, outlawing clan bards and severely limiting the consumption of strong liquor. Yet another forbade the use of firearms, even for killing game, thus encouraging recourse to the king's courts to resolve differences rather than by the traditional recourse to bloodshed.[81]

Although the islands of St Kilda, 40 miles to the west of Harris, are now part of the Hebrides, there is no record of the circumstances in which they were first colonised. However, by the eighteenth century they were inhabited by Scots and have been treated as British at least since then.

The Maid of Norway

Alexander's life came to a tragic end on 18 March 1286. That day he had been dining with many of his nobles in Edinburgh Castle. Notwithstanding the bad weather and the attempts of his nobles to dissuade him, after dinner he set off to visit his new wife, Yolande, the daughter of the comte de Dreux, whom he had recently married. She was then living at Kinghorn, on the coast of Fife between Burntisland and Kirkcaldy. Having been ferried over the Forth, the King lost his guides in the darkness near Inverkeithing. He pressed on nonetheless but, alone in the dark, he fell from his horse and broke his neck.

Alexander had no surviving child. Despite an attempt by Yolande to say that she was pregnant and later to pass off a changeling as her own child by the King, Alexander was succeeded by his granddaughter, Margaret. Known to posterity as the Maid of Norway, she was the three-year-old daughter by his own daughter, also called Margaret, and Eric II of Norway. The succession accorded with Alexander's wishes and was supported by the promise which had been made to him by thirteen Scottish earls and twenty-eight Scottish barons at Scone two years earlier. The irony is that not only was she the heiress to the throne of Scotland but, notwithstanding her grandfather's despatch of the Norwegians at Largs in 1263, she was also the heiress to the kingdom of Norway.

Three years later Eric approached the English King, Edward I, to discuss the affairs of his daughter. That led to a meeting between commissioners from Norway, Scotland and England at Salisbury where they concluded a treaty on 6 November 1289, by which they agreed that Margaret would not enter Scotland unless it was peaceful and that she would not be married without the consent of Eric and Edward.[82] Behind the scenes, however, Edward was in the process of procuring papal dispensation for the marriage of Margaret with his own son, the future Edward II. The dispensation was needed because, as first cousins once removed, they were within the prohibited degrees of consanguinity; but, notwithstanding the consanguinity, it was granted shortly afterwards.

The following year, in anticipation of the marriage between Margaret and Edward, a further treaty was concluded at Birgham and confirmed at Northampton between Edward I and the Guardians of Scotland on behalf of Margaret.[83] Although superficially it appeared to guarantee the

independence of Scotland from England in the event that there were no heirs
of the union between Margaret and Edward, it was so hedged about with
qualifications that it achieved nothing other than perhaps to preserve the
status quo in diplomatic language.

It is a curiosity that to this day no-one knows precisely where in, or near,
Birgham (pronounced 'Berjum' locally) the treaty was sealed, there being
no sign of any castle or other likely site nearby. Birgham is however close
to the Scottish bank of the Tweed, the traditional border, and therefore an
appropriate site for the making of such a treaty.

But the marriage was not to be, for Margaret died on 26 September 1290
whilst on her way from Norway to Scotland. She had sailed in a Norwegian
ship from Bergen bound for Leith. Driven by storms, the ship put into what
has been called ever since St Margaret's Hope on South Ronaldsay in Orkney.
There Margaret died, apparently from the effects of seasickness. Had she
lived and borne children by Edward, the history not only of Scotland but
of England too would almost certainly have turned out very differently.
However, with her death there were thirteen claimants to the Scottish throne
and the start of the most tempestuous and bloody relationship with England.

The contest for the crown and war with England

News of the rumour of Margaret's death was sent by the Bishop of St
Andrews to Edward I in a letter dated 7 October 1290, in which the Bishop
urged the King to look favourably on the claim to the throne of Sir John
de Balliol over that of Sir Robert de Brus.[84] The following year Edward
held court at Norham Castle, where he was presented with an offer by the
thirteen claimants to submit to his determination as to which of them was
the rightful heir.[85] To this Edward agreed, but subject to a condition which
was to have far-reaching consequences: the heir whom he chose had in effect
to agree to surrender the kingdom of Scotland to him so that he could then
re-grant it to the heir, the heir being required to do homage to Edward for
the kingdom; in other words, to accept that Edward was the sovereign not
only of England but also of Scotland too. In their desperation to succeed
to the Scottish throne, nine of the claimants signified their agreement
to the condition in a document drawn up the following day, 5 June 1291.
The document had so many seals attached to it by parchment ribbons
that it became known as the 'Ragman'.[86] Among the nine were Sir John de

Balliol, Sir Robert de Brus and Sir John de Hastynges, each a descendant respectively of one of the three daughters of David, Earl of Huntingdon, great-granddaughters of King David I. So it was that at Norham on 5 June 1291 Edward declared himself to be the Lord Paramount of all Scotland and received the homage of all his nobles.

After months of wrangling and reference to forty responsible persons (half from Scotland and half from England), on 17 November 1292 Edward chose Sir John de Balliol. Three days later Balliol swore fealty to Edward and, devastatingly for Scotland, on 26 December did homage to Edward at Newcastle, thus acknowledging that Scotland was a vassal state of the English King.

In 1294 Edward declared war on France to defend his duchy of Aquitaine against French incursions. To support his endeavour, he demanded Scottish levies. Balliol being too pusillanimous to deal with this, the reins of his Government were taken over by a council of twelve men, by whom Edward's demand was rejected. Faced by a common enemy, on 23 October 1295 the Scottish Council and King Philippe IV of France resurrected the Auld Alliance and concluded a treaty, known as the Treaty of Paris.[87] It was agreed that the Scots should attack the English, that the French would continue their war against England and that neither would make peace with England without the consent of the other. To cement the alliance, they also agreed that Balliol's eldest son, Edward, should marry the eldest daughter of Philippe's brother, Charles, comte de Valois et Anjou. This marked the beginning of three centuries of almost continual warfare between Scotland and England.

That same year the Scots attacked the English first in the east, devastating the area round Carham, and shortly afterwards in the west, forcing their way through Redesdale. Among many atrocities laid at the door of the Scots was the trapping of the children of Hexham in their school and burning them to death. English retaliation was not only inevitable but also swift. Edward moved north during that winter and in March 1296 he sacked Berwick-upon-Tweed. Having remained there for several weeks, he moved up the coast to reduce Dunbar Castle. On 27 April his army routed the Scots on Spottsmuir, just to the south of Dunbar. By the middle of June he had captured the castles of Roxburgh, Edinburgh and Stirling. In July he took Montrose Castle. Balliol was captured at Stracathro (a few miles to the north-west of Montrose). There, on 7 July, he was forced to renounce his treaty with France. Three days later in nearby Brechin Castle he was forced to abdicate his throne and to surrender to Edward not only himself but Scotland too. Finally, while at Montrose Castle, as a sign of his treachery and final degradation, Balliol's tabard, displaying his royal coat of arms, was stripped from him, giving rise to his nickname of Toom Tabard – the empty tabard. From Montrose he was taken as a prisoner to England where for the most part he was held in the Tower of London. Three years later he was exiled to France where he died in obscurity at the Château de Hélicourt, his ancestral home, in 1314.

As for Edward, he proceeded from Montrose as far north as Moray. To consolidate his conquest, on his return journey not only did he take what he wanted from the Scottish treasury held in Edinburgh Castle but, more importantly in the long run, he took the Stone of Destiny with him from Scone. The stone was then set in what became known as the Coronation Chair and placed in the chapel of St Edward the Confessor in Westminster Abbey. It was to be a formidable symbol of English domination and, save for a spirited attempt to return it in 1950 during which it was broken, it was to remain in Westminster Abbey until it was returned to Scotland in 1996.

The Scots did not take Edward's conquest lying down. Almost immediately there were outbreaks of rebellion against the English Government in occupation which Edward had imposed. By the following year two principal leaders of the Scottish uprising had emerged: one was William Wallace; and the other was an unsung hero called Andrew Moray who had been captured at the Battle of Dunbar, imprisoned at Chester and later escaped.

By the summer of 1297, the English had little control over Scotland north of the Forth. With a view to relieving the siege of Dundee Castle, Edward's Lieutenant in Scotland, the Earl of Surrey (who happened also to be Sir John de Balliol's father-in-law) mustered an army and marched from his stronghold in Edinburgh towards Stirling to cross the Forth by the wooden bridge, about a mile upstream from where the Old Bridge stands today. Wallace and Moray, having combined forces, marched to meet Surrey and pitched camp on Abbey Craig Hill to the north of the river awaiting developments. On 11 September, expecting the Scots to wait chivalrously until he had crossed the bridge and deployed his forces for battle, Surrey ordered his army to cross. The bridge was narrow and, when only part of the army had crossed, the Scots attacked. Isolated on the north side of the

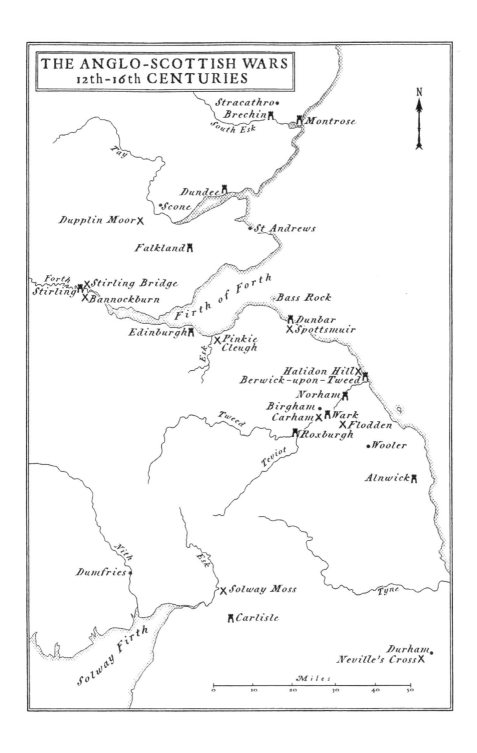

THE ANGLO-SCOTTISH WARS
12th-16th CENTURIES

N

Stracathro
Brechin
South Esk
Montrose

Tay

Dundee
Scone
Dupplin Moor
Falkland
St Andrews

Forth
Stirling Bridge
Stirling
Bannockburn
Firth of Forth
Bass Rock
Dunbar
Spottsmuir
Edinburgh
Esk
Pinkie Cleugh

Halidon Hill
Berwick-upon-Tweed
Norham
Birgham
Carham
Wark
Flodden
Roxburgh
Tweed
Wooler
Teviot
Alnwick

Nith
Dumfries
Esk
Solway Moss
Tyne
Carlisle

Solway Firth
Durham
Neville's Cross

Miles
0   10   20   30   40   50

river, the English vanguard was hacked to pieces. Reinforcement by the rest of Surrey's forces was hampered by the collapse of the bridge. Seeing what had happened, the remainder of the English fled.

Moray was mortally wounded in the battle and the Scots, now under Wallace's sole command, were unable to sustain the momentum of their victory. A year later, Edward invaded Scotland once more and on 22 July 1298 managed to engage the Scots in a pitched battle near Falkirk. Although the Scots were defeated, Wallace escaped, resigned his command and went on the run. His luck ran out in 1305 when he was captured, taken to London and barbarously executed as a traitor.

The void was filled on 25 March 1306 when Sir Robert de Brus, better known as Robert the Bruce, was crowned at Scone as King Robert I of Scotland. He was another of those who had claimed the throne in 1290 and who had fixed his seal to the 'Ragman' the following year. Not only had he done homage to Edward at that stage, but he had fought for Edward against the Scottish invasion which had led to the English conquest. However, by the summer of 1297 he had had a change of heart and joined the Scottish rebellion. In the light of Balliol's failings, he had been progressively recognised as having a better claim to the throne.[88] Finally, he disposed of his nearest rival by having him murdered, thus freeing his path to the throne. The victim was his cousin, John Comyn, whom he had lured to confer with him at the house of the Minorite Friars in Dumfries and there had him killed in the Greyfriars Church (slightly to the west of where the present church stands today).

In 1307 Edward I died and was succeeded by his ineffectual and divisive son, Edward II, who seven years later presided over the greatest defeat that the English were ever to suffer at the hands of the Scots.

In April 1314 Robert the Bruce's brother, Edward, Earl of Carrick, invaded England by way of Carlisle, laying waste to much of the surrounding country supposedly in retribution for the failure of the landowners to pay tribute due to the King of Scotland. Robert also recaptured Edinburgh and Roxburgh Castles and had laid siege to Stirling Castle, all formidable strongholds (Roxburgh commanding the confluence of the Tweed and the Teviot just west of Kelso, little of which remains today). King Edward therefore marched north and in June approached Stirling not only to relieve the English garrison but also to engage the Scots who were then assembled in strength in the wooded park which lay to the south of the castle. On 23

June an English advance guard entered the park and was attacked and put to flight by the Scots, Robert the Bruce among them killing Sir Henry de Bohun with his battle-axe. At the same time another detachment of the English army had made a detour on open ground round the east side of the park where they too were engaged and routed by the Scots. Dispirited by the events of the day, the English army spent the night on open ground between the River Forth and the Bannockburn to the east of the park.

The Scots had been on the point of striking camp and marching that night towards safer ground in the region of Loch Lomond, when Sir Alexander de Seton, having secretly deserted the English camp, found Robert the Bruce in the park, told him that the English had lost heart and encouraged him to attack. Thus it was that at sunrise the following day the Scots marched out of the park in three dense columns of infantry and went into the attack. The English rapidly mounted their horses, but were no match for the dense array of pikes presented by the Scots infantry (a formation known as a schiltron), the Scots having been trained to kill the horses with their pikes first so as to rob their riders of their advantage. Driven back by the Scots in confusion into the Bannockburn, huge numbers of the English were killed. Among those who managed to flee from the mayhem that followed was King Edward, who beat off the pursuing Scots with his mace. His charger having been impaled by a pike, the King was forced to change horses and with difficulty escaped, ultimately taking refuge at Dunbar with his wife's lover, Roger Mortimer (later created 1st Earl of March).

Despite this catastrophic defeat, hostilities continued sporadically until Edward II died, or at least disappeared, and was succeeded by his young son, Edward III, in 1327. Having been defeated by the Scots at Stanhope in Weardale that year, Isabella, the Queen Mother and Regent of England, together with Mortimer, opened negotiations for peace which culminated in the Treaty of Edinburgh-Northampton in 1328.[89] The treaty provided not only for peace between the two kingdoms but also for the marriage, when they came of age, of Robert the Bruce's son and heir, David, with Edward III's sister, Joan; for the recognition of Scotland as wholly independent of England; and for the payment of £20,000 sterling by the King of Scotland to the King of England over a period of three years. The prior deed of subjection and homage to be done by the King of Scots to the King of England, the 'Ragman' of 1291, was returned to the Scots; but, despite orders from the English Privy Council, the English refused to return the Stone of Destiny.[90]

As ever, the peace was short-lived. In 1329 Robert died and was succeeded by his then five-year-old son as David II, Scotland being ruled during his minority by a succession of guardians. In 1332 Edward Balliol, son of Sir John de Balliol (who had died in 1314) and thus a contender for the Scottish throne, raised a rebellion, invaded Scotland, defeated the Scots loyal to King David at Dupplin Moor and was crowned at Scone. Although he was driven out of Scotland a few months later, in the following year, with the support of Edward III and English forces, he routed the Scots loyal to David at Halidon Hill, just outside Berwick-upon-Tweed.[91] Faced by this setback, David was spirited away to France. There he sought the help of King Philippe VI to recover his kingdom, doing homage for it to Philippe in return, thus accepting Philippe's sovereignty over Scotland.

Meanwhile, fulfilling a promise previously made to Edward III in return for his support, Edward Balliol now claimed to be King of Scotland, acknowledged Edward III as the lord paramount of the whole of Scotland and, by a charter dated 12 June 1334, purported to cede to Edward with all regalities 'the town, castle and county of Roxburgh, the town, castle and forest of Jedburgh, the town and county of Selkirk, the forests of Selkirk and Ettrick, the town, castle and county of Edinburgh, with the constabularies of Haddington and Linlithgow, the town, castle and county of Peebles and the town, castle and county of Dumfries'.[92]

Not only had Edward Balliol purportedly handed over all of the Scottish border counties to England, ostensibly for all time, but in the space of a year the two rival Scottish kings had surrendered Scotland to another king, one French and the other English. However, that state of affairs was not to last long.

On St Andrew's Day 1335 Sir Andrew Moray, son of the erstwhile victor at Stirling Bridge and Guardian of Scotland, defeated forces loyal to Balliol at Culblean in Aberdeenshire and the tide of Scottish fortunes began to turn. Following Moray's death in 1338, he was succeeded as Guardian by Robert Stewart, a grandson of Robert the Bruce and future king. By 1340, Stewart had cleared the English from Scotland north of the Forth and on 17 April 1341 Edinburgh Castle was recaptured after Sir William Douglas (the Knight of Liddesdale) and his men gained entry hidden in haywains delivering fodder to the garrison. In June that year David II returned from France to take over his kingdom. Then over the next two years much of the border counties which had been ceded by Edward Balliol were retaken, leaving only Roxburgh Castle and Berwick-upon-Tweed in English hands, where they remained until the Wars of the Roses over a century later.

Following the resounding victory of the English over the French at Crécy on 26 August 1346, King Philippe, invoking the Auld Alliance, encouraged David to create a diversion by attacking the English on their home ground – encouragement that he took to heart, but with disastrous consequences. David marshalled an army, crossed the border into Cumberland and marched east, reducing Liddel Castle and sacking Lanercost and Hexham Priories as he went.[93] He arrived outside Durham on 16 October and pitched camp in the park of Beaurepaire (now Bearpark) to enjoy his success. From there he sent out plundering parties, unaware that a large English army had been rapidly assembled by the Archbishop of York at Bishop Auckland, only 8 miles to the south. The following day the English army pushed north-east to forestall an expected raid on Darlington and in dense fog at the little town of Merrington surprised a Scottish raiding party under the command of Sir William Douglas.

The Scots were put to flight, but Sir William managed to escape and to warn David of the danger he was in. Initially David refused to believe that an army large enough to pose a threat could have been mustered by the English so soon after Crécy. This delay allowed the English to take up an advantageous position on Red Hill where there was an ancient cross, known as Neville's Cross (coincidentally the same name as one of the English commanders, Ralph Neville), in sight of David's camp at Beaurepaire. Spurred into action, the Scots advanced towards the English position, but the terrain was such that they had to divide their forces either side of a small gully. Hampered by the gully and deserted by the division commanded by Robert Stewart, the Scots were routed. Whether Robert Stewart had deserted the battlefield to secure his own claim to the throne or simply to secure Scotland against the consequences of defeat may never be known.

David managed to escape from the field, unarmed and wounded by an arrow in his face, but he was captured shortly afterwards and spent the next eleven years as a prisoner of Edward III in the Tower of London. His captivity was finally brought to an end by an indenture made at Berwick-upon-Tweed on 3 October 1357 between commissioners acting respectively for Robert Stewart, as Guardian of Scotland, and Edward III by which David was ransomed for the enormous sum of 100,000 marks sterling payable over ten years, the payment being secured by hostages.[94]

A further indenture made at Westminster in 1363 recorded that the Privy Councils of Scotland and England had agreed that if David died without an heir he should be succeeded by the King of England. However, the agreement was rejected by the Scottish Parliament the following year.[95]

In 1371 David did die without an heir and, rather than being succeeded by the King of England, he was succeeded by the Guardian, Robert Stewart. Robert was the heir presumptive. He was the nephew of David and a grandson of Robert the Bruce, his mother, Marjorie, being the daughter of Robert the Bruce by Isabella of Mar. His succession accorded with a statute of the Scottish Parliament which had been enacted in 1318 during the reign of Robert the Bruce. Within months of his coronation he had renewed the Auld Alliance with France.[96] Thus began the reign of the House of Stewart (later Stuart) which, more than three centuries later, was to lead to the union between England and Scotland.

Robert Stewart, as Robert II, died in 1390 and was succeeded by his son John, known (confusingly) as Robert III. Robert III had been badly injured when he was kicked by a horse some years earlier and had withdrawn from affairs of state. In 1399 his heir, David, Duke of Rothesay, was appointed as Lieutenant of Scotland under the supervision of the King's jealous and manipulative younger brother, the Duke of Albany. Following a dispute between them, David was imprisoned by Albany in Falkland Castle where he died in 1402, leaving Robert III's eight-year-old son, James, as the only surviving heir. Following a clash with Albany's allies and fearing a plot by Albany to assassinate him, in February 1406 James fled to the Bass Rock in the Firth of Forth. Arrangements were then made for him to take refuge in France with his ally, Charles VI. Accompanied by the Earl of Orkney and the Bishop of St Andrews, he boarded a ship at the Bass Rock bound for France. As ill luck would have it, on 30 March 1406 the ship was seized by pirates off Flamborough Head. Although the Bishop managed to escape, James and the Earl of Orkney were taken to Windsor and delivered captive to the English King, Henry IV, later being transferred to the Tower of London. When Robert heard the news of his son's capture, he appears to have lost the will to live and died a few days later.

So it was that James I of Scotland spent the first eighteen years of his reign as a prisoner of the English King in the Tower of London. His release was purchased by the Treaty of London between James and Henry VI, which was executed on their behalf on 4 December 1423.[97] The treaty required James to pay a ransom of 'forty thousand pounds of good and legal money of England' in half-yearly instalments of 10,000 merks secured by hostages. This was yet another enormous debt to the English Crown with which Scotland was burdened. The catalyst for the treaty was the English desire for peace with Scotland to free up resources for her continuing war with France. It was augmented by the marriage between James and Lady Jane Beaufort, a cousin of Henry VI, the following year.

Much of the reigns of James I, James II and James III was devoted to the pacification of their own kingdom. However, the final piece of the jigsaw of Scotland was put in place during the reign of James III.

Orkney and Shetland

The names of Orkney and Shetland are derived from Old Norse, Orkney from *Orkneyjar* (meaning Seal Islands) and Shetland from *Hjaltland* (possibly a reference to the shape of the islands being like the hilt of a sword). Medieval documents referred to Orkney and Shetland as the *Nordr-eyjar* or Nordreys (Northern Isles) to distinguish them from the Hebrides and the Isle of Man, called the *Sudr-eyjar* or Sudreys (Southern Isles), a name still reflected in that of the diocese of Sodor and Man and in the county of Sutherland as lying to the south of the Northern Isles.

When Harald Fairhair, King of Norway, invaded Orkney and Shetland in about 874, he killed any of the Vikings who had not fled to sea, and established Ragnvald, Earl of Møre, as Jarl (earl – the word being derived from *jarl*) of Orkney and Shetland, albeit that Ragnvald then gave the lands and earldom to his brother, Sigurd. Sigurd, poor man, came to an unfortunate end: having slain the Scottish Earl Maelbrigte Tooth, and fastened Maelbrigte's head to his saddle straps, he grazed his leg on one of Maelbrigte's protruding teeth and died soon after from the infected wound.

Following Harald's conquest, Orkney and Shetland became part of the kingdom of Norway. In 1194 Sverre Sigurdarson, a Faroese opportunist who had taken the Norwegian throne, detached Shetland from the Orkney earldom and ruled it directly in reprisal for a rebellion led by the then Earl of Orkney, Harald Maddadarson, but the two were reunited in 1379 when Henry Sinclair (originally Henri St Clair) became Earl of Orkney and was invested with the title of Lord of Shetland by King Haakon VI.

As a result of a series of dynastic arrangements, the three kingdoms of Denmark, Norway and Sweden were united under one crown by virtue of the Union of Kalmar, so named after the coronation in 1397 of Margaret as Queen of the three kingdoms in the town of Kalmar in Sweden, close to the then border with Denmark. Margaret had thus become the sovereign of the islands of Orkney and Shetland. Between 1448 and 1450 Christian I (not a descendant of Margaret) was elected successively to the thrones of Denmark, Norway and Sweden. In 1468 his daughter, Margaret, was betrothed to James III of Scotland. To that end, a treaty was concluded in Copenhagen on 8 September 1468 for the payment by Christian of a dowry.[98] Christian, as King of Norway, agreed to forgive the debts of the King of Scotland long overdue under the Treaty of Perth (1266) for the acquisition of the Hebrides and the Isle of Man. He also promised to pay 60,000 Rhenish florins (gold coins of considerable value), 10,000 being payable to the Scottish procurators before their return to Scotland from Denmark and payment of the balance being secured by a pledge over all of his rights in Orkney.

Largely as a result of the cost which he had incurred to secure his three crowns, Christian was by this time seriously short of money and managed to pay only 2,000 florins out of the 10,000 florins which were then due. To secure the balance, on 20 May 1469 he pledged all of his rights in Shetland.[99]

Margaret and James were married at Holyrood two months later. Unfortunately for Norway, King Christian defaulted on his promises of payment and, as a result, his rights in Orkney and Shetland were forfeited to the Scottish Crown. A contemporary Scottish chronicler recorded that the Scots gained a good queen into the bargain: 'She deemed it a greater thing to be queen of Scotland than daughter of a king who wears three crowns.'[100]

Although Christian was the sovereign of Orkney and Shetland, under the Norwegian system of land tenure (known as udal tenure)[101] he did not have title to those parts of the islands which had been granted to the Earl of Orkney in 1379. Those parts were not, therefore, forfeited as a result of Christian's default. However, the Earl agreed to cede them to the King of Scotland in return for lands in Fife, effect being given to the cession by an act of annexation by the Scottish Parliament passed on 20 February 1472.[102]

Although various attempts were made by Christian's successors to redeem the pledge, they were always rebuffed and Orkney and Shetland have remained (questionably at least) part of the kingdom of Scotland ever since.

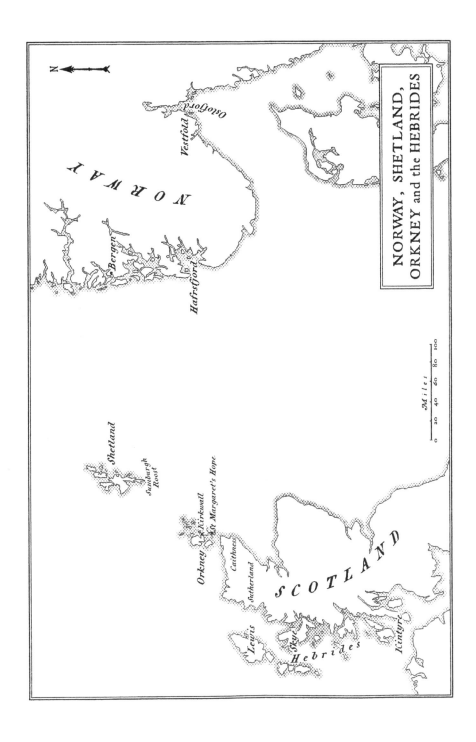

NORWAY, SHETLAND, ORKNEY and the HEBRIDES

Even now there is some vestigial doubt over whether sovereignty was ever effectively transferred. An Act of the Scottish Parliament of 1469 provided that the right to redeem the pledge would be lost by prescription after forty years, but a lingering doubt remains as to whether it could ever have had that effect.[103]

The surrender of Berwick-upon-Tweed

Berwick-upon-Tweed lies on the north bank of the Tweed estuary and was thus outwith the border of Northumberland. Its castle (now in ruins) stood on the hill that commands the final bend in the estuary, close to what is now the northern end of the magnificent Victorian railway bridge.[104] Both the town and the castle had been in English hands since Edward III's victory at Halidon Hill in 1333 and their formal cession by Edward Balliol the following year.

By 1460 the Wars of the Roses for the English throne between the Lancastrian faction of Henry VI and Richard, Duke of York, were in full swing. Taking advantage of the civil war in England, the Scots took the opportunity to secure their position in the north. In the summer of 1460 they laid siege to Roxburgh Castle, about 25 miles upstream from Berwick-upon-Tweed. It too had been ceded to the English by Edward Balliol in 1334. On 3 August, King James II was killed by an explosion of one of his own cannons engaged in the siege and was succeeded by his young son as James III. But redemption for the Scots was at hand, for a few days later Roxburgh Castle fell, leaving Berwick-upon-Tweed alone in English hands.

On 30 December 1460 Richard, Duke of York, was killed at the Battle of Wakefield and was succeeded by his son, Edward. The following year Edward avenged his father's death by crushing the Lancastrian army at the Battle of Towton. The battle had been fought in the snow on Palm Sunday, 29 March, and was the greatest and bloodiest ever fought on English soil. In the face of such defeat, Henry VI and his family fled to Scotland, where they were fortunate enough to be welcomed by the regency council acting for the young King James. Whether it was a condition of his refuge in Scotland or merely to find favour, Henry, as King of England, handed over the town and castle of Berwick-upon-Tweed to the Scots.[105]

With his victory at Towton, Edward seized the English throne and was crowned as Edward IV in Westminster Abbey on 28 June 1461. Not to be outdone, Henry's redoubtable wife, Margaret, sought help from her cousin, Pierre de Brézé, from her uncle, the King of France, and from the Scots. Although her endeavours received some support, they met with little success and came to an end after the Scots concluded a truce with England in December 1463, by the terms of which they agreed, among other things, to withhold support from Henry and his family.[106] The truce was then extended by the Treaty of York the following year and extended further the year after that by the Treaty of Newcastle.

Henry, now a fugitive, was captured. He was then held by Edward in the Tower of London, where, after a short-lived restoration to the throne, he died a prisoner in 1471.

In 1474, in furtherance of the truce which had been concluded a decade earlier, Edward and James agreed that James's infant son and heir, the future James IV, and Cecily, the youngest daughter of Edward, should, when they came of age, be married, the dowry being 20,000 marks of English money to be paid at once by instalments.[107]

By the spring of 1480, notwithstanding the plans for a royal marriage and the truce which was still in force, the border raids of the Scots had become intolerable and Edward also feared an invasion in the north following an alliance between James and Louis XI of France. So it was that on 12 May Edward appointed his brother, Richard, Duke of Gloucester (the future Richard III), as Lieutenant-General of the North with power to raise troops. That winter Gloucester reinforced every garrison on the border and raised levies ready for a campaign against the Scots. During 1481 James, anticipating an English attack, had also raised a large army and made three separate raids over the border, all of which in the event had been successfully repulsed.

Then in May 1482 James's younger brother and bitter rival, Alexander, Duke of Albany, having previously taken refuge from James in France, landed in England with a view ostensibly to aiding Edward's campaign against the Scots loyal to James, but in reality to wrest the crown of Scotland from his brother for himself. That same month, Gloucester swept north and sacked Dumfries. On 11 June a treaty was concluded at Fotheringhay Castle in Northamptonshire between Edward and Albany under which Edward agreed to help Albany to seize the crown of Scotland if Albany would procure the annulment of his recent marriage to Anne de la Tour and marry Edward's daughter, Cecily (notwithstanding Cecily's earlier betrothal to James's son), surrender Berwick-upon-Tweed and other border lands to Edward, recognise Edward's sovereignty over Scotland and renounce the alliance with France. The following day Edward appointed Gloucester as commander of the English army in Scotland.[108]

In early July Gloucester marshalled an army of 22,500 men at Alnwick and proceeded together with the Duke of Albany towards Berwick-upon-Tweed. When the townspeople saw the huge English army across the river, they surrendered the town without a fight, but not the castle. Having left 4,000 men to besiege the castle, Gloucester marched onward with the rest of his army towards Edinburgh.

To meet this English invasion, James mustered his forces and pitched camp at Lauder. It was while at Lauder that the Earl of Angus and other disaffected nobles seized six of the King's servants, whom they regarded as having a pernicious influence over the King, and hanged them from a nearby bridge. This barbarity led to mutiny among the Scots and their army melted away. The King therefore fled to what he hoped would be the safety of Edinburgh Castle and either shut himself away or possibly was held prisoner there by his uncle, the Duke of Atholl. When Albany and Gloucester reached Edinburgh at the head of the English army, they were unable to obtain any answer from the King to their demands that the terms of the previous truce should be honoured and that he should give redress for the previous violations of it. In the light of this impasse, the Earl of Argyll, the Archbishop of St Andrews and others assured Albany that, if he changed sides, he would be restored to his former dignities and possessions. Having accepted these assurances, Albany left Gloucester's protection, joined the Scottish nobles and was immediately declared by them to be the Lieutenant of Scotland. With his new-found power, Albany then concluded a truce with Gloucester. However, as the price for peace, Gloucester insisted on the surrender of Berwick Castle (not just the town) and the repayment of that part of the dowry for Cecily which had already been paid to James. Gloucester then withdrew to Berwick-upon-Tweed. Having withstood the siege, the castle was surrendered to him on 24 August 1482.[109] Berwick-upon-Tweed has remained an anomalous outpost of England ever since.

As for the Duke of Albany, he never succeeded in wresting power from James, having lost his greatest supporter with the death of Edward IV in April 1483.

Prelude to union with England

On 11 June 1488, James III was thrown from his horse during a battle against Scottish rebels at Sauchieburn, south of Stirling. Badly injured by his fall, he was carried to a nearby mill. There he called for a priest to give him absolution, but an assassin masquerading as a priest stabbed him to death. He was succeeded by his son, James IV.

Fourteen years later, to put an end to the constant skirmishing across the border with England and to Scotland's Auld Alliance with France, a Treaty of Perpetual Peace was concluded between James IV and Henry VII.[110] The bait was the promise of marriage between Henry's daughter, Margaret Tudor, and James. It was that marriage in 1503 which set the first scene of the union between Scotland and England.

The peace for which the treaty provided did not last long. In 1511 a Holy League was formed between the Pope, the King of Spain and the Doge of Venice which called for the partition of France. The League was then joined by Henry VIII, who had succeeded his father as King of England two years earlier. In July 1512, convinced that the stability of Europe depended on the survival of France, James renewed the Auld Alliance. The following year, Henry VIII invaded France, prompting the French King, Louis XII, to call on James to create a diversion by invading England, just as Philippe VI had called on David II following his defeat at Crécy, and with the same disastrous consequences for Scotland.

Having formally declared war on England some days earlier, on 22 August 1513 James crossed the border at Coldstream with a vast army which had been collected from every corner of Scotland, including the Western Isles. With them they brought heavy cannon, mainly of Flemish make. The footsoldiers had been equipped by the King of France with the Swiss pike, all of 15 feet long, instead of the old and much shorter spear and bill (or halberd). Philippe had also sent forty French officers to instruct the army in the Continental method of war. Initially all went well, the Scots successfully taking the border castles south of the Tweed at Norham, Etal, Chillingham and Ford. James took up quarters at Ford and the army pitched camp on the banks of the River Till close by. There they waited for the inevitable English reaction.[111]

Before his departure for France, anticipating trouble, Henry VIII had appointed the Earl of Surrey to defend the border against any trouble from the north. By 3 September, Surrey at the head of an English army had reached Alnwick and a few days later reached Wooler, only 6 miles from the Scottish camp. No doubt with the advice of the French officers, James then took up an almost impregnable position on nearby Flodden Edge, facing south-east towards Wooler. Given James's position, Surrey sent a message to him proposing in medieval fashion that they should fight on 'indifferent ground' between their two camps, a proposal that James rejected out of hand, saying that he would fight where and when he chose.[112]

Faced with James's rejection, Surrey made an astonishingly bold decision: he decided to attack the Scots from the rear, not only exposing England to a Scottish invasion but also risking his line of retreat and, worse still, being hemmed in by the formidable obstacle of the Tweed to what would then be his own rear. On 8 September the English marched north, leaving Flodden Edge 5 miles to their west, and sheltering for the night in Barmoor Wood. At dawn the following day in the pouring rain they resumed their march, the van under the command of Surrey's son, Admiral Thomas Howard, crossing the River Till at Twizel Bridge and the rear under Surrey's own command at Milford Bridge, both then turning south towards Branxton. Seeing the English approaching from the north, James shifted his position from Flodden Edge to the top of Branxton Hill, immediately to the north and almost as advantageous.

Although the Scots could readily have charged down Branxton Hill and attacked the English while they were still deploying, they did not do so, preferring to retain their strong defensive position. The English therefore formed up along the ridge at the foot of Branxton Hill and the battle was begun with an artillery bombardment from both sides. The defensive strategy of the Scots began to unravel when Lord Home's Borderers on the left wing, following up an early success, pursued their enemy down the hill, prompting the Scottish centre to be ordered forward too, leaving their right wing on the crest of the hill. The Borderers, more interested in looting the bodies of the fallen than continuing the fight, were successfully attacked by Lord Dacre's reserves, allowing Lord Dacre to join the mêlée against the Scottish centre. In the meantime, Sir Edward Stanley had managed to lead a flanking force to the top of the hill and to take the Scottish right by surprise before charging down the hill and attacking the Scottish centre from the rear. The Scottish centre, having been raked by cannon fire on their way down the hill, were now hemmed in on all sides and cut to pieces, their long Swiss pikes becoming more of a hindrance than an advantage at close quarters against the billhooks of the English. There they fought bravely to the last, the few survivors staggering as best they could from the field, including Lord Home who was subsequently executed as a traitor for his efforts.

Among the dead lay King James – the last king of either kingdom to die on the field of battle. Ironically, his widow, Margaret, was none other than the sister of the victor, Henry VIII. She now became the Regent for her one-year-old son, James V.

With the failure of the Treaty of Perpetual Peace culminating in the defeat of the Scots at Flodden, the Auld Alliance with France was renewed once more, this time by the Treaty of Rouen in 1517. The treaty not only provided for the mutual protection of both kingdoms against England but also for the betrothal of the eldest daughter of François I, King of France, to King James should her betrothal to the King of Spain or his brother fall through.[113] Twenty years later, on New Year's Day 1537, James married Madeleine, the elder daughter of François. The marriage had been arranged by a revision to the Treaty of Rouen the previous year. Although in an attempt to placate Henry VIII François had tried to substitute his younger daughter, Marie, for Madeleine under the arrangement, it was too late because James had already fallen in love with Madeleine. But the marriage was tragically short. Having been taken back to Scotland by her husband, the frail Madeleine was killed by the damp before the year was out.

Anxious to perpetuate the Auld Alliance, not least as support against his fractious relations, James V sent envoys to France with instructions to find a pleasing young woman of suitable rank and known fertility, capable of bearing healthy sons. By the end of the following year the envoys had selected a young widow of royal lineage who had already borne a son: she was Marie de Guise-Lorraine. Her marriage to James was celebrated by proxy in the cathedral of Nôtre-Dame in Paris in May 1539. Marie then sailed for Scotland, landing in Fife, where she was met by James. The two were married in person in St Andrews Cathedral that June. The marriage infuriated Henry VIII, who had himself lighted on Marie as a prospective bride, following the death of his third wife, Jane Seymour.

Provoked by the refusal of James to follow him and break with the Church of Rome and provoked too by an offer from some Irish Catholic chiefs of the crown of Ireland to James, Henry VIII proclaimed himself Lord-Superior of Scotland and invaded the country. James responded by invading England. But, unsupported by his nobles, his fractious and feebly led army was routed by a small and vastly outnumbered band of Borderers under the skilful command of the Warden of the English West March, Sir Thomas Wharton, at the Battle of Solway Moss, on the English side of the River Esk just south of Longtown on 24 November 1542. To make matters worse, the retreating Scots were mercilessly attacked and plundered by Scottish reivers as they fled north.

In the meantime, Marie had borne James two sons in quick succession, but tragically both of them died within days of each other: the second was either stillborn or died within two days of his birth in April 1541; and the first died supposedly of measles a few days later, inevitably fuelling rumours that both of them had been poisoned. Then, on 8 December 1542, Marie gave birth, not to a hoped-for son, but to a daughter, Mary. James, already ill and sick at heart following the humiliating defeat of the Scots at Solway Moss, died within a fortnight of hearing the news of his daughter's birth. So little Mary became Queen of Scots.

Determined to make himself master of Scotland and to secure an ally against Catholic France, Henry VIII lost no time in arranging for the marriage of his infant son, Edward, to Mary. The arrangement was contained in one of the two Treaties of Greenwich (the other providing for peace between the two kingdoms) sealed on behalf of Mary and with the great seal of Henry VIII on 1 July 1543 and ratified by the Earl of Arran, the Governor of Scotland, the following month.[114] However, Mary's mother, Marie de Guise, had other ideas. Before the year was out, she had procured Mary's coronation in the Chapel Royal in Stirling Castle, the renewal of the Auld Alliance with France and the repudiation of the relevant Treaty of Greenwich by the Scottish Parliament.

Thwarted by Marie's machinations, in the summer of 1544 Henry invaded Scotland, laying waste to the borders so viciously that it left an indelible scar on the Scots and became known euphemistically as 'the rough wooing'. Although Henry died in 1547, his war against the Scots was continued by the Duke of Somerset as regent for the young King, Edward VI. The war was ended with another humiliating defeat of the Scots, this time at Pinkie Cleugh on the banks of another River Esk, the one which flows into the Firth of Forth near Musselburgh, on Saturday 10 September 1547, a day known to the Scots ever since as 'Black Saturday'.

Thoroughly defeated, the Scots turned once more to France. On 7 July

1548 at the nunnery of Haddington a treaty was executed by the Earl of Arran on behalf of Mary and by André de Montalembert, sieur d'Essé, as envoy of the King of France, Henri II, by which it was agreed that, in return for French military support, Mary should marry the King's son, the Dauphin François, when he came of age.[115] Ten years later, on Sunday 24 April 1558, the two were married in Nôtre-Dame, as a result of which not only did Mary become the Dauphine of France, but François became the King of Scotland. The latter had been agreed by the formal contract of marriage which had been concluded a few days earlier and witnessed by Protestant and Catholic Scottish Commissioners alike. The contract also provided that, on the accession of François to the throne of France, the two kingdoms should be united under one crown, all Scots being granted the privileges of French citizens and all French the privileges of Scottish citizens.[116] This formal contract had been preceded by three secret documents, witnessed by Mary's family and the Catholic Scottish Commissioners alone, by the first of which Mary had agreed that, in the event of her death without children, her rights to the throne of England were to pass to the King of France.[117]

It was during her time at the French court that Mary adopted the French spelling of her name, signing herself 'Marie Stuart'. So the House of Stewart became the House of Stuart.

On 17 November 1558, the English Queen, a staunch Catholic and known by Protestants as Bloody Mary, died. In the eyes of the Catholic Church her legitimate successor was Mary, Queen of Scots – Elizabeth, Henry VIII's daughter by Anne Boleyn, being illegitimate. Nonetheless, Elizabeth succeeded to the English throne by virtue of an Act of the English Parliament.[118] However, so long as Elizabeth remained unmarried, Mary had the strongest claim to be Elizabeth's successor to the English throne, being a great-granddaughter of Henry VII and thus a first cousin once removed of Elizabeth.

Henri II died in 1559 and was succeeded by François. Mary was now not only Queen of Scotland and pretender to the English throne but Queen of France too. Early in 1560 her mother, who had been acting as Regent of Scotland in her daughter's absence since 1554, despatched a French army to Scotland to further the Catholic cause there; her Protestant opponents (among them notably the firebrand John Knox) had received support from the forces of Queen Elizabeth pursuant to a treaty between them which had been concluded at Berwick on 27 February 1560.[119] Mary's mother having died in June 1560, hostilities were brought to an end by a treaty concluded in Edinburgh on 6 July 1560 between commissioners representing the French and English Crowns, with the assent of the Scottish Lords of the Congregation.[120] Under that treaty, all foreign forces were to be withdrawn from Scotland, Mary and François were to abandon the arms and style of sovereigns of England, the Scottish Parliament was authorised to meet but not to deal with the religious question, which was reserved to the King and Queen, and various concessions were made to the Scottish people. Importantly, the treaty expressly recognised that Elizabeth was the lawful heir to the English throne. It was Mary's resolute refusal ever to ratify it,[121] at least without concessions on Elizabeth's part, that ultimately sealed her fate.

Notwithstanding the terms of the treaty, in August the Scottish Parliament (known as the Reformation Parliament) approved two Acts, one to break with Rome[122] and the other to establish the Protestant religion in Scotland,[123] Acts to which Mary also refused her assent.[124] It is a strange irony that, had Mary had her way and Scotland remained Catholic, it is almost inconceivable that her son, James VI, would have succeeded to the throne of England on the death of his cousin Elizabeth in 1603 and improbable that the two kingdoms would have been united in 1707.

In December 1560 François died, suffering from crippling earache. Five years later Mary married her cousin, the feckless Lord Darnley. Once her initial love for him had evaporated, Darnley's only virtues from Mary's perspective were that, as a grandchild (like Mary) of Margaret Tudor, he was next in line to the English throne after Mary, he was a Catholic and, in due course, he fathered her son and heir, James (the future James VI and I). However, within months of James's birth in 1566, Darnley was found dead after a mysterious explosion in the house where he was staying at Kirk o' Field outside Edinburgh, probably murdered by Mary's lover, the Earl of Bothwell, with Mary's connivance. It was the assumed murder of Darnley and Mary's subsequent marriage to Bothwell that precipitated her capture, imprisonment on Loch Leven by the Regent of Scotland (her half-brother, the Protestant Earl of Moray) and her abdication which she was forced to sign on 25 July 1567.[125] Four days later, her thirteen-month-old son was crowned James VI of Scotland in the Protestant church at Stirling.

Mary's first attempt to escape from Loch Leven disguised as a washerwoman was thwarted when the boatman spotted her implausibly white hands. Her second attempt, however, was successful, when a young accomplice managed to take the keys of the castle gate from her gaoler during drunken May Day festivities. Having escaped her captors, she sought to regain her throne, but without success. On 13 May 1568 forces loyal to her were marching north from Hamilton aiming to cross the Clyde to Dumbarton Castle, only to find that their path was blocked by troops under Moray's command at the hilltop village of Langside (now swallowed by the south of Glasgow but marked by a splendid Victorian memorial). After a brief but fierce engagement, Mary's forces were routed. Mary, who had watched the battle from nearby Cathcart Hill, was rescued by her retreating cavalry and escaped south. She spent her last ever night in Scotland at Dundrennan Abbey (the fine ruins of which still stand today). From there she crossed the Solway Firth to England on 16 May 1568 and somewhat naïvely sought protection from her cousin Elizabeth, but to no avail. As a rival for the English throne, suspected of complicity in the murder of Darnley, she was imprisoned, initially at Carlisle Castle.

Having been held in various castles and houses, Mary was moved to Chartley Manor in Staffordshire at Christmas 1585. It was whilst at Chartley that she wrote the fateful letter of 17 July 1586 in cipher to Anthony Babington asking about plans for her own escape, inciting him to raise a Catholic rebellion both in Ireland and in Scotland and implicitly condoning the planned assassination of Elizabeth. Although Babington destroyed the letter, he recounted its contents after he had been caught in a sting by agents of Elizabeth's principal secretary, Sir Francis Walsingham. Mary was then moved to Fotheringhay Castle just north of Oundle, where she was tried for treason, condemned to death and, on 8 February 1587, showing great dignity and courage, she was beheaded. She was buried first in Peterborough Cathedral, although even that was delayed by the political fallout for five months, her coffin at last being taken discreetly to the cathedral under cover of darkness. Finally, twenty-five years later, on the orders of her son, James VI and I, she was exhumed and buried in Henry VII's Chapel in Westminster Abbey. It is an irony of history that her temporary resting place in the south aisle of Peterborough Cathedral, now well marked, lies opposite the grave in the north aisle of another queen who fell foul of an English monarch, Catherine of Aragon, first wife of Henry VIII.

The border revisited

By the end of the eleventh century the border between England and Scotland was known to stretch between the Solway Firth in the west and Tweedmouth in the east. Between those two points it was ill defined, and any attempt to agree where it should be was bedevilled by the perennial warfare among the Borderers by whom the land was held, given, as they were, to reiving the property of their neighbours, even far-flung neighbours, at the slightest opportunity. Such was the lawlessness of the region that by the end of the thirteenth century it had been divided into three English and three Scottish Marches, East, Middle and West, each under the command of a Warden charged with keeping the peace and administering justice in accordance with the peculiar Laws of the Marches (*Leges Marchiae*).

Although in theory the border between England and Scotland had been established as the northern boundaries of the counties of Cumberland and Northumberland by the Treaty of York in 1237, there was at that stage no agreement as to where precisely the border lay. There had been an attempt to reach agreement in 1222 which had ended in blows. In 1249 a jury of twelve English knights and twelve Scottish knights reported their findings as to the laws and customs of the Marches from which it appears that the border was customarily defined in part (at least) by the Esk in the west and by the Tweed in the east, but without anything more being found about the area in between. With charming simplicity paragraph 9 of the report says (in translation from the Latin):

> if any inhabitant of either kingdom affirmed, in opposition to a claimant of the other, that a horse, ox, cow, or hog, in his possession, was his own, he should have the usual respite of days established between the kingdoms, before the matter was brought to a trial. And on the day fixed for that, if he chose to avoid a combat, and knew that the thing was not his own, he was obliged to bring it to the marches, and inform the opposite party that he was satisfied, upon enquiry, that the horse, &c., was the property of that party, and after this declaration he was bound to drive it into the water of the Tweed or Esk; and the defendant should then be free from the claim or challenge brought against him. But if it was drowned before it reached the mid-stream of the water, the defendant ought, according to the custom of the

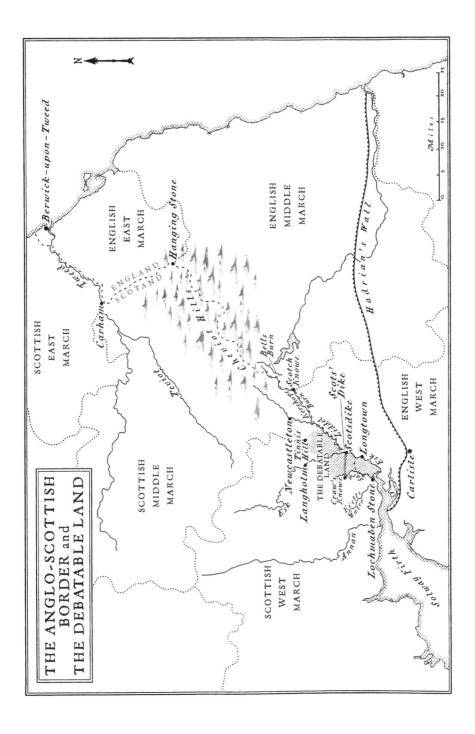

N

THE ANGLO-SCOTTISH
BORDER and
THE DEBATABLE LAND

Berwick-upon-Tweed

SCOTTISH
EAST
MARCH

ENGLISH
EAST
MARCH

ENGLAND
SCOTLAND

Hanging Stone

Carham

Tweed

Cheviot Hills

Teviot

Bells Burn

Scotch Knowe

Netherbie Burn

Newcastletons

Tinnis

Langholm Hill

THE DEBATABLE
LAND

Crawk
Knowe

Kirtle
Water

Scots'
Dike

Scotsdike

Longtown

ENGLISH
MIDDLE
MARCH

ENGLISH
WEST
MARCH

Hadrian's Wall

Carlisle

SCOTTISH
MIDDLE
MARCH

SCOTTISH
WEST
MARCH

Annan

Lochmaben Stone

Solway Firth

Miles
0 5 10 15 20 25

marches, to be still answerable for it; and this extended to an ox, cow, or swine, or other things, only nothing was established about a load.[126]

The cession of Berwick-upon-Tweed to England in 1482 extended the English border to include its bounds.[127]

Even then, there remained an area in the south-west which by that stage was known as the Debatable Land, over which neither kingdom claimed sovereignty. At its greatest extent it was about 13 miles long and 8½ miles wide and stretched from the Lochmaben Stone in the south-west to the foot of Tinnis Hill (between Langholm and Newcastleton) in the north-east. It was bounded by the Liddel Water and the Esk in the east and south and by the River Sark in the west. Although in the sixteenth century its name might have been an apt description of the lawless reiving to which it was then subject, the name appears to have reflected the ancient custom that permitted the grazing of animals on it between sunrise and sunset but it was to be deserted by night: in that ancient sense it was described as 'batable' or 'debatable'.[128]

Notwithstanding that the Scots had been roundly defeated by the forces of Edward VI at Pinkie Cleuch in 1547, the 'rough wooing' of Mary Queen of Scots was only formally ended by the Treaty of Norham between Edward, Mary and her prospective father-in-law, Henri II of France, in 1551. Under the treaty, the line of the border other than through the Debatable Land was agreed to be what it had been before the rough wooing and territory which had been taken in the recent hostilities was to be restored.[129] Unfortunately it did not specify precisely where that line was.

As a solution to the lawlessness of the Debatable Land, early in 1552 the French Ambassador to England, Claude de Laval, proposed that the whole of it should be evacuated and laid to waste. Dissatisfied with this proposal, it was later agreed between the two kingdoms that it would be better to divide the area between them. To that end commissioners were appointed, with the French Ambassador as arbiter, and on 24 September 1552 they agreed on a line to be marked by a ditch and march stones, subsequently known as Scots' Dike (or sometimes as March Bank or Dike).[130] The line is more or less straight and runs between the place named Scotsdike on the Esk in the east and Craw's Knowe on the River Sark in the west. To this day much of it can be seen as a low bank, bounded on each side by a ditch and marked (now somewhat irregularly) along the crest of the bank by pieces of roughly hewn sandstone much like milestones.

Whereas the border through the Debatable Land had now been fixed and marked, the same was not true of substantial parts of the rest of the border, beyond the agreement that it followed the line of the northern boundary of the counties of Cumberland and Northumberland. Surveys of the East and Middle Marches carried out under the supervision of Sir Robert Bowes in 1542 and 1550 identified the surveyors' understanding of the location of the border line between Kershope and Berwick-upon-Tweed but refer to numerous uncertainties.[131] A more definitive description of the line from coast to coast is to be found in Johnson and Goodwin's survey of 1604,[132] but even that is imprecise in some respects.[133]

Nevertheless, subject to that imprecision, from that day to this the border has followed the same somewhat extraordinary line. It begins on the east coast 3 miles north-west of Berwick-upon-Tweed, reaches the Tweed near Paxton, follows the Tweed to a point just beyond Carham and strikes off south-south-east to the watershed of the Cheviot Hills which it follows for 35 miles. It then follows the courses of the Bells Burn, the Kershope Burn, the Liddel and the Esk for short distances, before cutting across due west along Scots' Dike to the River Sark which it follows to its confluence with the estuary of the Esk opposite Sarkfoot Point and thence to the Solway Firth.

As might have been expected, the settling of the border line did not put an end to the reiving. That was left to Mary's son after he had acceded to the throne of England as James I in 1603.

Although much of the significance of the border as the boundary between the two sovereign states of England and Scotland disappeared following the Treaty of Union in 1707, it is striking that to this day the people living either side of it are governed by different laws, are educated in different schools, speak with different accents, practise different religions and forge few friendships across it. Strange as it may seem, the accents of the occupants of a farm on one side of the border are likely to be completely different from those of the adjoining farm on the other side of the border: the one broad Scots and the other Cumbrian or Northumbrian.

The accession of James I of England

With Mary's death, her son, James, acceded to the throne of Scotland as James VI. In an attempt to placate him and to assuage her own guilt, Queen Elizabeth sent a personal letter to him to express her regrets and to distance herself from the execution of his mother. However, such was the sense of outrage in Scotland at what had happened that James was unable to offer safe-conduct to Elizabeth's envoy, Sir Robert Carey, and the letter had to be handed over to James's emissaries at Foulden Kirk on the Scottish side of the border with Berwick-upon-Tweed.

The year before Elizabeth's own death in 1603, and no doubt in anticipation of it, a treaty had been concluded at Berwick-upon-Tweed between James and Elizabeth for a Protestant league, promising to encourage other Protestant princes to join in mutual support against invasion.[134] The treaty had been negotiated by Elizabeth's chief minister, Lord Burghley, concerned by the ever present fear of invasion by Catholic powers. James had tried to include in the treaty provisions to the effect that, if Elizabeth were to die without issue, he should succeed to the crown of England and Ireland,[135] but Elizabeth had refused to agree, although she did agree privately to support him with a pension of £4,000 a year.[136]

One of James's principal rivals for the crown of England and Ireland was his first cousin, Arabella Stuart (variously referred to as Arabella or Arbella), the daughter of Lord Darnley's younger brother and a great-great-granddaughter of Henry VII. (In 1603 Sir Walter Raleigh was condemned to death for plotting to depose James in favour of Arabella, for which he was finally executed fifteen years later.) No doubt spurred by Elizabeth's refusal to acknowledge that he was her presumptive heir, in 1601 James began secretly to exchange letters with Robert Cecil, Lord Burghley's son (the future Earl of Salisbury) and successor as Elizabeth's chief minister, to foster his claim to the crown of England and Ireland.[137]

Elizabeth died childless on 24 March 1603 and later the same day at Whitehall Gate James was proclaimed King James I of England and Ireland. The news of the Queen's death reached James at Holyrood two and a half days later by the hand of the same Sir Robert Carey who had carried Elizabeth's letter to James following the execution of his mother. Sir Robert was Elizabeth's first cousin (and possibly even her half-brother) and had been at her deathbed. Hoping to win favour with the new King, he had ridden post-haste all 397 miles from London in 60 hours (notwithstanding a bad fall during which he was kicked on the head by his horse), arriving at Holyrood after the King had gone to bed and giving him one of Elizabeth's rings as proof of her death. Although he had reached the King before Cecil's own envoys, his escapade caused resentment in London and his hopes of royal favour were disappointed at first, receiving no more than admission as one of the gentlemen of the King's bedchamber and even that he lost when the King went south. It was only later that he received preferment.

James was crowned as James I of England and Ireland in Westminster Abbey on 25 July 1603. Although often misunderstood, his coronation did not unite the crowns, let alone the kingdoms, of Scotland, England and Ireland: the two crowns (there being no crown of Ireland distinct from that of England), and indeed the two kingdoms, remained distinct until 1707.[138]

As elegantly summarised by Eileen Cassavetti, 'This culminating point in the rise of the House of Stuart held the stage to play out the concept of the divine right of kings. The century began with triumph, descended into chaos, was transformed into a brief blaze of splendour at the Restoration, and ended like a Jacobean tragedy with the leading players chased from the scene to France, to wait for the recall that never came.'[139]

The descent into chaos of the House of Stuart

James VI and I found himself in a difficult position as King of two countries which had been at each other's throats off and on for centuries. He hoped to solve that problem by uniting the two kingdoms, to put an end not only to the perennial hostilities between them but also to the lawlessness of the border. With that aim a treaty of union was agreed on 6 December 1604 by commissioners appointed under authority of both Parliaments. The Scottish Parliament passed an 'Act anent the union of Scotland and England' in 1607[140] to give effect to the treaty, but it was conditional on the English Parliament doing the same. In the event the English Parliament had the previous year passed an 'Act for the utter Abolition of all Memory of Hostility, and the Dependances thereof, between England and Scotland, and for the repressing of Occasions of Discord and Disorders in Time to come',[141] but, reflecting the objections by English merchants that there was no advantage to them, it did not give full effect to the treaty and was itself conditional on the Scottish Act being effective. With each Act being dependent on the efficacy of the other, neither took effect. The consequence was that the two kingdoms were not united as the King had hoped.

Nevertheless, James did manage to take two steps along the road to union. First, by royal proclamation he succeeded in removing some of the barriers to trade between Scotland and England; among other things and to their great advantage, the Scots and their ships were no longer treated by the English as foreign. Secondly, by 1610 he had rooted out the most lawless, not to say notorious, denizens of the border region by hanging some, exiling others and disarming the rest.

In Scotland the 'chaos' into which the House of Stuart descended was driven principally by religion. Protestantism had taken root in its Presbyterian form with the Reformation of 1560, the Church of Scotland being governed not by bishops or the king but by elders and, in time, by presbyteries and the General Assembly. Whereas James VI had managed the tensions to which they gave rise, including the Gunpowder Plot of 1605, with some degree of success, his son Charles I, by whom he had been succeeded in 1625, was, to say the least, confrontational. Within months of his father's death he married a staunch Catholic, Henrietta Maria, the daughter of Henri IV of France. He then attempted to revoke some of the consequences of the Reformation of 1560. That was followed in 1637 by his imposition of a Book of Common Prayer[142] contrary to the tenets of Presbyterianism. Its use was shouted down by the congregation of St Giles's Cathedral when first introduced; and so unpopular was it that the Bishop of Brechin felt constrained to conduct his service over a pair of loaded pistols.

The imposition of a Book of Common Prayer in turn provoked the disaffected Scots to sign the National Covenant of 1638 (thus becoming known as the Covenanters) rejecting episcopal government.[143] The reaction reached its apogee in the Solemn League and Covenant of 1643 between the Covenanting Scots and the English Parliament, seeking to impose Presbyterianism not only on Scotland but also on England and Ireland too.[144] It was by virtue of the Solemn League and Covenant that the Covenanters joined forces with the Parliamentarians against the Royalists in the Civil War that had broken out in England the year before – a war not between the two kingdoms as in the past, but between two factions which straddled both. In Scotland the Royalist forces were led by the turncoat James Graham, Marquess of Montrose, until his defeat by General Leslie at Philiphaugh in 1645.

The first stage of the Civil War ended in England the following year with the undignified escape by Charles I from the siege of Oxford dressed as a woman. On 5 May 1646 he surrendered to the Scottish Covenanters besieging Newark in the hope of arousing their loyalty – a hope that was dashed by his refusal to establish Presbyterianism. He was then handed over to the English Parliament under a deal with the Scots whereby the Scots agreed to leave England in return for a payment of £400,000.[145]

Although held under house arrest, Charles managed to escape and fled to the Isle of Wight. There, having misjudged the sympathy of the Governor, he was held in Carisbrooke Castle. Nevertheless, following secret negotiations with one faction of the Covenanters, culminating in a document known as the Engagement, which he signed at Carisbrooke on 26 December 1647, Charles promised to confirm the Solemn League and Covenant by Act of Parliament of both kingdoms, to give Presbyterianism a trial in England for three years and to endeavour to unite the two kingdoms so that they might become one, all in return for the raising of a Scottish army in support of his cause.[146] However, his cause was finally lost with the defeat of the Covenanters' forces at Preston in 1648, followed by his trial and, on 30 January 1649, his execution in Whitehall for treason.

The execution of Charles I had been ordained by the residue of the English Parliament, in which the Scots, of course, had played no part. Contact was therefore made with his eighteen-year-old son and heir, Prince Charles, who was then proclaimed King of Scotland by the leader of the Covenanters, the Marquess of Argyll, in Edinburgh. In return for signing the New Covenant and the Solemn League and Covenant at Argyll's behest, Charles landed in Scotland and, on New Year's Day 1651, was crowned by Argyll at Scone as King of Scotland (but not, of course, England or Ireland). With this new threat to the Parliamentary cause, Oliver Cromwell moved his forces to Scotland where they defeated the Scots under General Leslie at Inverkeithing on 20 July 1651. Charles then moved south with his army but was finally and utterly defeated by Cromwell at the Battle of Worcester on 3 September 1651. Unlike most of his comrades in arms, Charles managed to escape from the battlefield and, after hiding from one of Cromwell's search-parties in an oak tree at Boscobel House, fled to France.[147]

Following Cromwell's subjugation of England, Scotland and Ireland, in 1653 his Council of Officers adopted a written constitution for the government of what was to be called the Commonwealth of England, Scotland and Ireland, vesting supreme legislative power in the Lord Protector, being none other than Oliver Cromwell himself.[148] Then, on 12 April 1654, Cromwell, as Lord Protector, with the advice and consent of his Council and ostensibly with the agreement of the people of Scotland, issued an Ordinance for uniting Scotland into one Commonwealth with

England, abolishing the authority not only of the King of Scotland but of the Scottish Parliament too, albeit providing for Scotland to have thirty seats in the Commonwealth Parliament at Westminster.[149] Ironically, union had been one of the goals of the Engagement with Charles I, although not, of course, without a king. On this occasion it did not last long.

On 3 September 1658 Cromwell died. His death was followed by political turmoil which was brought to an end by General Monck, commander of the army in Scotland. The Rump Parliament (an English Parliament), having been recalled by Monck, dissolved itself and was succeeded, following an election, by another English Parliament known as the Convention Parliament in 1660. Although the House of Lords had purportedly been abolished by an Act passed by the House of Commons alone in 1649,[150] it nevertheless formed part of the Convention Parliament. In response to a series of loyal speeches in Parliament, in May 1660 Charles despatched to Parliament a document known as the Declaration of Breda[151] in which he promised to pardon offences committed during the Civil War, to require the return of property which had been confiscated, to ensure that General Monck's army was paid and freedom of religion. On receipt of this, Parliament declared that Charles II had been the lawful King of England since the execution of his father in 1649 and invited him to return from abroad. Charles landed in England on 25 May 1660. On 23 April 1661 he was crowned in Westminster Abbey as King of England, Ireland and France and later that year he was crowned for the second time at Scone as King of Scotland.

Although it did not come to light until over a century later, in 1670 Charles concluded a secret treaty with Louis XIV of France (known as the Treaty of Dover) by which he agreed to support Louis' invasion of the Dutch Republic with ships and men in return for a small share of the territory, an enormous payment and, importantly, his own public conversion to Catholicism. In the event, nothing was achieved by Charles because he was forced by Parliament to withdraw from the war against Spain that had started under the Commonwealth in league with France. Had Charles become a Catholic, or even had his promise to become a Catholic come to light, the Glorious Revolution might well have happened earlier, his younger brother, James, might never have succeeded to the throne of England or Scotland and the Jacobite (or in that event the Caroline) cause might never have flourished as it did.

The Glorious Revolution

Notwithstanding that he had been married to Catherine of Braganza for many years, Charles II died without any legitimate children in 1685. He was succeeded by his brother, James VII and II, already a Catholic convert. At that stage James had two surviving children by his first wife, Anne Hyde, both daughters, both Protestant and both married to Protestants: the elder was Mary, who was married to Prince William of Orange, and the younger was Anne, who was married to Prince George of Denmark. In 1673, after the death of Anne Hyde, James married a Catholic, Maria d'Este, the daughter of the Duke of Modena. Having suffered numerous miscarriages and stillbirths, on 10 June 1688 Maria gave birth to a healthy son, James Francis Edward, who thus became the heir apparent to the kingdoms of England, Scotland and Ireland.

To thwart the threat of a Catholic dynasty and to redress the growing discontent with the government of King James, a cabal of English conspirators approached William of Orange, the King's son-in-law. Having received favourable indications, they sent him a letter dated 30 June 1688 inviting him to invade.[152] This was an invitation that fell on fertile ground, because the Dutch Republic, of which William was by then the Stadtholder (the *de facto* head of state of the seven United Provinces of the Dutch Republic), was critically exposed to the territorial ambitions and Catholic zeal of the French King, Louis XIV, following the revocation in 1685 of the Edict of Nantes, which had granted toleration to Protestants in France. On 5 November 1688 an invasion force under William's command landed at Torbay. After some skirmishes, opposition in England rapidly collapsed and by the end of the year James and his entourage had fled to France, James having in the meantime dropped the Great Seal of England into the Thames in a fruitless attempt to put a spanner in the works of government. Although James endeavoured to recover his kingdoms, he never set foot in England again; his foray in Ireland was crushed at the Battle of the Boyne in 1690; and through lack of support nothing came of his brief return to Scotland in the winter of 1715–16.

On 22 January 1689 the English Parliament met and under considerable pressure from William agreed that he would rule as joint monarch with his wife, Mary. However, before they were offered the English throne, they were required to agree to the Declaration of Rights which had been drawn up the previous year, defining for the first time the boundaries between the powers of Parliament and the Crown on the one hand and the liberties of the subjects on the other. On 13 February 1689 William and Mary formally accepted the throne of England and on 16 December that year gave their royal assent to an Act of Parliament entitled 'Bill of Rights'.[153]

The Bill of Rights enshrined the Declaration of Rights in law, recited that James had abdicated the government and abandoned the throne, declared that William and Mary were the King and Queen of England, France and Ireland, provided for the future succession to the throne, barring Catholics for all time, and prohibited Catholics from sitting in Parliament.

In Scotland the revolution took a different course. On 10 October 1688 William issued a proclamation to Scotland in terms similar to, but shorter than, those of the English Declaration of Rights. Three months later, in January 1689, at the request of various Scottish nobles and gentry who had travelled to London to meet him, William agreed to undertake the administration of Scotland pending a convention of the estates of Parliament. On 11 April the convention adopted the Claim of Right,[154] which recited that James VII, being a professed papist, having failed to take the coronation oath and by virtue of numerous misdeeds, had forfeited the right to the crown such that the throne of Scotland was vacant; it declared that William and Mary were the King and Queen of Scotland; it provided for the succession to the throne, declaring that no papist could be king or queen; it abolished prelacy in the governance of the Church; and it protected the liberties of the people much along the lines of the English Bill of Rights. The Claim of Right was followed two days later by Parliament's adoption of the Articles of Grievances, listing various shortcomings of government which needed to be rectified.[155] Then, on 11 May, William and Mary, on accepting the crown of Scotland, swore an oath promising, among other things, to uphold the Presbyterian Church of Scotland. But that was not the end of the matter.

Resistance to the Glorious Revolution in Scotland crystallised round John Graham of Claverhouse, Viscount Dundee, leading to the first Jacobite rising. Having raised an army among the Highland clans, he made his headquarters at Blair Castle. On 17 July 1689 he positioned his army on the steep slope above Urrard House looking down on the River Garry in order to intercept the advance of William's army – the 'redcoats' – under the command of General Mackay as they emerged from the pass of Killiecrankie on their way north towards Blair Atholl. Realising too late that he had marched into a trap, Mackay deployed his forces on flatter ground at the foot of the slope and, recognising Dundee's commanding position above him but confident in his superior numbers and firepower, waited for Dundee to attack. Dundee also waited because the sun had been shining in the eyes of his men. At sunset he gave the order to charge.[156] The charge down the hill by the Highlanders was so rapid that the redcoats had no time to reload or to fix their bayonets and they were driven from the field, one of them reputedly leaping 18 feet to safety across the gorge through which the river flows, known to this day as the Soldier's Leap.

Despite the Highlanders' victory, Dundee himself died on the field of battle. With his death resistance dwindled, and it was effectively extinguished for the time being by the defeat of the Highlanders by the Cameronians under the command of Colonel Cleland in the streets of Dunkeld on 21 August 1689. The Highlanders were finally dispersed following an engagement with government troops at Cromdale, near Grantown-on-Spey, in May 1690.

After a fruitless attempt to reach a settlement with the Highland chiefs, on 27 August 1691 William issued a proclamation offering pardon to those who had taken part in the rising provided that before 1 January 1692 they had sworn an oath of allegiance to him in the presence of the Lords of the Privy Council or of the sheriff or his deputy in the shire where they lived. Failing that, they were threatened with the utmost extremity of the law. Before taking the oath required the chiefs sought a release from their oath of allegiance to King James, which was not received until the middle of December. Despite the difficult winter conditions, most took the oath in time. Some were permitted by the local sheriff to take it late but of one latecomer a shocking example was made.

The latecomer was McKean of Glencoe, a chief of a sept of the MacDonald clan. He had travelled to Fort William and asked the Governor, Colonel Hill, to administer the oath, but Hill had no authority to do so, so gave him a letter of protection and instructed him to proceed to Inveraray to take his oath before the Sheriff of Argyll. McKean finally took the oath on 6 January. Initially the Privy Council recorded that he had complied with the proclamation, but later deleted his name. On 11 January William authorised the severest of action against recalcitrant chiefs,[157] whereupon the Secretary of State, the Master of Stair, a Lowlander and bitterly hostile to the Highland clans, set about his task with a vengeance. He had already lighted on the MacDonalds as 'the only popish clan in the kingdom'[158] and on 16 January obtained William's explicit authority to take action against McKean of Glencoe.[159] To that end troops from Argyll's Regiment of Foot were billeted in Glencoe, ostensibly with a view to collecting property taxes. However, on 12 February 1692 Major Robert Duncanson issued the now infamous order to his subordinate, Captain Robert Campbell of Glenlyon, to fall on the MacDonalds at 5 am precisely and 'to putt all to the sword under 70. You are to have a speciall care that the old fox and his sones doe not escape your hands.'[160] And Captain Campbell did as he was ordered. McKean was killed in his bed and many of those who were not killed by the troops died of exposure in the snow while trying to escape. Such was the outcry at news of the massacre that an investigation was authorised. Three years later a commission of enquiry exonerated the King and Colonel Hill and attached most of the blame to Stair, who was then removed from office as Secretary of State.

Union with England

On 22 July 1706 a treaty was concluded between the kingdoms of Scotland and England for the union of the two as a result of which on 1 May 1707 the two kingdoms merged into the new kingdom of Great Britain and the two separate kingdoms of Scotland and England ceased to exist.[161] The treaty reflected a hard-fought and bitter compromise between the interests of the two kingdoms, to which there were two principal strands: one was the economic weakness of Scotland, and the other was the succession to the throne of Scotland.

Before the accession to the throne of England by James I in 1603, Scottish commerce had suffered badly from a lack of capital and was largely confined to trade with England's great commercial rivals, the Netherlands and France.[162] Inevitably the accession of the House of Stuart to the English throne gave rise to difficulties partly because in the eyes of the Dutch and French the Scots were tainted by association with the English competition and, more importantly, because in time of war between England and France (1627–29 and 1688–97) and England and the Netherlands (1652–54 and 1665–67), Scottish trade with England's enemies all but ground to a halt.

Although James I and Charles I had done much to remove barriers to trade between England and Scotland, and during the period of the Commonwealth, save for some limited protection of English interests, there were no barriers at all, Scotland was unable to take much advantage of that freedom, not only for want of capital but latterly also because it was verging on destitution both as a result of the Civil War and subsequently as a result of the protection afforded to the English by the English Navigation Act of 1651.[163]

To make matters worse, following the restoration of Charles II in England, the English Parliament passed the Navigation Act of 1660[164] which protected English shipping and overseas trade together with the shipping and overseas trade of the burgeoning English colonies from foreign competition, including therefore that of Scotland, greatly to its economic detriment. The adverse impact of the Navigation Act on Scotland was then exacerbated by a succession of other English Acts.[165]

The Scottish Parliament retaliated with a series of their own Acts, starting in 1681 with an 'Act for encouraging Trade and Manufacturies' which prohibited the import, among other things, of various types of foreign cloth, including therefore cloth from England or her colonies.[166] In 1693 a further Act was passed, this time 'for encouraging of foreign trade', which facilitated the formation of companies to carry on foreign trade and promised protection against the consequences of piracy.[167]

Notwithstanding the encouragement, by 1700 Scotland economically was on its knees. First, there had been a series of particularly bad harvests in 1695, 1696 and 1697. Secondly, the Nine Years' War (1688–97) between England, as part of the Grand Alliance, and France had effectively prevented any trade between Scotland and its important trading partner, France. Thirdly, and most importantly, there had been the catastrophic failure of the Darién Scheme.

In 1695 an Act was passed by the Scottish Parliament, founding 'The Company of Scotland Trading to Affrica, and the Indies', giving it a monopoly of trade with Africa, Asia and (for thirty-one years) America, exemption from almost all taxes and import duties for twenty-one years, a ten-year licence to build, fit out and navigate ships and the right to take possession of uninhabited territories.[168] This not only constituted a direct threat to the monopoly enjoyed by the English East India Company under English law but also conferred privileges on the Scottish Company which were far more extensive than those of the English Company.[169]

The Scottish Company's capital was to be raised by public subscription, with preference as to half being given to Scottish residents. Initially the capital of £600,000 was fully subscribed by a flood of investors largely from England. However, the English East India Company objected that its rights were being infringed and the English investors were forced to withdraw. Nevertheless, with a reduced capital of £400,000 the Company was fully subscribed by Scottish investors, sinking perhaps a quarter of Scotland's liquid assets in the enterprise. Part of the capital was then lost by embezzlement.

In 1698 five ships sailed from Leith bound for the Darién Peninsula in Panama. The purpose of the venture was to establish a Scottish colony which would have access not only to the Atlantic but also across the isthmus of Panama to the Pacific too.[170] The venture was funded by the Company and promoted by William Paterson, erstwhile founder of the Bank of England. The ships anchored in the Gulf of Darién in November 1698. The colony was named New Caledonia. The whole venture, however, ended in disaster, initially through sickness for want of fresh provisions and (so it was said) strong liquor[171] and then at the hands of the Spanish between whose colonies at Porto Bello and Cartagena Darién lay. On seeking relief from the English colony in Jamaica, it transpired that the English Governor of Jamaica, following instructions from the Government in England, had issued a proclamation prohibiting English subjects from assisting. Subsequent relief expeditions failed, the remaining colonists ultimately being driven out in 1700 by the Spanish who laid claim to the territory.

In 1699 the Scottish Parliament and the Company had begged the King for protection of New Caledonia. However, because the protection was needed not only from Spain (with whom England was then at peace) but also from the English Government, William had no choice but to refuse. However, he realised that the potential for conflict between the Governments of Scotland and England was such that a union between the two kingdoms was essential.

As time went by, the Scots became convinced that the union had been forced on them by England's bad faith: first, the withdrawal of the English subscriptions to the Company; secondly the refusal to assist New Caledonia; and thirdly the justifiable belief that the English had themselves been preparing their own scheme to colonise Darién ahead of the Scots. Whatever the truth of the matter, the Darién Scheme was not the only venture to fail:

Above: *The Battle of the Standard 22 August 1138* by John Gilbert, 1880. The Scots were roundly defeated by the forces of the Archbishop of York, partly because the animals which the Scots drove before them into battle turned tail among their own ranks at the sound of 'noisesome instruments' which the English had concealed on the battlefield, causing mayhem among the Scots. The standard was a ship's mast at the head of which hung a silver pyx (containing consecrated bread) and banners of the saints, filling the English with religious fervour. The Bishop of Durham, the English commander, is shown at the foot of the 'standard' celebrating the victory. The vanquished Scots surrender in the foreground.

Below: A tenth century Anglo-Saxon view of a Norse ship with a typical dragon prow. When anchored off Great Cumbrae during a storm immediately before the Battle of Largs in 1263, the gilded nostrils of the dragon-prow of King Haakon's ship were broken in a collision with a merchant ship.

Above: Largs Bay looking north, with the memorial to the battle of 1263 erected in 1912. The island of Great Cumbrae, where the Norwegian fleet had anchored, can be seen in the background on the left. Although the battle was inconclusive, it led to the purchase of the Hebrides and the Isle of Man by Alexander III of Scotland from Magnus IV of Norway under the terms of the Treaty of Perth in 1266.

Below: *Norham Castle, on the River Tweed* by J. M. W. Turner. c. 1822–23. The castle, which stands on the English bank of a great bend in the River Tweed, was the site of several meetings between the Scots and English kings. It was at Norham that the 'Ragman' was sealed by nine of the thirteen claimants to the Scottish throne submitting both their claims and themselves to Edward I in 1291.

Above: Two of the four panels of the *Trinity Altapiece* by Hugo van der Goes, 1478, depicting King James III of Scotland and his wife, Princess Margaret of Denmark, Norway and Sweden. As a result of the failure of Margaret's father, King Christian I, to pay her dowry in full, the security for it, consisting of all of King Christian's rights in Orkney and Shetland, was forfeited to King James.

Left: *Margaret Tudor, Queen of Scotland* by Daniel Mytens, c. 1620–38. Margaret was the wife of James IV of Scotland and the sister of Henry VIII of England. James was the last king of either kingdom to die on the battlefield, vanquished by his brother-in-law at Flodden in 1513. It was by virtue of Margaret's marriage to James that their granddaughter, Mary Queen of Scots, had (at least in the eyes of the Catholic Church) a better claim to the English throne than Queen Elizabeth I, and her great-grandson became James I of England.

Below: Part of the western section of Scots' Dike marking the border and dividing the Debatable Land between Scotland and England by agreement reached in 1552.

Left: Loch Leven Castle, seen from the west with the Lomond Hills in the background. Mary Queen of Scots was imprisoned in the castle between 1567 and 1568 and forced to abdicate in favour of her thirteen-month-old son, who became James VI.

Above: Dundrennan Abbey, where Mary Queen of Scots spent her last night in Scotland on 15 May 1568 before crossing the Solway Firth to England, imprisonment and finally execution.

Right: A silver half crown for the Commonwealth of England, Scotland and Ireland featuring Oliver Cromwell and struck in 1656, although never issued. The crown on the reverse is a curious paradox, as is the legend around it in Latin – 'Peace is sought by War'.

Above, top: The Palace of St-Germain-en-Laye near Paris, seen in an engraving by Adam Perelle, c. 1670. It was lent to the exiled Stuart kings by Louis XIV.

Above, bottom: *The Massacre of Glencoe* by James Hamilton, 1883–86 – a dramatic imagining of the grotesque punishment in January 1692 for a readily excusable shortcoming on the part of McKean of Glencoe.

Right: Castle Rushen and Peel Castle on the Isle of Man by Wenceslaus Hollar, from *A short treatise of the Isle of Man* by James Chaloner, originally published in 1656 as an appendix to *King's Vale Royal of England*. Magnus, the last of Godred Crovan's descendants to be King of Man, died in Castle Rushen in 1265. It was besieged by Robert the Bruce and fell in 1313: with its fall, the Isle of Man fell too. It is also where Charlotte, Countess of Derby, learnt of her husband's execution and surrendered to Parliamentary forces in 1651. Peel Castle stands on St Patrick's Isle in the precincts of a Celtic monastery, just off the west coast of the Isle of Man. It was also surrendered to Parliamentary forces in 1651.

Above: *James Stanley, Lord Strange, later Seventh Earl of Derby, with his Wife, Charlotte, and their Daughter* by Anthony Van Dyck, c. 1636. The Earl of Derby was the Lord of Man. He was executed in 1651 for his support of the Royalist cause in the Civil War. It was through the marriage of one of the daughters, Amelia Anna Sophia, that the Isle of Man passed to the Dukes of Atholl.

Above: Sir Henry Loch (seen here as Secretary to Lord Elgin in 1860) was Lieutenant Governor of the Isle of Man from 1863 to 1882. He did much to restore the fortunes of the island and to put it on a sound political footing. He led a particularly colourful life both before and after his period in office on the island. He was created 1st Baron Loch in 1895.

Above: Part of Offa's Dyke, on Llanfair Hill, near Knighton, Powys, with Mercia on the left and Wales on the right. It was constructed during the reign of Offa, King of the Mercians (757–796), as a boundary against the Welsh. The dyke consisted of a ditch and rampart, with the ditch on the Welsh side, and stretched much of the way between Prestatyn near the estuary of the Dee in the north and Chepstow on the Wye near its confluence with the Severn estuary in the south; the gaps in it were generally where there was a natural boundary, such as a river or dense forest.

Below: The stone marking the place where Llywelyn ap Gruffudd was reputedly stabbed in the back with a lance and killed in 1282 by the forces of Edward I. It stands above the River Irfon, a tributary of the Wye, near Builth Wells. Llywelyn was the first and last Welsh Prince of Wales recognised by the English Crown.

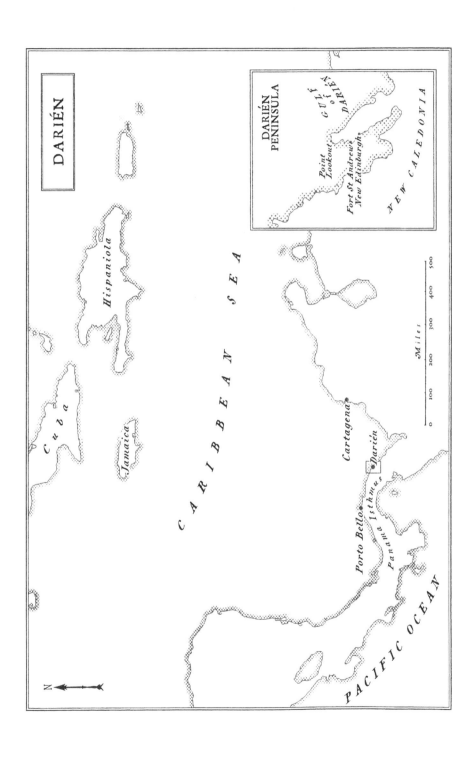

swept up in the fever of speculation around the turn of the century were the French Compagnie des Indes and its ruinous investment in Louisiana and the English South Sea Bubble which burst in 1720.

Whereas the Scots were driven to union with England primarily for economic reasons, the English were driven primarily by fear of the restoration of the House of Stuart and Catholicism. While the Company of Scotland was being established, the Nine Years' War with France was drawing to a close. It was in anticipation of that war that William had been invited to invade England in 1688. The following year he had taken England into the Grand Alliance with the Dutch Republic and the Holy Roman Empire against France to prevent Louis XIV from realising his territorial ambitions.[172] Hostilities had been halted finally by the Treaty of Ryswick, concluded on 20 September 1697.[173] By Article IV of the Treaty, Louis both for himself and for his successors as kings of France promised not to disturb, or to support any disturbance of, William in the possession of his kingdom of Great Britain, and William made a like promise to Louis in respect of France.

William's wife, Queen Mary, died childless in 1694. As matters stood, therefore, the heir to the throne of England and to the throne of Scotland following the death of William would be Anne, Mary's sister, and her heirs, by virtue of the English Bill of Rights and the Scottish Claim of Right. Anne's only surviving son and heir died in 1700, prompting the English Parliament to pass the Act of Settlement the following year, by which the succession was assigned to a granddaughter of James I, Sophia, Electress and dowager Duchess of Hanover, and her heirs, provided that they were Protestant.[174] William died in 1702 and was therefore succeeded by Anne as Queen of England, Ireland and Scotland.

The Scottish Parliament took a different and fiercely independent course. In 1703 it passed an 'Act anent Peace and War', arrogating from the Crown to itself the right to determine whether to declare war on behalf of Scotland and also to determine the terms of any treaty of peace.[175] It then approved an 'Act for the security of the kingdom' (known as the Security Act 1704), to which royal assent was initially withheld by the Queen's Commissioner, his authority to assent to it having been specifically excluded.[176] Ultimately, under pressure to retain Scottish troops for the War of the Spanish Succession which had broken out three years earlier, Queen Anne assented to the Act personally on 15 August 1704, being unaware of the English victory at Blenheim two days earlier.

The Act gave the Scottish Parliament the power to nominate the successor to the Scottish throne provided that he or she was

always of the Royal line of Scotland and of the true protestant Religion Providing always that the same be not successor to the Crown of England unless that in this present Session of Parliament or any other Session of this or any ensuing Parliament during her Majesties reign there be such conditions of Government settled and enacted as may secure the honour and sovereignty of this Crown and Kingdom, the freedom frequency and power of Parliaments, the religion liberty and trade of the Nation from English or any foreigne influence With power to the said Meeting of Estates to add such further conditions of Government as they shall think necessary the same being consistent with and no ways derogatory from those which shall be enacted in this and any other Session of Parliament during her Majesties reign ...[177]

The Act demonstrated the determination of the Scottish Parliament to prevent English domination, particularly in the context of trade. Indeed, there is some suggestion that the terms of the Act approved by the Scottish Parliament were more forthright in that respect, but that they were watered down surreptitiously before they received the royal assent.[178]

Hard on the heels of the passage of the Security Act there followed an outrageous miscarriage of justice, motivated by enmity and fomenting the bitterness between the two kingdoms, which almost certainly prompted the Queen to press for union between them.

The prelude was the seizure by English customs officers on 31 January 1704 of a ship named the *Annandale* when she was anchored off the Downs (just off the east coast of Kent). The *Annandale* was at the time under charter to the Company of Scotland Trading to Africa and the Indies and the seizure was at the behest of the Scottish Company's latest rival, the new English East India Company,[179] on the ground that the *Annandale* had been intending to trade east of the Cape of Good Hope without a licence from the English Company and thus in breach of the monopoly which the English Company enjoyed under its charter granted by the English Crown. Although she was under charter to the Scottish Company, carried a letter of marque from the Queen's Commissioner for Scotland authorising her to capture ships of the

Queen's (that is the Queen of Scotland's) enemies as prize and, at the time she herself was seized, was bound for Glasgow before proceeding to the East, she fell foul of the English Company's monopoly because her master, almost certainly in collusion with the English Company, had been fitting her out and recruiting English crew for the voyage in English waters. On 28 June 1704, together with her cargo, she was condemned by the English Court of Exchequer[180] as prize lawfully taken by the English Company. Although the Scottish Company mounted an appeal against the Court's decision, it had been required in the meantime to put up security for the value of the ship and her cargo.[181]

It so happened that, soon after the security had been put up and before the appeal had been heard, an English East Indiaman, the *Worcester*, put into the Firth of Forth on 28 July 1704 and a fortnight later, while riding at anchor off Burntisland, was seized by agents of the Scottish Company. The crew were arrested and ultimately charged with piracy in the East Indies and the murder of the crew of a Scottish ship, the *Speedy Return*, which (despite her name) had failed to return from the east. On 16 March 1705 a jury in the High Court in Edinburgh returned a verdict of guilty against the whole crew of the *Worcester* except one who had been ashore at the time of the supposed attack and another who had become a witness for the prosecution. That verdict had been reached notwithstanding that the evidence of piracy was obviously untenable: two members of the crew of the *Speedy Return* had reached Scotland and given evidence at the trial to the effect that there had been no piracy nor had any of her crew been murdered. However, that was not enough to deflect the jury from their lust for revenge. Although the Queen managed to procure a short reprieve, she dared not in the circumstances be seen to interfere with the administration of justice, with the result that the master of the *Worcester*, Captain Green, and two other members of the crew were hanged before a huge crowd on Leith Sands. Mercifully, the Queen's Commissioner in Scotland, the Duke of Argyll, managed to procure the release of the remainder of the crew and, out of his own pocket, paid for their return to England. The *Worcester* herself was declared to be lawful prize of the Company of Scotland in reprisal for the seizure of the *Annandale*.

Stung by the Scottish Security Act of 1704 and the drama surrounding the fate of the *Worcester* and her crew, the English Parliament passed an 'Act for the Effectual Securing the Kingdom of England from the apparent Dangers that may arise from several Acts lately passed in the Parliament of Scotland', known as the Alien Act.[182] It provided for the appointment of Commissioners by the Queen of England to treat with such Commissioners as the Queen of Scotland (albeit the same person – Queen Anne) might be authorised by the Scottish Parliament to appoint for the union of the two kingdoms, but, in the meantime and unless and until the Scottish Parliament brought the succession to the Scottish throne into line with the succession to the English throne by 25 December 1705, and subject to some exceptions, native Scots were to be treated in England and English dominions as aliens, incapable of inheriting property in England or English dominions, and they were also prohibited from exporting cattle, sheep, coal or linen from Scotland into England, Ireland, Wales or Berwick-upon-Tweed.

Union was opposed in Scotland by the Country Party, headed by the Duke of Hamilton, and by the New Party of the Marquess of Tweeddale. However, in September 1705, in an astonishing volte-face, Hamilton stood up in Parliament and moved 'that the nomination of the commission should be left to the Queen herself'. The motion was carried. The game had been won by union. There were suspicions that Hamilton had been bribed. Thus, by an Act for a Treaty with England 'for extinguishing the heats and differences that are unhappily raised betwixt the two nations',[183] the Scottish Parliament authorised the Queen of Scotland to appoint Commissioners to treat with English Commissioners for the union of the two kingdoms. The English Parliament reciprocated the following year by repealing the Alien Act.[184]

On 22 July 1706 the Commissioners appointed by the Queen concluded a treaty for the union of the two kingdoms, to which, subject to some revisions, effect was given by the Scottish Parliament on 16 January 1707 (1706 in the old calendar)[185] and, subject to the same revisions, by the English Parliament shortly afterwards.[186] The treaty, entitled the 'Articles of Union', provided for the union of the two kingdoms into one kingdom on 1 May 1707 and for it to be named Great Britain (Article I); it repeated the arrangements for the succession to the throne of the new kingdom which had previously been contained in the English Act of Settlement of 1700, including the exclusion of papists for all time (Article II), leading in due course to the succession of Prince George of Hanover on the death of Queen Anne in 1714; it provided that there should be only one parliament (Article III); it enabled all subjects of the new kingdom to enjoy the same freedoms of commerce (Articles IV–VII); it made substantial economic concessions to the Scots (Articles VIII–

XIV); it provided for the receipt by the Scots of a lump sum of £398,085 10s and such increase of the share of the customs and excise revenue as was required to compensate the Scots for the standardisation of the coinage, the losses from the Darién Scheme, the public debts of the Scottish Crown and a seven-year subsidy for wool, fisheries and other commercial enterprises (Article XV); it preserved the Scottish legal system and laws which had previously been applicable in Scotland[187] (Articles XIX–XXI); it allowed for sixteen Scottish peers to sit and vote in the House of Lords and for forty-five representatives in the House of Commons (Article XXII); and finally it provided for the annulment of any existing laws inconsistent with the treaty (Article XXV).

Thus it was that both the Scottish Parliament and the English Parliament voted themselves out of existence and the two kingdoms merged into one.[188]

Neither the Channel Islands nor the Isle of Man were, or ever had been, part of the kingdom of England (or indeed Scotland): rather, they were dominions of the Crown of England. Thus, by providing for union between the kingdom of Scotland and the kingdom of England, neither the Treaty of Union nor the Acts of Union included the Channel Islands or the Isle of Man.

One curiosity arising from the Union is the regnal number of the monarch. When William IV was crowned in 1831, he had been preceded by three kings of that name in England, one in Scotland and none in Ireland, but he adopted the regnal number IV. It so happens that the number adopted is a matter of royal prerogative[189] – choice of the monarch – although, as a matter of constitutional convention, it is taken to be the highest of those which would apply in any constituent state.[190] (There is of course another, older, curiosity as to why the regnal numbers start with the Norman Conquest: there were, after all, several kings of England named Edward before Edward I (r. 1272–1307).)

The aftermath of the Union

In 1701 James VII and II had died. But for the English Bill of Rights of 1689, the English Act of Settlement of 1701 and the Scottish Claim of Right of 1689, he would in the ordinary course have been succeeded by his son, James Francis Edward, as James VIII of Scotland and James III of England and Ireland, who subsequently became known as the Old Pretender. He, like his father before him, was living in exile with his court in the enormous palace made available by Louis XIV at St-Germain-en-Laye, a few miles north-west of Paris.

At the time of the Union, France had been engaged for the past five years in the war of the Spanish Succession against the Grand Alliance between the Holy Roman Empire, Austria, the Dutch Republic and England. One of the consequences of the Union was that, in theory at least, the Scots were now at war with France. The Union was deeply unpopular among differing factions in Britain, causing riots on both sides of the former border, a situation from which Louis XIV of France thought he might well profit.

In March 1707 Louis gave one of his agents, Colonel Nathaniel Hook, plenipotentiary powers to treat with the Scottish Jacobite sympathisers. In May that year eight Scottish nobles arrived secretly at the exiled Jacobite court at St-Germain-en-Laye to try to persuade James to return to Scotland as their king. James was not difficult to persuade. More importantly, however, he appeared at least to have the full support of Louis. By early March 1708, Louis had assembled a substantial invasion fleet at Dunkirk together with 4,000 French troops and had given James the enormous sum of 100,000 *louis d'or* as well as linen, plate and clothes.

By this stage Queen Anne had heard of the preparations for invasion and, in order to be ready to defend her kingdom, held back the fleet and troops which had been destined for the war against Louis in Spain. James arrived at Dunkirk on 9 March. The French fleet was expected to sail the following day, but on 11 March, with Machiavellian cunning, Louis sent a letter to James countermanding the whole expedition. Whether or not he received the letter, James embarked at Dunkirk and, in spite of Louis' orders, the French fleet sailed on the evening of 18 March. Although it was intercepted by the British fleet with the loss of one ship, the French fleet reached the Firth of Forth, where it anchored. However, the French Admiral, Forbin, refused to let James go ashore, thus from James's perspective defeating the whole purpose of the expedition. Louis, on the other hand, had achieved his goal of diverting substantial numbers of British ships and troops from the war in Spain. Humiliated, James had no choice but to sail back to France without a shot being fired.

As between France and Great Britain, the War of the Spanish Succession was brought to a close by the Treaty of Utrecht, which was signed by their respective ambassadors on 11 April 1713.[191] The treaty was a further nail in the coffin of the Jacobite cause, for not only did Louis for himself and his heirs agree to recognise the succession to the British Crown prescribed by Article II of the Articles of Union between England and Scotland, but he also agreed for himself and his heirs never to allow James (who was then abroad in Lorraine – not at that time part of the kingdom of France) to return to France (Article IV) or to give succour to anyone who sought to oppose the prescribed succession to the British Crown (Article V).

Undaunted, the following year James embarked on correspondence with sympathisers in England. However, circumstances changed fast. On 8 June 1714 Princess Sophia, the dowager Electress of Hanover and heir presumptive to the British throne, died, leaving her son, Prince George, the Elector of Hanover, as the heir presumptive. Then, on 1 August, Queen Anne, James's half-sister, died. Although she had been heard in her final days to murmur repeatedly 'my brother, my poor brother', suggesting that she wanted James to succeed her, nevertheless the very day that Anne died the son of the Electress was proclaimed King George I of Great Britain and Ireland.[192] George was not popular and there was pro-Jacobite rioting in several cities. His first act as British King was to persuade Parliament to put the colossal price of £100,000 on James's head.

In July 1715, there was consternation when the commander of the British army, the Duke of Ormonde, defected to France to support the Jacobite cause. On 10 September, following the death of Louis XIV, the Earl of Mar, having summoned all the Jacobites he could muster, raised the Stuart standard at Braemar, proclaimed James King and marched south – but to no avail: on 13 November he was roundly defeated by Government forces on a bleak stretch of moorland south-west of Perth called Sheriffmuir. The following day, other Jacobites under the command of Thomas Forster surrendered to Government forces at Preston. Seeking to join the uprising, James proceeded to Dunkirk, where he was told that a gift of 200,000 gold crowns from the King of Spain had been shipped ahead of him to Scotland. On 22 December he stepped ashore at Peterhead, only to be told that the ship carrying the Spanish gold had been wrecked. Finally, in February 1716, finding his support dwindling and faced with the advance of the Duke of Argyll at the head of a large Government force, he boarded a French ship at Montrose and sailed away from Scotland for ever.

Still smarting from the terms of the Treaty of Utrecht, by which they had lost Gibraltar, Sicily and Sardinia, the Spanish sought once again to make common cause with the Jacobites against their common enemy, the King

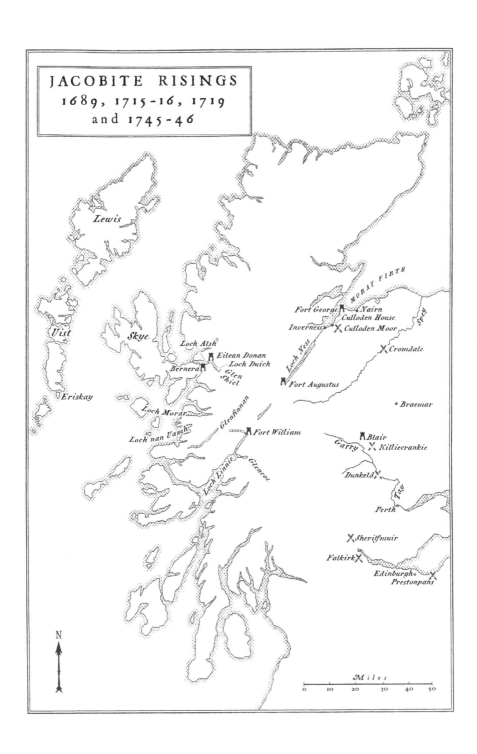

JACOBITE RISINGS
1689, 1715-16, 1719
and 1745-46

Lewis

Uist

Skye

Eriskay

Loch Alsh

Eilean Donan
Berneral
Loch Duich

Glen Shiel

Loch Morar

Loch nan Uamh

Glenfinnan

Fort William

Glencoe

Loch Linnie

Fort George
Culloden House
Inverness
Nairn
Culloden Moor

MORAY FIRTH

Spey

Loch Ness

Cromdale

Fort Augustus

Braemar

Blair
Garry
Killiecrankie

Dunkeld

Tay

Perth

Sheriffmuir

Falkirk

Edinburgh
Prestonpans

N

Miles
0   10   20   30   40   50

of England, but it was no better fated than the last. The plan hatched by the
Duke of Ormonde and Cardinal Alberoni of Spain was to invade the south-
west of England and at the same time to support a large scale uprising in
the Highlands. In March 1719 the Duke of Ormonde set sail with a Spanish
fleet of 29 ships and 5,000 Spanish troops from Cadiz, but, like the Armada
a hundred and thirty years earlier, the fleet was wrecked in a storm and the
surviving ships limped home. The loss of the Spanish fleet caused many of
the Highlanders to lose heart, and much of the support for an uprising in the
Highlands fell away. Nevertheless, in April George Keith, the Earl Marischal
of Scotland, having sailed from the north of Spain, landed in Lewis with 300
Spanish troops, together with arms and ammunition. From there he joined
forces with a contingent of Highlanders under the Marquess of Tullibardine
at Eilean Donan Castle which commands the confluence of Loch Alsh with
Loch Duich. In June Tullibardine with his force of about 1,000 men was
caught in a pincer movement. In the west Eilean Donan had been bombarded
by three British frigates and from the east General Wightman had marched
with a contingent of 970 redcoats from Inverness. On 10 June Tullibardine
took up a defensive position in the narrow confines of Glen Shiel beyond the
head of Loch Duich in an attempt to stop Wightman's advance. But it was an
attempt that failed. With the advantage of four mortars, Wightman put the
Highlanders to flight. The Spaniards, made of sterner stuff, held out until
they surrendered the following day.

Although defeated for the time being, the Jacobites remained a cause
of concern to the Government in London, not only because of the threat of
rebellion in Scotland which they posed but also because they kept open the
door to the unpredictable ambitions of the French King. To address that
concern, the possession of arms by anyone in the Highlands (except the
King's army officers and their men, officers of the law and (paradoxically)
peers, the sons of peers and commoners of substantial means) was
forbidden,[193] Roman Catholics were obliged to register their names and
landed estates so that they could be identified[194] and in 1724 Major-General
George Wade was despatched to Scotland to find a lasting solution.

The solution that General Wade proposed was to establish a series of
well-manned forts in strategic positions and to link them together by well-
paved, well-drained and, so far as practicable, straight roads. The proposal
was adopted by Parliament the following year and Wade was appointed as
Commander-in-Chief of North Britain. At the time there were no roads to

speak of in the Highlands at all. Under Wade's command, the most northerly road was that built along the Great Glen, linking Fort George on the Moray Firth, Fort Augustus in the centre and Fort William on the west coast. Although farther north than Fort William, the fort which had recently been built at Bernera on the west coast to control the crossing to Skye was not at that stage linked by a new road. New forts and new roads were subsequently built farther south, first by Wade and then by his successor, Major William Caulfield. It was to keep the peace that in 1725 Wade formed from among loyal Highlanders the regiment that would later become known as the Black Watch (so called after the dark tartan which they adopted).

The final throw in the Stuart cause was that of James's elder son and heir, Charles Edward Stuart, known as the Young Pretender or Bonnie Prince Charlie, a quarter of a century later. By the summer of 1745, most British troops were engaged with their allies on the Continent in the War of the Austrian Succession against France, Prussia and Bavaria. Seizing the opportunity, on 2 August 1745 Charles landed with seven supporters on the Isle of Eriskay in the Outer Hebrides. Supported by some of the clans, he raised his standard at Glenfinnan a fortnight later. Gathering further support on his way, he captured Perth and then, in the middle of September, Edinburgh, where his elderly father was proclaimed King James VIII. On 21 September Charles's Highlanders routed a Government force under Sir John Cope at Prestonpans on the southern shore of the Firth of Forth to the east of Edinburgh.

Encouraged by Charles's success, on 24 October 1745 the last military alliance between France and Scotland was concluded by the Treaty of Fontainebleau, signed by the marquis d'Argenson on behalf of Louis XV and by Colonel O'Bryen on behalf of Charles as Prince Regent of Scotland acting for his father. As a result, supplies and money came from France, but in the event no men until a few joined forces the following year.

To meet the growing Jacobite threat, large numbers of troops were recalled from Flanders, where they had been engaged in the Continental War. Together with troops from Hanover, Dutch auxiliaries and regular troops already in England, they were formed into three army groups, one to be deployed on the south-east coast to counter any French invasion, another to proceed to Lancashire against any Scottish invasion from the north-west and the third to Newcastle to protect the north-east. Wade, now a Field Marshal, was in command of the troops mustering at Newcastle, where he arrived on 29 October. It was around this time that two anti-Jacobite verses were added to the patriotic song which was later to become the British national anthem. Sung with patriotic enthusiasm at the time, they ran as follows:[195]

> *God grant that Marshal Wade*
> *May by thy mighty aid*
> *Victory bring.*
> *May he sedition hush,*
> *And like a torrent rush,*
> *Rebellious Scots to crush.*
> *God save the King.*
>
> *From France and Pretender*
> *Great Britain defender,*
> *Foes let them fall:*
> *From foreign slavery*
> *Priests and their knavery,*
> *And Popish reverie,*
> *God save us all.*

In the event, the Highland army marched south by Carlisle, sidestepping Wade in Newcastle. (It was the inadequacy of the roads for the movement of artillery between Newcastle and Carlisle that led to the construction between 1751 and 1758 of the military road – now the B6318 – between Heddon-on-the-Wall and Greenhead and the wholesale pillaging of material from substantial sections of Hadrian's Wall for that purpose.) Having successfully outmanoeuvred the Government's army intended to defend the north-west, now under the command of the King's younger son, the Duke of Cumberland, the Highlanders had by early December reached Derby, only 125 miles from London. This, together with the build-up of French forces at Dunkirk, caused panic in London, with rumours flying about that the King and his family had chartered a yacht to take them back to Hanover. Although Charles had wanted to press on, he was dissuaded by his advisors, led by Lord George Murray, and, much against his better judgment, he turned back. In January the Highlanders put a Government force under General Hawley to flight at Falkirk, the latter greatly handicapped by the difficulty of firing their muskets in driving rain. Then, notwithstanding their victory, the Highlanders retreated to Inverness, where they proceeded to establish their headquarters.

In the meantime, the Government had been bringing back more and more troops from Flanders. These were assembled at Aberdeen under the command of the Duke of Cumberland. On 8 April they left Aberdeen going north and west towards Inverness with a view to engaging the Highlanders. By 14 April they had crossed the formidable barrier of the River Spey unchallenged and reached Nairn, about 16 miles to the east of Inverness.

Charles had moved his headquarters to Culloden House, a few miles to the east of Inverness, the day before. On 15 April he drew up his Highlanders on Culloden Moor, a short distance away, expecting Cumberland to attack. He had chosen the site for the battle himself. Relatively flat, open ground, it was well suited for regular troops supported by cavalry and artillery, such as Cumberland's, but singularly unsuitable for Highlanders, who were best on hilly, broken ground. However, nothing happened, because, unknown at the time to Charles, Cumberland was celebrating his birthday with his men. Later that day, when Charles learnt of the celebrations, he decided to make a surprise attack on Cumberland's camp at Nairn that very night under cover of darkness. Although the Highlanders started on their march to Nairn, the planned attack was abandoned in disarray when those in the rear failed to keep up, making it impossible to reach Cumberland's camp before dawn. Tired and hungry, the Highlanders returned to Culloden to snatch some sleep.

However, there was little sleep to be had, because news soon reached Charles that the enemy were advancing fast. By midday the Highlanders had taken up their battle lines on the Moor, but in an even less advantageous position than the day before. It was a cold wet day and they were under-strength, under-fed and exhausted by their march the previous night. Cumberland's redcoats, well-fed, well-rested and well-trained, were drawn up about 500 yards away. The battle began with a barrage of Cumberland's artillery about an hour later. The Highlanders were no match for the redcoats. They were hopelessly outnumbered, decimated by enemy artillery and grapeshot, unable effectively to break through the well-ordered lines of redcoat infantry and in disarray as a result of confusion and squabbling among their commanders. In the end the survivors among them were driven to retreat and, as they retreated, they were cut to pieces, Cumberland having given the order that no quarter was to be given. So ended the last battle on British soil: 'it was the bloodiest and most discreditable in the history of the British army'.[196] With Cumberland's victory at Culloden, the sovereignty of the house of Hanover over the whole of Great Britain was established once and for all.

There remained, however, the task of pursuing and capturing the Highlanders who had escaped from the massacre at Culloden. It was that task which brought home to the Government that there were no reliable maps of the Highlands, let alone of Scotland as a whole, to assist in the pursuit. This prompted a topographical survey of the Scottish mainland by William Roy (then a civilian but later a major-general) between 1747 and 1755 which resulted in the production of what became known as the Great Map and, towards the end of the century, the establishment of the Ordnance Survey. At the time, the Highlands were a vast wilderness into which the rebels vanished, particularly north of General Wade's roads. Confronted by this problem, the Government's solution was ruthless, adopting a policy of occupation, devastation, starvation and massacre, requiring the surrender of arms by everyone in the Highlands (except those previously exempted and Members of Parliament) when summoned to do so, forbidding the wearing of Highland dress anywhere in Scotland (with an exception for Highland regiments, the formation of which had started with the Black Watch in 1725 and grew shortly afterwards with the regiments raised to fight in the Seven Years' War)[197] and abolishing all hereditary jurisdictions in Scotland, which was directed particularly to those of the Highland chiefs.[198]

Principal among the escaping rebels were Charles Edward Stuart and Lord Lovat. Notwithstanding that there was an enormous price of £30,000 on his head, the Young Pretender did manage to get away, pursued by redcoats, first to the Outer Hebrides, then with his celebrated passage to Skye disguised as 'Betty Burke' in company with Flora MacDonald, and finally on 19 September 1746 embarking on a privateer, named *L'Heureux*, at the head of Loch nan Uamh (a sea loch due west of Fort William), by which he was carried safely to France – like his father before him never to return. Lord Lovat was less fortunate. After two months on the run, he was caught hiding in a hollow tree on an island on Loch Morar. From there he was taken to London where he was tried for high treason and condemned to death. He was executed on Tower Hill on 9 April 1746, the last person in Britain to be publicly beheaded.

Home Rule

The defeat of the Jacobites at Culloden did nothing to quell the dissatisfaction of many Scots with the Union: if anything, it made it worse. However, enthusiasm to end the Union was kept in check for much of the next century and beyond by a variety of circumstances. First, there was a massive expansion of the armed forces recruited initially from the Highlands and then more generally from Scotland to fight three great wars: the Seven Years' War in Europe and North America (1756–63), the American War of Independence (1775–83) and the Napoleonic Wars (1793–1815), giving employment to many who might otherwise have been unemployed and disenchanted, particularly as a result of the clearance of much of the population from the Highlands to give the land over to sheep. Secondly, there was widespread emigration either to exploit the opportunities available in the rapidly growing British Empire (witness the numerous streets named after Scots in far-flung corners of the world) or at least to escape poverty, particularly that brought about by the Clearances, with the result that the emigrants had little further interest in the Union as such. Thirdly, until the passing of the Scottish Reform Act[199] in 1832, political power lay principally with the landed gentry who tended to be part of the British Establishment. With the passing of the Act, however, the number of Scottish seats at Westminster was increased from 45 to 53 and much of the middle class were enfranchised, bringing new vitality to Scottish politics. This was followed by the Second Reform Act in 1868[200] and the Third Reform Act in 1884,[201] which, together with the Redistribution of Seats Act of the following year,[202] increased the number of seats to 60 and 72 respectively and extended the franchise to many of the working class.

It was in 1853 that the first concrete signs of Scottish nationalism emerged with the founding of the National Association for the Vindication of Scottish Rights. This had gained sufficient support to prompt the Government to establish the Scottish Office and to appoint a Secretary for Scotland in 1885. Three years later the Scottish Labour Party was founded advocating Home Rule for Scotland, followed by the Scottish Home Rule Association in 1894. Then in 1913 William Cowan, the MP for Aberdeenshire Eastern, presented a Private Member's Bill for a devolved Scottish Parliament to deal with those matters which concerned Scotland alone. In May of that year the House of Commons passed the second reading of the Bill, but, as with Irish Home

Rule, it fell by the wayside as a result of the outbreak of the First World War.

From 1928 Scotland gained greater administrative independence with the establishment of the office of Secretary of State for Scotland. The Scottish National Party was founded in 1934 and in the general election of 1945 gained its first seat at Westminster. With the discovery of oil in the North Sea in the 1970s, economic independence became a real possibility and the SNP gained traction claiming 'It's our oil.' Finally, in 1998 Scotland acquired its own Parliament with devolved powers under the Scotland Act 1998.[203] The Scottish Parliament met for the first time on 12 May 1999. Winnie Ewing, presiding over the first session, opened with the words: 'The Scottish Parliament, adjourned on the 25th day of March in the year 1707, is hereby reconvened.'

Although further powers have been devolved since then, including limited powers to raise income tax, complete independence is still a goal of many Scots and, whatever the wisdom of it, this may yet be achieved.

The Isle of Man

The Isle of Man lies midway between the coast of Cumbria and the coast of Northern Ireland, well placed strategically for access to any of Ireland, Scotland, England or Wales.

From the sixth century the island had been colonised and ruled by Celts initially from Wales bringing with them their Brythonic language (known as P-Celtic) and later by Celts from Ireland and Scotland whose Goidelic (known as Q-Celtic) displaced the Brythonic and from which much of the Manx language was derived. Then, by the end of the ninth century the Vikings had started to settle on the island.

In about 874, when Haraldur Hárfagri (Harald Fairhair), King of Norway, invaded Orkney and Shetland to put an end to the pestilential Vikings who had been troubling his kingdom, he had continued his conquest first in the Hebrides and then in the Isle of Man. The Hebrides and the Isle of Man were known in Old Norse as the *Sudr-eyjar*, or Southern Isles, in contrast with the Northern Isles (*Nordr-eyjar*) of Orkney and Shetland. From the *Sudr-eyjar*, the name of the diocese of Sodor and Man is derived, originally a suffragan of the archdiocese of Nidaros (Trondheim) in Norway.

The inhabitants of the Isle of Man, having heard of the retribution exacted by Harald Fairhair among the islands further north, had fled before the arrival of his fleet taking most of their possessions with them. What was left, he laid to waste.

It was under early Norwegian rule that the parliament known as the Tynwald was instituted. Although it has undergone various constitutional changes, it is the oldest continuous parliament and is still the parliament of Man to this day. Its name is derived from the Old Norse *thing völlr* meaning 'parliament field', characterised by its meetings being held in the open on a hill. For centuries the meeting has been held on a mound outside the village of St John's on what had been St John the Baptist's Day, 24 June, but later, with the adoption of the Gregorian Calendar, on 5 July. Originally it consisted of twenty-four Keys, the name coming from *keise*, those 'chosen' as representatives of the people, presided over by a deemster (a judge). Today the twenty-four Keys constitute the lower chamber of Tynwald, known as the House of Keys: the upper chamber is the Legislative Council. Even now the validity of legislation passed by Tynwald depends on it having been proclaimed in the open from St John's Hill.

A century after the conquest by Harald Fairhair, the Dublin dynasty of Vikings appears to have had control of the island. The picture becomes distinctly clearer however a century later with the arrival of Godred Crovan.

The dynasty of Godred Crovan and the sovereignty of the kingdom of Norway

Having fought for the Norwegian King, Harald Hardrada, and been defeated at Stamford Bridge in 1066, a Norseman called Godred Crovan (*Crobhan* meaning White Hands, the colour of his battle gauntlets) took refuge on the Isle of Man, the island being ruled at that time by the Dublin Vikings. Then in 1079 and somewhat ungraciously towards his erstwhile hosts, at the third attempt he conquered the island. He assembled a large war-band and brought them ashore at Ramsey by night, hiding 300 men in a wood to ambush the defending Vikings and Manxmen who (like the British in Singapore in 1942) were expecting any attack to come from the sea. At daybreak, Godred's men attacked the defenders from the rear, trapping them against the flood tide. Realising that they could not escape, the defenders begged for mercy. Gracious at least at the end, Godred spared their lives, allowing his men either to plunder the island and return home to Norway or to settle on the southern half of the island, leaving the other half to the survivors among the defenders on condition that they did not question his hereditary right to the whole island. Ultimately, Godred's field of conquest and alliance, like that of Harald Fairhair, included not only the Isle of Man but all of the Hebrides too.

Although Godred's conquest was not perhaps itself out of the ordinary, it was significant because, subject to two short interludes, his descendants

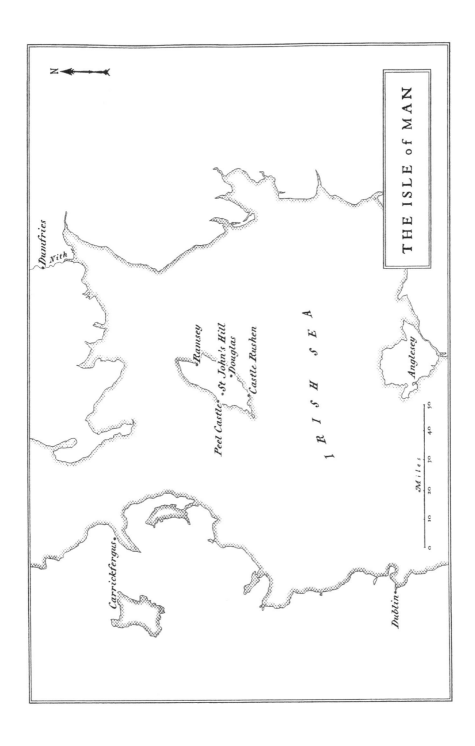

ruled as kings of Man briefly as sovereigns in their own right and subsequently as vassals of the kingdom of Norway until the island was ceded to the King of Scotland by the Treaty of Perth in 1266.

Godred died in 1095 leaving three sons, Logmann, Harold and Olaf. He was succeeded initially by Logmann who put paid to a challenge by his brother Harold by blinding and emasculating him. Three years later, filled with remorse for the way in which he had treated his brother, Logmann resigned his kingdom and joined a crusade to Jerusalem from which he never returned. Hearing of Logmann's death, the nobles of Man sent envoys to the King of Ireland asking him to send someone 'energetic' and of royal blood to rule over them until Olaf, the youngest of Godred's sons, should come of age.[204] Unfortunately the King of Ireland made a disastrous choice, sending Donald son of Tadc. Donald turned out to be not only energetic but a tyrannical monster and was soon evicted by the chiefs of the island.

In 1098 Magnus III, otherwise known as Magnus Bareleg, King of Norway, following a dream in which he was told to choose between losing his life and kingdom in thirty days or leaving Norway never to return, set sail with a fleet of 160 ships and, having subdued Orkney and the Hebrides, proceeded to the Isle of Man where, finding how pleasant it was, he decided to settle for the time being, building castles with timber imported from Galloway. Notwithstanding the dream, Magnus did return to Norway and in 1102 he set out on another expedition to the island. Although he was killed by the blow of an axe in a skirmish in Ulster with the forces of the King of Dublin the following year, he had in the meantime established Norwegian sovereignty over the Isle of Man, Godred's descendants as kings of Man thereafter holding the island, albeit tenuously at times, as a fief of the kingdom of Norway.

Following Magnus's death, the chiefs of the island sent for Olaf, Godred's youngest son, who reigned peacefully as King of Man for the next fifty years until he was murdered by one of his nephews. In 1153 the three sons of his brother Harold (who had been brought up in Dublin) came to the island and demanded that Olaf should give half of it to them. Olaf prevaricated by arranging for a council to discuss their demand. At the meeting of the council in Ramsey on 29 June 1153, Harold's second son, Ronald, stood apart and, when summoned by Olaf, turned as if saluting him and struck off his head with a single blow from a gleaming axe.

Olaf was succeeded by his son, Godred, who, like his father before him, enjoyed a long albeit a less peaceful reign, not least because it was interrupted by the conquest of Man by Somerled in 1158, who then held the island until his death in 1164. At an early stage Godred did homage for the island to the King of Norway. On his return, he avenged his father's death by killing all three of his cousins, having put out the eyes of two of them. He died in 1187 and was succeeded by his illegitimate son, Rögnvald.

It was during Rögnvald's reign that Norwegian sovereignty over the island was briefly interrupted by England's King John. After Hugh de Lacy together with Matilda de Briouze and her family had escaped pursuit by John's forces in Ireland in 1210, they had taken refuge on the Isle of Man for four days before fleeing onward to Galloway. In retribution and notwithstanding the brevity of the fugitives' stay, John's forces invaded the island and in the space of a fortnight laid it to waste. So it was that two years later Rögnvald ended up doing homage for his kingdom to King John and in 1219 imitated him by surrendering the island to the Holy See.[205] The circumstances in which the island ceased to be a fief of the Holy See are obscure. However, the transfer of the diocese of Sodor (later named Sodor and Man) from the province of Nidaros (Trondheim) to the province of York was recognised in a Papal Bull of 1458 and by an English statute of 1542.[206] From then on at least, the severance of the Church of England from the Church of Rome would effectively have terminated any vestigial subjection of the island to Rome.

In 1217, a year after the death of King John, Haakon IV succeeded to the throne of Norway. It was during his long reign that the Norwegian empire reached its zenith. Among other things, he reasserted his sovereignty over the Isle of Man, requiring succession to the kingdom of Man to be subject to confirmation by the King of Norway.

In 1229 Rögnvald was killed and was succeeded as King of Man by his half-brother, Olaf ('the Black', their father's legitimate son). In 1231 Olaf visited Norway and attended Haakon's court. In the light of what happened subsequently, it seems likely that he was confirmed as King of Man on that occasion. Following his death in 1237, his fourteen-year-old son and heir, Harald, made the mistake of refusing to attend the Norwegian court or to seek confirmation of his succession. Retribution was swift, Harald being driven from the island by Haakon's henchmen and the royal tribute of the island being taken for Haakon's benefit. Notwithstanding his bad start, Harald redeemed himself by sailing to Norway in 1239 where he stayed for the next three years. While he was there not only did he win Haakon's approval but also Haakon's confirmation of his right to the kingdom of Man. Indeed, Haakon's approval was such that at a magnificent feast in Bergen in the summer of 1248 he gave his daughter, Cecilia, in marriage to Harald. Tragically, that autumn the newly married couple and all of their companions were drowned when their ship, bound for the Isle of Man, was wrecked in Sumburgh Roost, the tide race off Sumburgh Head at the southern tip of Shetland.

Harald was succeeded by his brother, another Rögnvald, the second son of Olaf, but within weeks Rögnvald had been murdered, in a meadow near Rushen. The kingdom was then seized by an interloper, Harald Guorodarson, who, two years later, unwisely answered a summons from Haakon to Norway, where he was taken prisoner. Before his ill-fated voyage to Norway, he had received a letter from Henry III permitting him to visit Henry in England. The letter was significant because it recognised Harald as the sovereign of a foreign state – no such permission being required had he not been a foreign sovereign.[207]

Then in 1254, after a contested interlude, Magnus, the youngest son of Olaf, was appointed King by Haakon. Possibly conscious of a looming threat to his kingdom from Scotland, Magnus sought comfort from the English King, being received honourably at the English court and being knighted by Henry in 1256. He then supported Haakon in his engagements with the Scottish King, Alexander III, which culminated in the Battle of Largs in 1263. Unfortunately for him, however, the Scottish threat was ultimately to be his undoing. Taking advantage of the death of Haakon that year and the impotence of the English King in the hands of his barons, Alexander saw the opportunity to seize the Isle of Man. He assembled a large army at Dumfries and prepared to despatch a fleet to the island. On receiving news of the planned invasion, Magnus, no doubt wisely, capitulated and offered his submission. With the benefit of a safe conduct from Alexander, he sailed to Dumfries (the River Nith being navigable in those days) where he swore an oath of fealty to Alexander, promising to provide him with ten longships whenever needed in return for protection against any retribution from the King of Norway.

Magnus, the last of Godred Crovan's descendants to be King of Man, died at Castle Rushen on 24 November 1265. The following year the Treaty of Perth was concluded between Haakon's successor, Magnus IV of Norway, and Alexander, formally ceding the Isle of Man and the Hebrides to the kingdom of Scotland, albeit for a price.

The contest for Man between the Scots and the English

The next sixty-seven years saw possession of the island change hands between the Scots and the English on several occasions. In the autumn of 1275 a rebellion led by an illegitimate son of Magnus Crovan was suppressed by an overwhelming display of force by the Scots: the rebels, having foolishly rejected a generous offer of peace, were attacked at dawn and routed.

Immediately following the death of Alexander III in 1286 it is unclear who had control of Man. However, in 1290 an assembly of the islanders bound themselves to submit to the King of England, Edward I, in return for his protection, which he granted on 4 June that year. From Edward's perspective the island was particularly valuable as a source of much-needed lead for his relentless castle-building in Wales. Two years later, in the chaos of competing claims to the Scottish throne following the death of the Maid of Norway, Edward was recognised as the sovereign overlord of Scotland. Having resolved the contest for the Scottish throne in favour of Sir John de Balliol, Edward recognised the rights of Balliol over the Isle of Man. Then, having paid off the arrears of the annual fee of 100 marks due to the King of Norway under the terms of the Treaty of Perth, Edward handed over the island to Balliol's control on 5 January 1293.

The recognition by Edward I of the rights of Balliol over Man did not prevent several other competing claims, not least by Robert the Bruce, who had been crowned as King of Scotland in 1306, a year before Edward's death. Seven years later, on 18 May 1313, Robert landed with a large force at Ramsey on the north-east coast of the island and after some days proceeded to the south coast to besiege Castle Rushen. The castle fell on 12 June and with its fall Man fell to the Bruce faction too. Then in February 1315, following the defeat of the English at Bannockburn the previous year and with the imminent threat of a Scottish invasion of Ireland, Edward II took the precaution of seizing Man and expelling Bruce. However, that was not enough to prevent the invasion of Ireland by Robert the Bruce's brother, also called Edward, in May 1315. Two years later, while Edward Bruce was devastating Ireland, the Isle of Man was recaptured by the Scots, whereupon Robert the Bruce appointed his nephew, Sir Thomas Randolph, 1st Earl of

Moray, as the lord, and subsequently king, of Man, where he remained in control until his death on 20 July 1332.

Although Scottish sovereignty over the island had been recognised in the short-lived peace treaty between England and Scotland, known as the Treaty of Edinburgh-Northampton, in 1328,[208] the tables were turned again five years later. With the death of Robert the Bruce in 1329 and the seizure of control of the English Government by Edward III from his mother, Isabella, and her lover, Roger Mortimer, in 1330, hostilities between the two kingdoms erupted once more. In 1332 Edward Balliol (the son of Sir John de Balliol), supported by Edward III, laid claim to the Scottish throne, defeating the Scots at Dupplin Moor the following year and being crowned subsequently at Scone.

With the death of the 1st Earl of Moray a few weeks before the battle and of the 2nd Earl during the battle itself, Edward III determined to recover the Isle of Man. It is possible that it was to that end that three large warships were fitted out in Bristol. At all events, on 30 May 1333 Edward announced that Man had been taken into his hands, his grandfather (Edward I) having been legitimately seised of the island in 1290 and implicitly, therefore, that John, the 3rd Earl of Moray, had no title to it.

Although in the years that followed it appears to have been assumed by the kings of Scotland on occasion that the island was a Scottish dominion, Edward's claim was never effectively displaced.[209]

The transfer of sovereignty

On 8 June 1333 the island was committed by Edward to the custody of Sir William de Montacute (Montagu), later the 1st Earl of Salisbury. Sir William was a grandson and heir of Sir Simon de Montacute, to whom a lady named Aufreca or Alfrica had quitclaimed (surrendered) the Isle of Man claiming that she was the heiress of Magnus, the last Crovan king (however this part of the history is obscure). More immediately and more importantly, he was a close friend and staunch supporter of King Edward. He had been the protagonist of the coup against Edward's mother and Mortimer. It was he who had led a handful of knights through a secret passage at Nottingham Castle on 19 October 1330 to seize Mortimer, which led to Mortimer's execution for treason at Tyburn six weeks later. He then distinguished himself in the wars with the Scots that followed.

The transfer of custody of Man was followed on 9 August 1333 by letters patent under the great seal of England by which Edward, with the assent of the prelates, barons, earls and other magnates attending him, quitclaimed his right in the island to Sir William proclaiming Sir William's hereditary and absolute rights to ownership of it.[210] This put paid to the petition which Sir John de Waldeboef had issued to Edward I in 1305 claiming possession of the kingdom of Man as a descendant of the Crovan dynasty.[211]

In reality, neither Edward nor Sir William had control of the island at that stage. Although Sir William was reputedly crowned as King of Man in 1343, it was not until after his death in 1344 that control was effectively wrested from the Scots. Scottish aspirations were finally dashed by the defeat and capture of King David by the English at Neville's Cross in 1346. The 3rd Earl of Moray, John, was killed in the battle, leaving no heir of his own to such rights to the kingdom as he might have enjoyed. In all of the negotiations for the release of David that followed, there was no suggestion that the Scots had any continuing rights over the island. The final nail in the coffin of the Scottish claim was hammered home by the terms of the Treaty of Berwick by which David was ransomed in 1357.[212] The treaty, between Robert Stewart, as Guardian of Scotland, and King Edward, refers to the Isle of Man as falling outside the kingdom of Scotland – that is clear.

On the face of it, the quitclaim of Man to Sir William without any requirement for homage or service in return would have transferred sovereignty of the island to him. In other words, he would have become King of Man, not as a vassal of the King of England, but as a sovereign in his own right. This, had it been as it appears, would have been unique. There is certainly no evidence that Sir William or his immediate successors ever did homage in respect of Man. Although the Treaty of Berwick of 1357 refers somewhat ambivalently to the Isle of Man as though its people were subjects of King Edward, the Truce of Leulinghem of 1389, which brought the second phase of the Hundred Years' War with France to a temporary close, clearly treated the Isle of Man as a sovereign state separate from both England and Scotland.[213]

Sir William had died in January 1344 as a result of wounds which he had suffered in a tournament at Windsor. He was succeeded by his son, the second Sir William and 2nd Earl of Salisbury. Tragically, on 6 August 1382 the second Sir William managed to kill his only son in a tournament. Unable to recover the valuable lordship of Denbigh which had been granted to his father by the King, beset by costly litigation and possibly out of spite for the nephew who was the heir to his titles and all that went with them, Sir William sold substantial parts of his property. In 1389 he agreed to sell the Isle of Man 'with the crowne' to Sir William le Scrope. The price was the sum of 5,000 marks, payable by instalments, the last of which was due on 25 April 1392, and was secured by a bond from le Scrope and his brother, Stephen, for 10,000 marks.[214]

The English conquest and the grant to the Stanleys

Sir William le Scrope, later Earl of Wiltshire, was an ambitious man who progressively acquired great estates and offices of state under Edward III's successor, Richard II, becoming Treasurer of England in 1397 and a close confidant of the King. He was deeply involved in the King's tyranny at the close of the century and was the leading member of the cabal that ruled England during Richard's absences in Ireland, becoming one of the most hated men in England. Then in 1399, when the King was in Ireland once again, Henry Bolingbroke, the King's first cousin (both being grandsons of Edward III), launched his claim to the English throne, rallying support throughout England. Recognising the inevitable, Richard returned to England and, having failed to find his own support, surrendered at Conwy Castle, finally relinquishing his claim on 29 September 1399.[215] Bolingbroke, the first of the Lancastrian line of Plantagenets, was crowned as Henry IV on 13 October 1399. Meanwhile, the wretched Richard was imprisoned at Pontefract Castle where (conveniently) he died of starvation in February the following year.

   Sir William le Scrope was one of the first victims of the Lancastrian coup, being arrested and summarily executed at Bristol in August 1399. In the first Parliament of Henry's reign, Scrope's lands, other than the Isle of Man, were declared forfeit. Whereas Henry had acceded to the English crown, so he said, by inheritance, he had acquired the Isle of Man by conquest. The fact of conquest was recited in the grant of Man by Henry to the Earl of Northumberland on 19 October 1399 as a reward for his support. The grant was made in return for the feudal service of carrying the Lancaster Sword at the King's coronation. However, the Earl's tenure was short-lived. Having led an unsuccessful rebellion against the King in 1403, he was attainted and his lands were forfeited to the Crown two years later.

On 3 June 1405, the King instructed Sir John de Stanley to take the island over and to keep it until further orders. Although Sir John had served Richard II in high office, he had wisely submitted to Henry in August 1399, contributing to the collapse of the previous regime. Then on 6 April 1406 Henry granted the Isle of Man to Sir John and his heirs. By letters patent under the great seal dated that day,[216] the island was granted with all rights to Sir John de Stanley as Lord of Man 'by liege homage, and the service of rendering to the said king two falcons once only; ... and of rendering to his heirs, Kings of England, two falcons on the days of their coronations, instead of all other services ...'[217]

In other words, by virtue of the feudal service to be given in return for the grant, first to the Earl of Northumberland and then to Sir John de Stanley, sovereignty was firmly asserted by the English Crown. Whereas the two Sir Williams de Montacute, father and son, and Sir William le Scrope held, or at least appear to have held, the Isle of Man uniquely as sovereigns, that sovereignty, whatever precisely it may have been, had been terminated once and for all by the King's so-called conquest. Although the island thereafter enjoyed, and continues to this day to enjoy, a unique status, it was from the time of Henry IV subject to the sovereignty of the English, and later the British, Crown: importantly, it was not part of the realm of England, but a dominion of the Crown. But that is by no means the end of the story relating to the title to the island.

To begin with there was a problem with Sir John de Stanley's title because, as a court was later to find, the attainder of the Earl of Northumberland and the forfeiture of his lands had not been completed when the grant was made to Sir John, so the King had had no title to grant. Sir John's great-grandson, Thomas, was created Earl of Derby by his stepson, Henry VII, following Henry's victory over Richard III at the Battle of Bosworth Field, a victory secured in part by Thomas withholding support for Richard. Several generations later, the 5th Earl of Derby, Ferdinando, had three children, all girls, so that when he died in 1594 (as a result, so it was believed, of having been bewitched[218]) he was succeeded by them as his heirs general, but the title passed to his brother, William, as the heir male. There was then a dispute between William and his three nieces as to who had title to the Isle of Man. In 1609 a court decided that title was vested in the three nieces, but even then it was not plain sailing. Because the original grant to Sir John de Stanley had been defective, title would have been vested in the Crown;

however, in the course of the proceedings, the Crown surrendered its claim in return for £2,000. Following the decision and for a price, the nieces agreed to transfer their title to the island to William and also agreed to a private Act of Parliament to give effect to the transfer.

On 7 July 1609 James I, as King of England, issued letters patent under the great seal by which he granted to William, his countess, Elizabeth, and their son, James, and James's heirs in perpetuity what amounted, save in one respect, to sovereign rights over the Isle of Man, excluding the rights of various religious houses.[219] The one respect in which the rights granted were not those of a sovereign, unlike those granted to Sir William de Montacute by Edward III in 1333, was that they were feudatory: they were held by homage and allegiance to the English Crown and by the service of presenting two falcons immediately and on every successive coronation.[220] The private Act of Parliament was passed about a year later:[221] importantly for what followed, it made clear that neither James nor his heirs could dispose of the Isle of Man to anyone else without the consent of the Crown.

The surrender of the island to the Commonwealth

The tenure of the Earls of Derby was briefly a casualty of the Civil War. James, the 7th Earl, having tried initially to remain neutral, had espoused the Royalist cause in 1642. In July 1649 he contemptuously declined an offer by General Ireton to restore his sequestrated estates in England in return for the surrender of the Isle of Man. Then in August 1651 he sailed from the island to join forces with King Charles II. On leaving he had handed over his sovereign rights to his wife describing them in the most extravagant of terms.[222] His wife, Charlotte de la Trémoille (a Huguenot and daughter of the duc de Thouars), had first shown her mettle in 1644 when, in her husband's absence, she had stoutly resisted the Parliamentarian siege of his castle near Ormskirk in Lancashire, known as Lathom House.

With the King, the Earl was defeated at the Battle of Worcester on 3 September 1651. Although he managed to escape and guided the King to safety with his friends, the Penderels, at Boscobel House, he subsequently gave himself up to Parliamentarian troops. He was arraigned for high treason before a court martial for having corresponded with the King. Unfortunately one member of the court was a Colonel Rigby who had been in command of the siege of Lathom House all those years before and who had not only been worsted but treated with contempt by Charlotte. Notwithstanding that the Earl had been promised quarter when he surrendered, he was condemned to death and on 15 October 1651 was beheaded at the market cross in Bolton.

Ten days later, Colonel Duckenfield arrived with a considerable force of Parliamentarian troops off the coast of Man. While lying at anchor waiting for the weather to improve, he received a message from Deemster Christian that there would be no opposition to his landing, save only that Peel and Rushen Castles still held out. On 29 October, Duckenfield's force went ashore and laid siege to the two castles. It was then that Charlotte, who was in Rushen Castle, learnt for the first time of her husband's death. With the defection of part of the garrison at Rushen, she decided to surrender both castles; however, she was permitted to sail with her family and servants to England to make whatever application to Parliament she thought fit.

A month later Parliament decided to take over the government and defence of the island and that it 'should be taken as part of England, yet retaining such laws already established, as are equitable and just, and more suitable to the condition of the People than any other that can be imposed'.[223]

General Fairfax was appointed as Governor with the same jurisdiction that the Earl had enjoyed as Lord of Man. His governance did nothing to improve the condition of the Manx people and it was with exuberant clamour that the restoration of Charles II was welcomed on the island at the end of May 1660.

Six weeks later, the 8th Earl of Derby resumed his father's dominion of Man and lost no time in prosecuting the erstwhile Deemster, Christian, for surrendering the island to the rebel forces of the Commonwealth without the consent of his mother. With the approval of the Keys and based on their advice as to the Lord of Man's powers, Christian was convicted, condemned to death and shot as a traitor. However, that, unfortunately for those concerned, was not an end of the matter.

Before his conviction, Christian's sons had appealed to the Privy Council in London invoking the English Act of Indemnity and Oblivion forgiving all offences committed under colour of governmental authority between 1637 and 1660.[224] In a conspicuous demonstration of English imperial sovereignty, the Privy Council directed Lord Derby to appear before them together with his prisoner, Christian. Having learnt that it was too late for Christian to be produced, the Privy Council decided that the English Act applied to the Isle of Man and ordered not only that full reparation should be made to Christian's heirs but also that the two deemsters, by whom Christian happened to have been condemned, should be prosecuted so as 'to receive condign punishment'.[225]

The dukes of Atholl

One of the daughters of the 7th Earl of Derby and Charlotte de la Trémoille was Amelia Anna Sophia. She married John Murray, the 1st Marquess of Atholl. On the death of the 10th Earl of Derby without a male heir in 1736, the Isle of Man passed to James Murray, the 2nd Duke of Atholl, a great-grandson of the 7th Earl of Derby. That, in turn, gave rise to yet more litigation. As against the Duke, two claims were made: one was by the 11th Earl of Derby for all of the rights over the island under the will of the 10th Earl; the other was by the Bishop of Sodor and Man for possession of some rectories on the island which had been leased by the 7th Earl of Derby to the diocese for 10,000 years and from which the Duke had evicted the occupants. In the litigation that ensued, Lord Hardwicke, the Lord Chancellor, found against the 11th Earl, because the island, as a feudatory dominion of the Crown, could not have been disposed of by will without the consent of the Crown, and against the Bishop, because the leases were void as contrary to the private Act of Parliament to which the daughters of Ferdinando, the 5th Earl, had agreed over a century before. Importantly, in the course of his judgment given in 1751 Lord Hardwicke explained that the Isle of Man was not part of the realm of England but a possession of the Crown, to which the law of England did not as such apply, just (as he said) like the Plantations, Jersey and Guernsey: it was, he said, a 'feudatory dominion by liege homage of the Kings of England'.[226]

The 2nd Duke died in 1764 and was succeeded by his only surviving child, his daughter Charlotte. Confusingly, Charlotte happened to be married to her cousin who was also the heir to the dukedom. No sooner had the new Duke and Duchess come into their inheritance, than the British Government started to put pressure on them to sell their rights over the island in order to put a stop to the smuggling of contraband through the island into Britain. Since the outbreak of the war between England and France in 1688, swingeing duties had been imposed in England on French imports, particularly wine and brandy, and to a lesser extent on imports from elsewhere too. There was therefore easy money to be made by Manxmen from importing such goods into the Isle of Man and then smuggling them into England. Under threat of losing all of their rights over the island, the Duke and Duchess agreed to sell their rights to the customs revenues and other seigneurial rights (known as regalities) to the Crown for £70,000. Effect was given to the agreement on 10 May 1765 by an Act of the British Parliament known as the Isle of Man Purchase Act (or the Revestment Act) 1765, by virtue of which King George III and his successors became Lords of Man.[227] Five days later import duties in the Isle of Man were drastically increased by another British Act known as the Mischief Act 1765 which also empowered British customs officers to stop and search vessels in Manx waters and to seize any contraband.[228] That was followed two years later by yet another Act imposing even greater duties. Even then the smuggling did not come to a complete stop.

The attempt by the Government to stem the tide of contraband reflected its pressing need to raise revenue in the wake of the Seven Years' War with France which had ended with the Treaty of Paris in 1763. The treaty had been followed by a series of British Acts to meet that need (among them the Sugar Act of 1764 and the Stamp Act of 1765 designed to raise money from the thirteen American Colonies, which culminated in their Declaration of Independence in 1776).

In 1774 Charlotte's husband, the 3rd Duke, died and their son, John, promptly set about trying to improve on the bargain which his parents had made in 1765. After thirty years of rebuffs by Parliament and the Privy Council, his importunity paid off. Having persuaded Pitt, who had returned to power in 1804, that he deserved more, an Act was passed the following year by which Parliament appropriated the customs revenues of the island to the Consolidated Fund, without earmarking them for the benefit of the island, and, to add insult to the injury of the islanders, granted the Duke and his heirs in perpetuity an annuity equal to a quarter of those revenues – an enormous amount.[229]

The 4th Duke's rapaciousness did not end there. Fed up with the trouble that his nephew, the Bishop of Sodor and Man, had caused in the island with disputes over tithes, in 1823 he intimated to the Government his willingness to sell the remainder of his rights over the island. Two years later Parliament passed an Act which enabled the Treasury to buy the rights at a price to be determined by arbitrators.[230] In 1829 the price was fixed at the eye-watering sum of £416,114, grossly overvaluing the rights that were to be transferred.

Fortunes restored

Although since 1805 the Manx people had not enjoyed the benefit of the island's customs revenue, having lost it through the machinations of the 4th Duke to the Consolidated Fund, that shortcoming was put right in in 1866. Three years earlier Henry Loch (later Sir Henry and then 1st Baron Loch) had been appointed as Lieutenant Governor of the island. He was a remarkable man. In his long and colourful life of service, he had among many other things been adjutant of the irregular corps known as Skinner's Horse, he had raised a body of irregular Bulgarian cavalry during the Crimean War and he had served on Lord Elgin's embassies to China where at one stage he was imprisoned and brutally treated. Some time after he had left the Isle of Man in 1882, he was Governor of Cape Colony and High Commissioner in South Africa where he set in motion the coup that culminated after his departure in the Jameson Raid and then the Boer War, for which he was instrumental in raising what became known as Loch's Horse.

Not long after his arrival in the Isle of Man, with a view to increasing the revenue of the island, Loch had embarked on a great series of harbour works for which the island needed public funds. That problem was then solved in 1866 by an Act of the British Parliament which, subject to payment of £10,000 per annum to the Consolidated Fund and some other costs, permitted the Government of the Isle of Man to apply one ninth of the customs revenues of the island to harbour works and to keep the balance for public purposes of the island.[231] Although the 1866 Act was repealed in 1958,[232] a similar regime has been continued by agreement between the Government of the Isle of Man and the Government of the United Kingdom ever since.[233]

By the end of the nineteenth century, responsibility for the external affairs, defence and residual good government of the island lay by constitutional convention with the Crown, as advised by the Privy Council, but in all other respects the island was autonomous, having its own legislature (the High Court of Tynwald) and legal system. And so it continues to be to this day, with the British monarch as Lord of Man.

Wales

After the abandonment of Britain by the Romans and the early migration of Germanic tribes into eastern Britain, most of western Britain was populated by Celts. The Germanics referred to them as *welsch* (Old English *wælisch*) meaning 'stranger' or 'foreigner'.[234] In what is now Wales, the language they spoke was Brythonic (P-Celtic) from which the Welsh, Cornish and Breton languages developed. When walking by the River Severn near Berriew (south-west of Welshpool) in the late sixth century, St Beuno heard the hunting cries of a Germanic migrant from across the river, whereupon with remarkable prescience he is reputed to have told his followers (no doubt in his own Brythonic tongue) 'put on your clothes and shoes and let us leave this place, for the nation of the man with the strange language, whose cry I heard beyond the river urging on his hounds, will invade this place and it will be theirs, and they will hold it as their possession.'[235]

Before the English conquest of the Welsh in the thirteenth century, their lands were ruled to a greater or lesser extent as parts of various principalities or kingdoms, the territories of which fluctuated with the fortunes of their rulers. Of those, the three greatest were Gwynedd in the north-west, embracing all of what is now known as Snowdonia, Deheubarth in the south-west and between them to the east Powys. There were other, lesser, principalities too, among which were Gwent, Morgannwg and Brycheiniog clustered in the south-east.

There were only brief periods when the Welsh united as a nation and, no doubt in part for that reason and unlike the Scots, few occasions when they invaded England, notably the invasions by Cadwallon ap Cadfan in 632, Gruffudd ap Llewelyn in 1057 and Llywelyn ap Iorwerth in 1210 and again in 1215.

There was a resurgence of Brythonic power which reached its apogee when Cadwallon ap Cadfan, King of Gwynedd, conquered the kingdom of Northumbria, killing the Northumbrian King, Edwin, in 632, only to lose his own life two years later in a battle against Oswald of Bernicia. From then on, as the kingdom of Mercia, in the midlands of what would become England, expanded into the valleys of the Dee, the Wye and the Severn, it was the western border of Mercia that came to determine the eastern border of what would become Wales. At that stage the border was effectively defined by Offa's Dyke, constructed during the reign of Offa, King of the Mercians between 757 and 796. The dyke consisted of a ditch and rampart, with the ditch on the Welsh side, and stretched much of the way between Prestatyn near the estuary of the Dee in the north and Chepstow on the Wye near its confluence with the Severn estuary in the south; the gaps in it were generally where there was a natural boundary, such as a river or dense forest. Whether through political wisdom or bargain, it lay to the east of territory which would have been obviously desirable, and so vulnerable, to the Welsh, for example giving the kingdom of Gwent access to the lower reaches of the Wye.

For a brief period in the tenth century most of Wales fell under the sway of one king, known as Hywel Dda. At the time of his death in 949 or 950 he ruled over the whole of Wales except for the kingdoms of Gwent and Morgannwg in the far south-east. He had achieved this by a combination of inheritance, marriage, the fortuitous deaths of rivals and violence. He ruled the kingdom of Deheubarth in south-west Wales from 903 or 904 and annexed Gwynedd in the north in 942. On his rise to power, he submitted to Edward the Elder, King of the Anglo-Saxons, at Tamworth in 918 and subsequently to Æthelstan, King of Britain, at Eamont Bridge in 927. Remembered as Hywel Dda (Hywel the Good), he was reputed to have been responsible for the codification and promulgation of customary Welsh law[236] which, no doubt as an effective means of tightening his control, was applied throughout his kingdom.

Following Hywel's death, his kingdom fell apart. When reunited over a century later it formed part of a kingdom that encompassed the whole of Wales. The King in question was Gruffudd ap Llywelyn, who ruled over the entire country from about 1057 until his death in 1063. His ascent to power was brutal and relentless: in 1039 he seized the thrones of Gwynedd and Powys, their King, Iago ab Idwal, having been killed by an unknown hand; in 1055 he finally took possession of Deheubarth, having killed its King, Gruffudd ap Rhydderch, in battle; and about two years later he seized Morgannwg on the north coast of the Bristol Channel, having driven out its ruler, Cadwgan ap Meurig. Gruffudd's ambition was not even confined to Wales: he attacked Mercia, driving out the English settlers from the border to the east of Offa's Dyke; and he married a high-born Mercian lady, Ealdgyth, a granddaughter of Lady Godiva, Countess of Mercia. Although allied with Mercians opposed to West-Saxon hegemony, in 1062 he was finally driven back into Wales and defeated by Harold Godwinson, the future King of England and casualty of the Norman Conquest. Gruffudd was murdered in Snowdonia on 5 August 1063 by the son of Iago ab Idwal, one of his erstwhile victims. His widow, Ealdgyth, then married Harold; so, having been Queen of Wales, she became Queen of England, but not for long. Harold, having been crowned as King of England on 6 January 1066, was dead within the year, killed by William the Conqueror's invading forces at the Battle of Senlac Hill near Hastings.

Following his conquest, William made large grants of land in the borderlands between his new kingdom and Wales, known as the Welsh Marches. The grants were made to over 150 of his most valued supporters, partly of course by way of reward but principally for the subjugation of the Marches themselves and the protection of his new kingdom from the Welsh. These new Lords of the Marches (or Marcher Lords) were granted not only the land but almost all of the perquisites of royalty too: they were entitled to build castles and towns without a licence from the King, to wage war, to administer the law to the exclusion of the King save for cases of treason, and even to enjoy the more arcane perquisites of salvage, treasure-trove, plunder and royal fish.

In due course numerous castles were built or rebuilt in the Marches, leading to the greatest concentration of motte-and-bailey castles in Britain, principal among which were Chester, Shrewsbury and Hereford. Although in time the Marcher Lords encroached westwards building more castles on the way, they never penetrated far into the mountain fastness of Snowdonia and, more importantly, they never succeeded in subjugating the Welsh. The overall effect of the Norman onslaught was not, therefore, to subdue Wales, but to partition it: thereafter the distinction between *Marchia Walliae* (the Welsh Marches) and *Wallia Pura* (Welsh Wales) was clearly drawn, although the boundary between the two shifted with the encroachment.

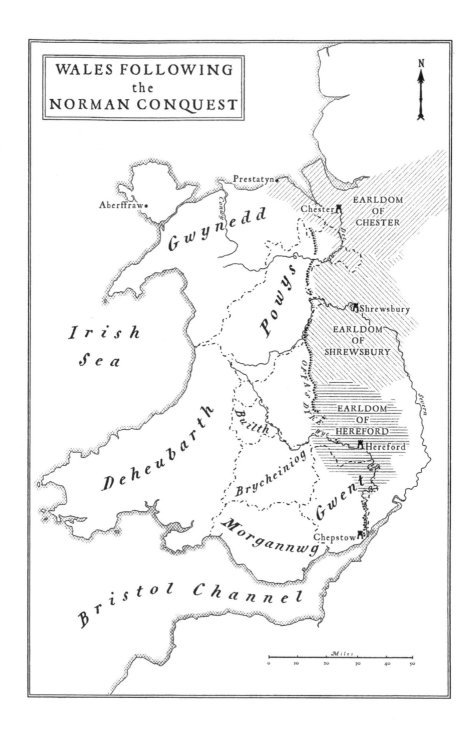

At the feet of their castles, the Norman invaders established fortified colonies, with settlers from England, France and Flanders. To the colonists they granted mercantile privileges. From their settlements and surrounding land, the Welsh were firmly excluded.

During the anarchy of Stephen's reign in England (1135–54) the Lords of the Marches consolidated their own powers, refusing to recognise the legitimacy of Stephen's rule. So too did the Welsh rulers, pre-eminent among whom were Owain ap Gruffydd, ruler of Gwynedd in the north-west, and Rhys ap Gruffydd, ruler of Deheubarth in the south-west. All of that changed, however, with the accession of Henry II to the English throne in 1154.

Henry II's attempted conquest

In 1157 Henry invaded Wales hoping to conquer it, directing his forces initially in the north against Owain ap Gruffydd, and subsequently in the south against Rhys ap Gruffydd. His invasion culminated with the submission of all of the major Welsh princes, including Owain and Rhys. At Woodstock on 1 July 1163 he received their homage and oaths of fealty secured – significantly for what was to follow – by hostages. Rebellion against such humiliation followed swiftly. It began in the autumn of 1164 with Rhys recapturing territory that he had lost in the south and was followed by Owain's son, Dafydd, further north at the beginning of 1165. Having gathered a large army in Shropshire, in July of that year Henry advanced with his forces to Oswestry where he halted.

The Welsh, in the meantime, had gathered at Corwen, 18 miles to the north-west of Oswestry, at the northern end of the Berwyn Mountains. Henry then proceeded west into the mountains, presumably intending to approach Corwen from the south. In the wooded valley of the River Ceiriog (Dyffryn Ceiriog in Welsh) he was ambushed, leading to heavy fighting with casualties on both sides. He therefore moved up onto the more open high ground, moorland then as much of it is today. There he was defeated not by the Welsh, but by the weather. Although it was August, there were high winds and torrential rain. It was bitterly cold and the transport of supplies became impossible in the mud and peat. Henry's men were dying from exposure and lack of food, forcing him to abandon the expedition and to retreat to England. In his anger at defeat, Henry turned on his hostages, blinding and possibly castrating many of them, including the sons of Owain and Rhys whom he held.

The vengeance exacted on the hostages did not deter Owain or Rhys. In November 1165 Rhys captured and sacked Cardigan. The following year Owain captured and destroyed the castle at Basingwerk on the Dee estuary. Then together in 1168 they laid siege to Rhuddlan and, after three months, took it and sacked it too, Prestatyn falling around the same time. From then on, however, co-operation between the Welsh began to fall apart, enabling Henry eventually to make peace with them, but not to subdue them.

Owain died in 1170 and his son, Dafydd, by whom he was succeeded as ruler of Gwynedd, made peace shortly afterwards and went on to marry Henry's half-sister, Emma, in 1174. More pressing for Henry was the need to reach some accommodation with Rhys to enable him not only to secure a base in south-west Wales from which to mount his expedition to Ireland in 1171 but also to take control of the lands of the Marcher Lords who had on their own initiative invaded Ireland, particularly Richard de Clare, erstwhile Earl of Pembroke, who had joined the invasion the previous year. Thus it was that Rhys was appointed Justiciar (the King's lieutenant) in south Wales.

Having secured peace in Wales, suppressed a rebellion by three of his own sons and achieved a tenuous conquest of eastern Ireland, Henry returned to Wales in 1177 and was attended by great feudal pomp and ceremony. It was on that occasion that Dafydd, as ruler of Gwynedd, swore an oath of allegiance to Henry. The Welsh princes, like the Scottish barons, were being systematically locked in to the feudal network.

Llywelyn ap Iorwerth

Matters in Wales came to a head once more in the quixotic reign of King John (r. 1199-1216). In 1208 John had thwarted an attempt by William de Briouze to re-take the castles at Radnor, Brecon and Hay which had been forfeited as security for a debt due to the King, leading to de Briouze's flight to Ireland. Gwenwynwyn, the ruler of southern Powys (Powys Wenwynwyn) and rival of de Briouze, somewhat unwisely then seized Brecon, only to be faced by the army which the King had marshalled for his invasion of France. Gwenwynwyn submitted without a fight, saved his life in return for hostages but forfeited all of his lands to the King. That in turn provoked Llywelyn ap Iorwerth, Prince of Gwynedd, to invade Powys, notwithstanding that he had sworn an oath of allegiance to the King in 1201, done homage to him in 1204 and either then or shortly after had married the King's illegitimate daughter, Joan. The King, however, was indulgent on this occasion and, having secured Llywelyn's submission in January 1209 with the threat of invasion, allowed him his liberty and to keep all of his lands, including his recent conquests. For the moment, at least, Wales was at peace.

But it was a peace which was not destined to last. In 1210, while John was occupied suppressing a rebellion in Ireland, Llywelyn, probably in concert with de Briouze, had launched attacks across the English border, although by the end of the year he had been driven back by the Earl of Chester into Snowdonia. His previous indulgence having been tested too far, John sought to retaliate by reinstating Gwenwynwyn in Powys, assisting Llywelyn's enemy, Rhys Gryg, to recover Llandovery Castle and then mustering a vast army with which to destroy Llywelyn completely. John's first attempt ended in failure, Llywelyn having retreated with his forces into the mountain fastnesses of Snowdonia, taking everything with them and depriving John's army of much-needed supplies. The following year, however, John returned with an even greater army, and pressed on into Snowdonia. It was only through the good offices of his daughter, Joan, Llywelyn's wife, that bloodshed was prevented and peace agreed. Although Llywelyn was spared his life and liberty, they came at a great price, consisting of thirty hostages (among whom was Llywelyn's illegitimate son, Gruffudd, at that stage his only son – a boy of eleven), all of his lands except in Snowdonia, a huge tribute of cattle and other animals and his submission, which he made on 12 August 1211.[237]

Having returned from Snowdonia, King John despatched his army to the south of Wales where the only princes who had not already submitted to him were forced to surrender and forfeited their lands to the Crown. To consolidate his hold on Wales, John built several more castles (among them Aberystwyth – not the one the ruins of which are visible today – and Mathrafal near Welshpool).

The following summer, dissatisfied with their treatment by the King, all of the princes of Wales, including the King's former allies Gwenwynwyn and Rhys Gryg, joined Llywelyn in rebellion, capturing many of the King's castles which had so recently been built. To that end Llywelyn concluded an alliance of mutual support with Philippe II of France.[238] When John learnt of the rebellion at the end of June, he determined to conquer Wales once and for all. He called off his plans to invade France and mustered a large army, surprising the Welsh rebels and retaking his new castle at Mathrafal. He then moved with his army to Nottingham, intending to proceed from there to Chester. While he was at Nottingham, not only were twenty-eight of the hostages given by Llywelyn the previous year hanged (including a seven-year-old boy) but, more ominously, he learnt both from the King of Scotland and from his own daughter, Joan, that some of his barons were plotting to kill him.[239] Fearful for his own life, he postponed his plans for conquest and in the short term devoted his attentions to identifying and dealing with the plotters.

From then on such luck as John might previously have enjoyed ran out. Notwithstanding the protection he had sought to gain by the surrender of his kingdom to the Pope in 1213, his army was routed by King Philippe at Bouvines the following year, putting an end to his hopes of recapturing any of his territory in France. He then had to confront his rebellious barons, culminating in his acceptance of the terms of Magna Carta in June 1215.

One of the events that had driven John to accept the terms of Magna Carta had been the capture of Shrewsbury by Llywelyn in May 1215. Of two terms of immediate relevance to Wales, one was the agreement that lands unjustly seized by the Crown from the Welsh should be restored[240] and the other was that Llywelyn's son, together with the other hostages from Wales (or such of them as had survived) and other security which had been given for peace in 1211, should be released.[241]

John died in October 1216. He was succeeded by his nine-year-old son, Henry III – a half-brother therefore of Llywelyn's wife, Joan. The following summer, Llywelyn took the opportunity to invade south Wales and captured Swansea. At the urging of the young King's advisers, particularly that of the Papal Legate, Guala Bicchieri, a settlement with Llywelyn was reached at Worcester in March 1218. As part of the settlement, the Crown recognised Llywelyn's pre-eminence in Wales, the King accepting his homage not only on his own behalf but also on behalf of all the Welsh magnates; and Llywelyn's territorial gains were confirmed, he being allowed to keep the royal castles of Carmarthen and Cardigan until the King came of age and to hold Powys Wenwynwyn until Gruffudd ap Gwenwynwyn came of age.[242]

Yet again, however, the peace did not last. Starting with the seizure of the castles of Carmarthen and Cardigan by the Earl of Pembroke on behalf of the King in 1223, there were intermittent outbreaks of hostility until 1231, when Llywelyn embarked on a sustained campaign to recover the position that he had enjoyed at the end of the reign of King John. His campaign lasted until 1234, when on 21 June he achieved his goal by the terms of the Peace of Middle (a village in Shropshire), following which he styled himself Prince of Aberffraw (the principal seat of the kings of Gwynedd on Anglesey) and Lord of Snowdonia. The terms of the Peace which lasted initially for two years were then renewed annually until his death in 1240.[243]

Dafydd ap Llywelyn

Llywelyn had had two sons – Gruffudd, who was illegitimate, and Dafydd by his wife, Joan. As Llywelyn had wished, he was succeeded by Dafydd. Summoned by Henry III to Gloucester, in May 1240 Dafydd was knighted by the King, did homage for Gwynedd alone and reluctantly agreed that the territorial rights of other magnates, including Gruffudd, should be determined by arbitration for which they would then do homage directly to the King, not to Dafydd. On his return to Wales, Dafydd took no chances. He lured Gruffudd and Gruffudd's eldest son, Owain, into a trap and imprisoned both of them in Criccieth Castle (on the north coast of Cardigan Bay). He then procrastinated over the arbitration to which he had agreed at Gloucester, provoking the King to invade north Wales the following year and to force Dafydd to agree to even harsher terms. The agreement was concluded on 29 August 1241 at Gwern Eigron on the banks of the River Elwy near St Asaph.[244] Dafydd agreed not only to surrender to their erstwhile lords the lands which his father had conquered and to yield to the Crown the north-eastern part of Gwynedd between the River Clwyd and the Dee but importantly to hand over Gruffudd and Owain to the King and to accept the judgment of the King's court as to Gruffudd's territorial rights, thus exposing Dafydd to the risk that the remainder of Gwynedd might be divided between them.

Gruffudd and Owain were duly handed over and held in the Tower of London. Although they were treated honourably, their imprisonment by the King flouted an agreement that the King had made only a few weeks earlier with Gruffudd's wife, Senana, for their release in return for 600 marks.[245] Senana was to be disappointed once more because Gruffudd died on 1 March 1244 when trying to escape from the Tower. Others had managed to escape before him using a rope made from bed-linen. Unfortunately he was a very large man, the rope broke and he fell, breaking his neck when he hit

THE ENGLISH
CONQUEST of WALES
12th - 13th Century

N

Anglesey Deganwy
Beaumaris   Conwy   Diserth
                    Rhuddlan
         Perfeddwlad   Flint
              Hawarden   Chester
Caernarfon   Ruthyn   Caergwrle
         Gwynedd
         Uwch   Powys
         Conwy   Fadog
                         Dee
Criccieth   S N O W D O N I A   Dyffryn Ceiriog
   Harlech   B E R W Y N   Oswestry
                   MOUNTAINS

Castell y Bere   Mathrafal
              Powys   Maes Moydog
           Wenwynwyn

I r i s h

S e a   Aberystwyth

                         Severn

                    Radnor

     Llywelyn's Stone   Builth
Cardigan   Newcastle   Aberedw
         Emlyn   Hay
         Llandovery   Wye
              Tywi
   Dryslwyn   Dinefwr   Brecon
Carmarthen   Irfon
                    Usk
                    Usk
                    Chepstow

              Cardiff

B r i s t o l   C h a n n e l

                    Miles
              0   10   20   30   40   50

the ground. The King was disappointed too, being deprived of his principal hostage. Although Owain was released later that year with a view to him luring support away from Dafydd, he played no further part at that stage.

Llywelyn ap Gruffudd and the conquest of Wales by Edward I

Meanwhile, Gruffudd's second son, Llywelyn ap Gruffudd, had joined forces with Dafydd. However, before Henry had had an opportunity to crush any further resistance, in February 1246 Dafydd died without any direct heir. He was succeeded by Gruffudd's two elder sons, Owain and Llywelyn, together. Although the succession was confirmed by the King in the Treaty of Woodstock on 30 April 1247, unfortunately for Owain and Llywelyn the treaty entailed the surrender of any semblance of sovereignty and confined their succession to the land centred on Snowdonia west of the River Conwy, known as Gwynedd Uwch Conwy, with the surrender of the eastern part of Gwynedd, known as Perfeddwlad, to the King. No provision was made at that stage for the two younger sons of Gruffudd, Dafydd and Rhodri.

Attempts to agree provision for Dafydd and Rhodri foundered on the King's refusal to hand over any part of Perfeddwlad and on Llywelyn's refusal to hand over any part of Gwynedd Uwch Conwy. Then in 1255 Llywelyn took matters into his own hands. Taking up arms against two of his brothers, Owain and Dafydd, he defeated them at Bryn Derwin on the Caernarfon peninsula and imprisoned both of them, thus consolidating his hold on Gwynedd Uwch Conwy. Whereas Owain remained his prisoner for the next twenty-two years, Dafydd was released shortly afterwards and initially allied himself with Llywelyn. The following year Llywelyn recaptured Perfeddwlad, except for the two castles at Diserth and Deganwy, and then annexed Meirionydd (at the head of Cardigan Bay), so completing the reintegration of the patrimony of his grandfather, Llywelyn ap Iorwerth. At Oxford on 17 June 1258, a truce was concluded with the King by emissaries on behalf of Llywelyn, essentially preserving the *status quo* but allowing the King and his men access to the castles of Diserth and Deganwy and, in the event that the castles could not be supplied by sea because of storms, requiring Llywelyn to conduct the supplies by land.[246] The truce was elaborated and extended first in August 1260 and then in June 1262.[247]

Notwithstanding the truce that had been agreed, Llywelyn attacked the royal castle at Builth twice in 1260 and by the end of 1262 had resumed his campaign against the King. The following spring, Dafydd defected and allied himself with the King's son, the future Edward I and conqueror of Wales. In the turmoil that ensued, Llywelyn gained a formidable ally when Gruffudd ap Gwenwynwyn joined forces with him and did homage to him for all his lands (essentially southern Powys).[248] The turmoil was compounded in 1264 when civil war broke out between the forces of Simon de Montfort, Earl of Leicester, and the King, known as the Second Barons' War. On the 14 May that year de Montfort captured the King and Prince Edward at the Battle of Lewes.

It was while the King was de Montfort's prisoner that on 17 June 1265 an agreement was concluded at Pipton between Llywelyn and envoys of de Montfort acting ostensibly on behalf of the King. By its terms, Prince Edward was to be released and Llywelyn and the heirs of his body were granted the principality of Wales and the lordship of all of the barons of Wales in return for a fine of 30,000 marks. Unfortunately for Llywelyn, only a few weeks later, on 4 August, Simon de Montfort was killed at the Battle of Evesham against the forces of the Crown and the King was rescued, immediately calling into question the effectiveness of the Pipton Agreement. However, all was not lost because on 29 September 1267, through the good offices of Cardinal Ottobuono de' Fieschi (later Pope Adrian V), Llywelyn and the King concluded the Treaty of Montgomery.[249] In return for homage and another huge fine – this time of 25,000 marks payable in instalments, the King (specifically with the agreement of Prince Edward) granted to Llywelyn the hereditary right to the principality of Wales and the homage of all of the Welsh lords except for Maredudd ap Rhys Gryg.

It was by virtue of the Treaty of Montgomery that Llywelyn became the first Prince of Wales recognised by the English Crown. His overlordship included the former principalities of Powys and Deheubarth. He retained the lands of Gwynedd Uch Conwy and Perfeddwlad but was required to cede his other conquests, except for Gwrtheyrnion, Builth, Brecon, Ceri, Cedewain, Whittington and, if he could establish his right to it, Maelienydd. He was specifically required to make provision for his brother, Dafydd, not least by restoring to him the lands which he held before he went over to the King.

Ten years later, however, Llywelyn's remarkable achievement fell apart. Henry III died in 1272 and was succeeded by Prince Edward as Edward I, a man of a very different mark. Edward was at that stage on crusade and did not return until August 1274. In his absence, Llywelyn had been storing up trouble for himself: he had made war on various Lords of the Marches, among them Gilbert de Clare, Earl of Gloucester, Humphrey de Bohun, Earl of Hereford, and Sir Roger de Mortimer; he had failed to pay one of the instalments of the fine which were due under the Treaty of Montgomery; and he had failed to swear fealty to the King as required.

After the King's return, Llywelyn's relationship with him grew steadily worse. First, the King had given shelter to Llywelyn's brother, Dafydd, and Gruffudd ap Gwenwynwyn following their conspiracy to assassinate Llywelyn and their flight to England. Almost certainly in retaliation for the shelter given to his would-be assassins, Llywelyn had promptly married by proxy Eleanor (to whom he had long been betrothed), the King's cousin and daughter of the King's enemy, Simon de Montfort. Although Eleanor had embarked on her voyage to Wales from France to join Llywelyn, on the King's orders her ship had been captured off the Isles of Scilly and she had been taken prisoner. The King had also failed to ensure compliance with the terms of the Treaty of Montgomery, of which Llywelyn complained bitterly not only to the King but also to the Pope. Summoned on several separate occasions to do homage to the King, Llywelyn had refused to comply unless the King would guarantee his safety (not least from his would-be assassins), release Eleanor and confirm the terms of the treaty, none of which (of course) had been acceptable to the King.

Infuriated by Llywelyn's conduct towards him and deeply dissatisfied with the terms of the Treaty of Montgomery, Edward marshalled a huge army and invaded Gwynedd in July 1277 with the aim of depriving Llywelyn of his entire patrimony. Following the defection of several of his supporters particularly in west Wales, Llywelyn surrendered and submitted to the humiliating terms of the Treaty of Aberconwy on 9 November, by which he acknowledged the hereditary right of his treacherous brother, Dafydd, to Gwynedd Uwch Conwy, albeit that he was permitted to keep it during his own lifetime, and he lost all his other lands except for Anglesey.[250] Although he was allowed to retain the title of Prince of Wales and the homage of five minor lords, he was obliged to pay £50,000 for reparations and for the King's grace (although subsequently waived), to continue the payments due under the Treaty of Montgomery and to continue annual payments for Anglesey. Provision was also made for his other two brothers – Owain, who was released from prison where he had languished since 1247, and Rhodri.

He swore fealty to the King at Rhuddlan two days later and did homage in London at Christmas that year. Finally on 13 October 1278, having released her from prison, Edward gave Eleanor in marriage to Llywelyn at Worcester Cathedral and graciously provided the wedding feast.

However, even that state of affairs was not destined to last. On Palm Sunday, 22 March 1282, Llywelyn's brother, Dafydd, led an attack on the royal stronghold of Hawarden Castle, about 5 miles west of Chester, leading rapidly to an uprising against the Crown in other parts of Wales. Initially Llywelyn took no part in the rebellion, but, following the death of Eleanor when giving birth to their only child, Gwenllian, on 19 June, he joined his brother. An attempt by the Archbishop of Canterbury, John Peckham (Pecham), to mediate between Llywelyn and the King failed, the two principal bones of contention being the application of English law to Wales and the ceding of Llywelyn's territories to the Crown. Although the insurgents enjoyed early success against the forces of the Crown, following the failure of the Archbishop's mediation the King redoubled his efforts to conquer Wales.

With the reinforcement of the King's army being marshalled at Chester, Llywelyn and Dafydd had fallen back to the west of the River Conwy. By the summer of 1282 Anglesey had been taken by the King with two aims in view: one was to cut off Llywelyn's most important source of grain supplies; and the other was an ambitious plan to build a bridge of boats across the Menai Strait to mount an attack on Llywelyn's rear at the same time as the King crossed the Conwy and attacked his front. The timber for the bridge was taken from a forest above St Asaph, just south of the King's stronghold at Rhuddlan. The bridge was built out from the Anglesey shore and was finally connected to the mainland on the morning of 6 November (the exact site is uncertain, although traditionally it was said to have been at a point south-west of today's bridges). Around midday when the tide was slack, English troops under the command of Luke de Tany began to cross the bridge. Forewarned, Llywelyn's men mounted a ferocious attack from the mainland, forcing the English back both onto the bridge and into the sea. The bridge broke under the weight of numbers and the stress of what was by then the ebbing tide race. Those of the English who had not already fallen or drowned or managed to re-cross the bridge fled east along the coast of the mainland to the safety of the royal castles at Rhuddlan, Flint and Caergwrle (also known as Hope). Why Llywelyn failed to follow up this victory is a mystery.

Instead, he left Dafydd in charge of Gwynedd and went south to gather further support. Whether for strategic reasons or, more probably, because he had been deceived by a letter from Sir Edmund de Mortimer (son of his erstwhile enemy Sir Roger), Llywelyn proceeded towards Aberedw Castle at the confluence of the River Edw and the Wye a few miles downstream from Builth Wells to receive the homage, so he was led to believe, of various powerful defectors from the King's cause, including some of his own relatives. On 11 December, whilst waiting at Aberedw, he was surprised by the sight of a squadron of knights and immediately fled with his small escort for what he hoped would be the safety of Builth Castle on the far side of the Wye. Disastrously, the Wye was too swollen by winter rains and snow to be forded, so they had to abandon their horses in order to cross by a footbridge. Disaster was compounded when the 'traitors of Builth' refused them entry, so they proceeded on foot. Not wanting to be trapped between the swollen River Irfon and its confluence with the Wye just north of Builth, they walked upstream and, near the village of Cilmery, crossed the Irfon by a footbridge which they then destroyed. With a barrage of arrows, Llywelyn's escort prevented their immediate pursuers from crossing the Irfon, but unknown to them there were others on their tail who had managed to cross the river further downstream. Llywelyn and his secretary (a priest) were standing apart in a wood looking down on the engagement on the riverbank below, when Llywelyn was stabbed in the back with a lance.

A standing stone marks the spot where Llywelyn is thought to have fallen. A copy of the letter by which it is probable that he was deceived was found by his assailants tucked beneath his clothes against his inner thigh, as reported to the King by Archbishop Peckham. His body was decapitated and his head, having reputedly been washed in the well which is still to be found in the gully nearby, was sent to the King at Rhuddlan (or possibly Caergwrle) Castle as proof of his death. The head was later taken to the Tower of London, where it was impaled on a spear over Traitors' Gate. The only survivor was the priest, every member of the escort having died in defence of their prince – the first and last Welsh Prince of Wales recognised by the English Crown.

After Llywelyn's death, his brother Dafydd assumed the title of Prince of Wales and Lord of Snowdon and continued the struggle, but he lacked the support that his brother had enjoyed. Castell y Bere, the last stronghold loyal to him, fell on 25 April 1283. Two months later he was captured, when his hiding place was betrayed to the English, and taken to Rhuddlan Castle

where the King was in residence. On 30 September he was taken in chains
to Shrewsbury and charged with high treason. Following a state trial, he was
condemned to death and on 2 October was hanged, drawn and quartered,
bringing to an end all hope of Welsh independence from the English Crown.
His head was then taken to London and displayed above Traitors' Gate
alongside his brother's.

Edward's conquest was consolidated by his elaborate and extensive
castle-building. After his victory in 1277, new castles were built at Flint,
Rhuddlan, Builth and Aberystwyth. Following the crushing of the second
uprising in 1283, he now added Conwy, Caernarfon and Harlech and an
extension to the former Llywelyn stronghold of Criccieth. For that purpose
he engaged a Savoyard master mason called Jacques de St-Georges
d'Espéranche (known in English as James of St George) who introduced
Savoyard designs: concentric fortifications and, in the case of Caernarfon,
polygonal towers – the latter included decorative bands of darker masonry,
copied perhaps from the walls of Theodosius at Constantinople, magnificent
stretches of which can be seen today. In all they formed the finest system of
self-supporting castles in medieval Europe, many of which still stand either
as picturesque – and much painted – ruins or in some cases well preserved,
having been adapted to changing needs over the ages. The first to be built
was at Flint, starting in 1277, a ruin now standing somewhat isolated
from the sea in which it once stood at the mouth of the Dee. The last was
Beaumaris, started in 1295 but never fully completed. Although Llywelyn's
stronghold at Castell y Bere was altered after it was captured in 1283, it
was abandoned in 1294 following the failure successfully to establish an
English colony there: to this day the crag on which its ruins stand is as wild
and remote as it was when Llywelyn first arrived there. The construction of
these castles required lead, which was readily to be found in the Isle of Man,
prompting Edward's interest in the island from 1290.

Together with the castles, new towns were built and fortified, the castle
and town dependent on each other for protection and trade, like the *bastide*
towns in Edward's dukedom of Gascony. The new towns, along with those
already at Criccieth and Castell-y-Bere, were to be colonised by English
settlers, the Welsh only being permitted to enter by day and even then not to
trade, let alone to carry arms (it was not until the eighteenth century that the
Welsh had towns which they could call their own). The colonisation did not
stop at the new towns: it included the displacement of the Welsh inhabitants

by English immigrants elsewhere too and, from 1291, the imposition of taxes to fund the Crown.[251]

Neither the conquest itself nor the castle-building nor even the garrisoning of the castles could have been achieved without the necessary finance, and that was found in large part by borrowing from bankers, pre-eminent among whom were the Riccardi of Lucca. Although the English Crown had had recourse to Italian bankers from early in the thirteenth century, Edward developed an ingenious relationship with the Riccardi enterprise over the first twenty-two years of his reign, so close indeed that the Riccardi almost became a branch of government. They provided the King with much needed liquidity, not only from their own resources but also by acting as guarantors for the repayment of loans from other Italian bankers. They were in return repaid from the revenues of the Crown, including those from Ireland and Gascony. The most important source of revenue for this purpose was the customs duties which the Riccardi collected on behalf on the Crown, particularly the duties on the export of wool which the King had introduced in 1275.[252] For twenty-two years the Riccardi enjoyed all the benefits of royal favour: safe conducts, lucrative business opportunities, pardons for violations of regulations and governmental assistance in collecting their debts. However, the relationship foundered with the outbreak of war against Philippe IV of France in 1294. When the Riccardi were unable to meet Edward's demands to finance the war, he removed the collection of customs duties from their control, then Philippe confiscated their assets in France and the Pope demanded repayment of debts owed by them to the Holy See, culminating in their bankruptcy in 1301.

In order more effectively to colonise Wales, Edward imposed an English system of administration and justice on those parts of Wales under direct royal control and replaced and extended many of the Marcher lordships while at the same time seeking to constrain their power.

The imposition of an English system of administration and justice was achieved by the Statute of Rhuddlan (also known as the Statute of Wales) of 1284.[253] It created the five shires (or counties) of Anglesey, Caernarfon, Flint, Merioneth and Cardigan (broadly the north-western half of Wales), each administered by a sheriff.[254] It provided for the application of English law, rather than Welsh law, to the most serious criminal offenses, for the endowment of married women, for inheritance by women in the absence of a male heir and for the disinheritance of bastards. It prescribed remedies for most civil causes similar to those available in England (differing fundamentally from the remedies available in Wales) which, importantly, would have included the collection of tax.[255] Although the Statute opened with a somewhat grandiose declaration, it is clear from what follows that it only applied to the five counties. It declared:

> The Divine Providence ... which hath vouchsafed to distinguish Us and our Realm of England, hath now of its favour, wholly and entirely transferred under our proper dominion, the Land of Wales with its Inhabitants, heretofore subject to us, in Feudal Right, all obstacles whatsoever ceasing; and hath annexed and united the same unto the Crown of the aforesaid Realm, as a Member of the same Body.[256]

As to the Marches, a more extensive English buffer was created between western Wales and England by giving Denbigh to Henry de Lacy, Earl of Lincoln, Ruthyn to Reginald de Grey, Bromfield and Yale to John de Warenne, Earl of Surrey, and Chirk to Roger Mortimer de Chirk (uncle of Roger Mortimer, 1st Earl of March). Although Edward lacked the pretext or the resources to abolish the extraordinary privileges of the Marcher Lords, he seized every opportunity to undermine them: he imposed taxes on them, he undertook direct military recruitment from within the Marches, he extracted Wigmore from the March and restored it to England and he intervened to restrain the habitual warfare between neighbouring Lordships.

Notwithstanding the firm grip which the King had taken of Wales, he was confronted by two rebellions. The first was by Rhys ap Maredudd, Lord of Drylswyn, on the River Tywi in the south-west. Having been loyal to the King both in 1277 and in 1282, Rhys had been disappointed by the King's refusal to re-grant nearby Dinefwr Castle to him, having in the first place surrendered it to the King in 1277; he had been publicly rebuked by the King for taking possession of lands granted to him before he had been formally invested with them; and he had been irked by his treatment at the hands of English officials. In June 1287 he overran the lands of a rival and ravaged parts of west Wales. However, his castle at Drylswyn was taken by royal troops in September and his castle at Newcastle Emlyn in January 1288. He was then on the run as an outlaw until he was captured and executed in 1292.

The other, and potentially far more serious, rebellion broke out in 1294. It was sparked off partly by resentment at the English colonisation, partly by the collection of the burdensome tax which had been imposed in 1291, and most immediately by the mutiny of a large number of Welsh troops refusing to obey an order to proceed to Portsmouth to embark for service on Edward's campaign against the King of France – the same campaign that led ultimately to the bankruptcy of the Riccardi bankers. The rebellion took the form of a widespread popular national uprising which began at the end of September 1294 and was led most prominently by Madog ap Llywelyn, a distant cousin of Llywelyn ap Gruffudd.

As in the past, Edward responded by mobilising a vast army. Abandoning his planned campaign in France, he reached Chester in early December, by which stage many of his castles had fallen into rebel hands, with the notable exceptions of Criccieth and Harlech which he was able to provision by sea. At the end of December Edward moved to Conwy Castle where for a short period in January he was besieged, suffering from short supplies until relieved by sea. By March the forces led by Madog had moved south. Alerted by English spies of Madog's position at Maes Moydog, near Castle Caereinion, the Earl of Warwick mustered troops and on 5 March, from his base at Montgomery nearby, mounted a surprise attack on Madog's camp under cover of darkness. In the battle that ensued the rebels were severely defeated and, as a result, the rebellion began to collapse. Although Madog himself escaped from the battlefield, he was hunted down and captured that summer, spending the rest of his life as a prisoner in the Tower of London. Strange though it may seem, he was never executed as a traitor.

In the meantime Edward had managed to occupy Anglesey with little resistance, making his base at Llanfaes on the eastern promontory. It was at Beaumaris (pronounced Beaumairs locally) on the coast nearby that the last of his castles was built, guarding the Menai Strait, the final mark of his conquest of Wales. Work began immediately and once again it was masterminded by James of St George. Although for want of funds the castle was never fully completed, much of it still stands today, a formidable fortress of remarkable beauty.

The first English Prince of Wales

At a ceremony in Lincoln in 1301 the King invested his seventeen-year-old son, the future Edward II, as the first English Prince of Wales, together with all the territories of the Crown in Wales and the allegiance of all of those lordships by which allegiance had previously been owed to Llywelyn ap Gruffudd. Singling out Wales in this way, the King was acknowledging to the Welsh that Wales was in some respects distinct from England.

Edward II succeeded his father in 1307. Most of his reign was dogged by his relationship first with Piers Gaveston and then, following Gaveston's murder in 1312, with Hugh Despenser (the younger), which culminated in the abdication and probably also the murder of the King himself. The baleful influence of both Gaveston and Despenser was opposed by much of the nobility, led by the King's first cousin, the Earl of Lancaster, and latterly by the Queen, Isabella, and her lover, Roger Mortimer (whom she later created 1st Earl of March), leading ultimately to civil war. Lancaster, Mortimer and Despenser held great swathes of territory in Wales, Despenser having been conspicuously acquisitive while the King was in his thrall. However, in the ebb and flow of hostilities, Lancaster was captured by the King and, given that he had been responsible for the death of Gaveston, was unsurprisingly executed as a traitor in 1322. Then in 1326, in company with the King, Despenser, who had retreated into Wales from the invading forces of Isabella and Mortimer, was captured and met a particularly gruesome end at Hereford Castle on 24 November that year.

In January 1327 the King was forced to abdicate and was succeeded by his fifteen-year-old son, who was crowned as Edward III in Westminster Abbey the following month. In September the erstwhile King, now known as Sir Edward of Caernarfon, was being held as a prisoner at Berkeley Castle and was reported to have died. The new King told of his father's death in a letter to his cousin dated 24 September, but he did not identify the cause. The chronicles of the time suggest a host of different causes, including the story of a red-hot poker rammed up his backside. The first report of murder was to Parliament in 1330. But speculation did not stop at the cause of death. Although there was a funeral for Sir Edward at Gloucester three months later, there were those who reported that he had in fact been rescued from Berkeley Castle and been spirited abroad.

Three years later the tables were turned again when Isabella and Mortimer were cornered in Nottingham Castle by a handful of the young King's knights who had gained access to the castle undetected by a secret passage. Whereas Isabella was allowed by her son to live in honourable retirement until her death in 1358, Mortimer was tried under one of his own laws, which ironically allowed of no defence, and subsequently executed as a traitor at Tyburn on 29 November 1330. So it was that the lives of the principal actors in the reign of the first English Prince of Wales, other than that of his mother, came to an abrupt end.

Annexation of the Marches

The long reign of Edward III (1327–77) saw one significant blow struck by the English Crown, not against the Welsh on this occasion, but against the Lords of the Marches. In 1354 a statute was passed which, without more ado, annexed all of the Welsh Marches to the English Crown.[257] Although the Marcher lordships had originally been granted by the King, the independence of the Marcher Lords had been growing and their allegiance to the Crown, as opposed to any allegiance to the recently created principality of Wales, might in the future have been open to doubt. The annexation was at the very least a timely reminder of the ultimate sovereignty of the Crown over the Marches.

Owain Glyn Dŵr's rebellion

Edward III was succeeded by his grandson, Richard II. In 1399 Richard was deposed and succeeded by another grandson, his cousin Henry IV. Within a year the new King was faced by an uprising in Wales led by Owain Glyn Dŵr, an uprising which was to last for the whole of his reign and beyond.

Owain Glyn Dŵr was a landed squire of the Welsh Marches and scion of the Princes of Powys. His part in the rebellion of which he became the leader was precipitated by his disgust at the failure of the English Parliament to give him redress in respect of a territorial dispute with Lord Grey de Ruthyn and by the potential forfeiture of his estates for failure to respond to a royal summons to a general muster for service in Scotland, the transmission of the summons having been delayed by none other than Lord Grey. On 16 September 1400 Glyn Dŵr, his son, two of his brothers-in-law, the Dean of St Asaph and many other Welshmen had gathered at Glyndyfrdwy on Glyn Dŵr's estate, intending the death of the King and the obliteration of the English language. Two days later they attacked, plundered and burnt the town of Ruthyn, part of Lord Grey's estate, and from there proceeded to attack and despoil the 'English towns' of Denbigh, Rhuddlan, Flint, Hawarden, Holt, Oswestry and Welshpool. Although on 24 September the rebels were checked by forces of the Crown near Welshpool, Glyn Dŵr escaped and lay low for the winter.

Early the following year Parliament passed several punitive statutes with a view to suppressing the rebellion, essentially excluding the Welsh from any English town.[258] These only inflamed the situation. On 1 April 1401 two of Glyn Dŵr's cousins, Rhys and Gwilym ap Tudur, captured Conwy Castle, followed by Glyn Dŵr's victory at Hyddgen Mountain to the east of Aberystwyth. By May Glyn Dŵr's success had led to a major escalation of the rebellion. In the spring of the following year Glyn Dŵr attacked Ruthyn for a second time, captured Lord Grey and succeeded in extorting a ransom of 10,000 marks for him from the King.

In the summer of 1402 Glyn Dŵr led a raid deep into the Mortimer lordships in east-central Wales. He took up a position on a hill called Bryn Glas near the village of Pilleth, north-west of Presteigne. Sir Edmund Mortimer, who was then at Ludlow nearby, raised the men of Herefordshire and marched against Glyn Dŵr. On 22 June battle was joined on Bryn Glas: Mortimer's force was routed and Mortimer himself was taken prisoner. Although a ransom was sought for his release, unlike with Lord Grey, the King refused to play ball, rightly suspecting that Mortimer had defected to Glyn Dŵr's cause and also troubled by the superior claim of the Mortimers to the English throne, the 5th Earl being a great-grandson of Lionel, Duke of Clarence, and thus a great-great-grandson of Edward III. Not only did the King refuse to ransom Mortimer, but he started to confiscate his estates. In the event his suspicions as to Mortimer's loyalty turned out to be well-founded, because that November Mortimer married Glyn Dŵr's daughter, Catherine, and in December he declared that he had joined Glyn Dŵr with a view to vindicating Richard II's claim to the throne or, if Richard was dead, the claim of his own nephew, Edmund Mortimer, 5th Earl of March.[259]

In an attempt to turn the tide, further punitive statutes were enacted by Parliament in September 1402 (and remained in force for the next two centuries), this time prohibiting, among other things, assemblies by the Welsh in Wales except by licence, the bearing of arms by the Welsh in public, the importation of victuals or armour into Wales, other than to provision English castles or towns or by special licence, and the keeping of castles or the holding of almost any public office by Welshmen.[260] Nonetheless, come the summer of 1403 Glyn Dŵr had taken Carmarthen and the castle at Newcastle Emlyn. Then in the autumn attacks were launched from French and Breton ships on Kidwelly (to the south of Carmarthen) and on Caernarfon.

In 1404 Aberystwyth, Harlech and Cardiff Castles fell to Glyn Dŵr, making him master of west Wales from sea to sea. Following a treaty of mutual solidarity between Glyn Dŵr and the King of France which had been concluded in 1404, French troops under the command of Marshal Jean de Rieux landed at Milford Haven in August 1405 and in conjunction with Glyn Dŵr's forces reached Worcester, only to withdraw to Wales on finding insufficient support from the English. The south-west of Wales also came under pressure with attacks on Haverfordwest, Carmarthen and Cardigan. The rebels even managed to seize the King's baggage train as royal forces advanced to relieve the siege of Coity Castle north-east of Porthcawl.

Supposedly buoyed up by the success of the rebellion, in February 1405 an indenture (of uncertain authenticity and known as the Tripartite Indenture) was executed by emissaries of Glyn Dŵr, Mortimer and the Earl of Northumberland in which they agreed to divide the kingdom into three parts between them, with Glyn Dŵr taking everything to the west of the Severn, Mortimer most of the south of England and Northumberland the rest.

However, the rebellion was not without its setbacks. In 1405 alone, the rebels were heavily defeated in March. Having burnt part of the town of Grosmont (between Hereford and Abergavenny), a small force under the command of Lord Talbot is reported to have killed between 800 and 1,000 of the rebels. Worse still, on 5 May Glyn Dŵr's son, Gruffudd, led an attack on Usk Castle, badly underestimating the strength of the fortifications, the size of the garrison and the experience of its commander, Lord Grey of Codnor. Having failed to breach the defences of the castle, the rebels withdrew towards Monk Wood only to be pursued by the castle garrison and driven towards the River Usk where many were cut down or drowned and others captured. Among the dead was reputed to have been Glyn Dŵr's brother, Tudur, and among the captives was Gruffudd. Whereas Gruffudd was held in the Tower of London until his death in 1411, 300 other captives were beheaded in front of the castle, no doubt as a salutary warning to others. The battle is known by the name of the 'yellow pool' – 'Pwll Melyn' – which lay to the north-west of the castle and to the east of the river, part of which exists today as Castle Oak Pond, where numerous skeletons were found in the nineteenth century. The Battle of Pwll Melyn marked the end of the rebellion in south-east Wales.

From then on Henry IV slowly gained the upper hand, having far greater resources, command of the sea and, increasingly, command of the lines of supply by land. The French withdrew their support in 1406 and so too did the inhabitants of Anglesey and the southern coastlands. By April 1407 only Caernarfonshire, Merionethshire and northern Cardiganshire continued solidly to support Glyn Dŵr; his main hope then was for support by sea to the castles which he still held at Aberystwyth and Harlech. However, that hope was finally dashed in December 1407, when the French concluded a peace treaty with the English.

Aberystwyth fell in September 1408 after withstanding a siege for sixteen months during the course of which the defenders are reputed to have catapulted the severed heads of hostages among the English below. The end came in February 1409 when Harlech fell. Mortimer had perished in the siege of the castle. Among the survivors were Glyn Dŵr's wife, two daughters and four young grandchildren, all of whom were captured and imprisoned in the Tower of London, where, over the miserable years that followed, all of them died.

Notwithstanding the loss of Aberystwyth and Harlech, Glyn Dŵr continued to make sporadic attacks on the English. However, the last of his movements which is known for sure is his involvement in the capture and ransom of the King's personal esquire, Dafydd Gam, in 1412.

In 1413 Henry IV died and was succeeded by his son, Henry V. The new King adopted a more conciliatory approach to the Welsh not only as a means of placating them but also to free up resources for his planned invasion of France. Within days of his coronation he had offered a pardon to the rebels, albeit that they would forfeit their lands, and he also commuted some of the fines which had previously been imposed. Within two years the rebellion had petered out. On 25 October 1415 Henry won his great victory over the French at Agincourt, a victory in which the Welsh archers had played no small part and among whom were many of the former rebels.

Although the last record of Glyn Dŵr himself is in 1412, legend as to what became of him abounds: he was never captured or betrayed; and there is even some suggestion that he lived for the rest of his days masquerading as an itinerant friar under the protection of his daughter, Alice Scudamore, at her husband's home at Kentchurch Court or his property at Dorstone just over the English border in Herefordshire.

The Tudor revolution

Henry V died in 1422 and was succeeded by his son, Henry VI. In about
1431 Henry V's widow, Catherine of Valois, married a first cousin once
removed of Owain Glyn Dŵr – Owain ap Maredudd ap Tudor, otherwise
known as Owen Tudor. There were two sons of the marriage, Edmund and
Jasper. Edmund married Margaret Beaufort who was the great-great-
granddaughter of Edward III, her great-grandfather being John of Gaunt,
Duke of Lancaster. Edmund died in 1456 leaving the thirteen-year-old
Margaret pregnant. Margaret's child, born the following January, was
Henry Tudor, a Lancastrian.

Henry VI was deposed in 1461 and was succeeded by Edward IV. In
1483 Edward IV died, leaving two young sons, Edward (Edward V, albeit
never crowned) and Richard. Although their uncle, Richard, Duke of York,
was nominally their protector, he seized the throne on the basis that both
Princes were illegitimate, and was crowned as Richard III. The illegitimacy
of the Princes and Richard's right to the throne had been declared in a
petition addressed to Richard by both Houses of Parliament, known as the
Titulus Regius. It was later that same year that both Princes disappeared
mysteriously from their quarters in the Tower of London (famously
portrayed both by Delaroche and by Millais), giving rise to the suspicion
that they had been murdered at the behest of their uncle.

With the disappearance of the Princes from the Tower, one of the
many obstacles to Henry Tudor's claim to the throne through his mother,
Margaret, was removed, leaving as principal obstacles the eldest sister of the
Princes, Elizabeth, and their uncle Richard.

To make good his claim, in August 1485 Henry Tudor landed at Milford
Haven with an army of about 2,000 Frenchmen together with some
Lancastrian exiles. He marched unhindered through Wales and on reaching
England was joined increasingly by supporters, including at a late stage the
forces of Lord Stanley and his brother, Sir William Stanley. In the meantime,
alerted to Henry's progress, Richard proceeded south from his base at
Nottingham to a muster of levies at Leicester and from there marched
west to intercept Henry. On 21 August Richard pitched camp at Sutton
Cheney, just to the south of Market Bosworth, and Henry at White Moors,
about 2 miles to the south-west of Richard's camp. The following day battle
was joined. Reliable details of the engagement are sparse. Richard's army

gained the crest of Ambien Hill overlooking Henry's advance towards them skirting the bog at the foot of the hill. When Richard realised that both of the Stanleys had joined the rebel cause and that his rearguard commanded by the Earl of Northumberland had not moved forward to support him, he charged his enemy and died like a king. It was in that charge that he lost his horse (probably in the bog) and, as Shakespeare imagined, cried 'A horse, a horse! My kingdom for a horse!'[261]

With Richard's death the Wars of the Roses and the Plantagenet dynasty came to an end. On 30 October 1485 Henry Tudor was crowned as Henry VII in Westminster Abbey. Then, a year later, he consolidated his hold on the Crown by marrying Elizabeth (sister of the Princes in the Tower).

By the end of his reign in 1509, little had changed in Wales, save that much of the Marches had fallen into Henry's hands: his uncle Jasper had died childless such that his lordships of Pembroke and Glamorgan passed to the Crown; and Sir William Stanley, notwithstanding that he had fought on Henry's side at Bosworth, had been executed as a traitor, so forfeiting his lordships to the Crown. It was, however, his heir, Henry VIII, who was to revolutionise the constitution of Wales.

In 1534 Rowland Lee, Bishop of Coventry and Lichfield, was appointed as President of the Council of Wales and the Marches, an office which he held until his death in 1543. He embarked on a ruthless suppression of the lawlessness endemic to much of Wales and particularly in the Marches. Brutal though his administration may have been, so efficient was it that the Council became fully established as the means by which Welsh affairs came to be administered.

Bishop Lee's tenure of office coincided with the enactment of a whole series of statutes which were to transform the governance of Wales, notwithstanding that initially there were no representatives of Wales in Parliament. Of those, the two most important were 'An act for laws and justice to be ministered in Wales in like form as it is in this realm'[262] and 'An act for certain ordinances in the king's dominion and principality of Wales'.[263]

The first of those two Acts was the creature of Henry's remarkable chief minister, Thomas Cromwell. It was passed in 1536 and has sometimes been referred to as the Act of Union. It opened grandiosely as follows:

Albeit the Dominion Principality and Country of Wales justly and righteously is, and ever hath been incorporated annexed united and

subject to and under the Imperial Crown of this Realm, as a very
Member and Joint of the same, whereof the King's most Royal Majesty
of mere Droit, and very Right, is very Head King Lord and Ruler ...

It continued by enacting

that his said Country or Dominion of Wales shall be, stand and
continue for ever from henceforth incorporated united and annexed
to and with this his Realm of England; and that all and singular
person and persons, born and to be born in ... Wales, shall have enjoy
and inherit all and singular Freedoms Liberties Rights Privileges
and Laws within this Realm, and other the King's Dominions, as
other the King's Subjects naturally born within the same have enjoy
and inherit ...

In other words, not only was there to be no distinction between the
citizens of Wales and the citizens of England but also, unlike the union with
Scotland in 1707 or Ireland in 1800, Wales was to form part of the realm
of England. The Marches were to be divided up, parts being ascribed to
shires in England[264] and the remainder to shires in Wales, the whole of Wales
being divided into shires. Thus, in addition to the eight shires which already
existed,[265] five more were created.[266] Each shire was to be represented in
Parliament by one knight, except Monmouth being represented by two; and
each shire town, except Merioneth, was to be represented in Parliament
by one burgess.[267] The inheritance of land was to be governed by English,
not Welsh, law,[268] thus enabling land to be inherited by the eldest son
alone;[269] and English law was to be applied for all purposes in the shires of
Glamorgan, Carmarthen, Pembroke and Cardigan,[270] save to the extent that
it was subsequently determined by a King's Commission that the application
of Welsh law in any given respect would be expedient.[271] Although the
lordships of the Marches were abolished, some peculiar manorial rights were
preserved[272] and so too were all of the liberties of the Duchy of Lancaster,[273]
now vested in the Crown. Most importantly, the administration of justice
and government was to be conducted in English, not Welsh,[274] and that
remained the position until 1993.[275]

Thomas Cromwell did not live to see the enactment of the second of the
two statutes, for he was executed in 1540. The 'act for certain ordinances

in the king's dominion and principality of Wales' was passed in 1543 and made lengthy and detailed provision for the administration of justice and government.[276] There were however two provisions of fundamental importance. One was the establishment of the President and Council of Wales and the Marches,[277] which had until then existed solely by virtue of the royal prerogative. The role of the Council was not defined, but it was in practice a court with jurisdiction over the most serious crimes, maladministration and claims by those too poor to afford recourse to ordinary courts. The other was the establishment of the court called the King's Great Sessions in Wales,[278] as distinct from the King's courts at Westminster. There was one particular oddity created by the Act which related to the treatment of Monmouthshire: it was left up in the air whether it was part of Wales or part of England,[279] an anomaly which was only resolved in 1972 when it landed in Wales and became known as Gwent.[280]

Subject to the oddity relating to Monmouthshire, the border between England and Wales had now been fixed along the boundaries of the shires. Nevertheless, as with the border between England and Scotland, there may be parts where there is room for debate as to where precisely it lies.

Although Henry VIII had gone a long way to assimilate Wales into England, there was one glorious exception introduced by his daughter, Elizabeth, shortly after she came to the throne. Following the Catholic Counter-Reformation of her half-sister, Bloody Mary, and no doubt concerned by the threat to her kingdom from Catholic Spain, in 1563 Elizabeth directed that the whole of the Bible and the Book of Common Prayer were to be translated into Welsh by March 1567 and that parts of the church services in Wales were to be conducted in Welsh as well as English with copies of the books to be supplied in both languages.[281] Part of the idea behind the latter was that the Welsh would learn to speak English and abandon their Welsh. By 1567 partial translations had been produced by William Salesbury and Richard Davies. Then, in 1588, consolidated translations were provided by Bishop William Morgan. Like King James's Bible which followed in English in 1611, Morgan's translation of the Bible was a work of great beauty and it continued in use until the twentieth century. Paradoxically it is thought to have been one of the principal reasons for which the Welsh language is so widespread and well preserved.

The changeable winds of Home Rule

Wales finally lost any semblance of separate identity first by the abolition of the Council of Wales and the Marches in 1689[282] and then by the abolition of the King's Great Sessions in 1830.[283] And, as if its assimilation with England had not been clear enough since 1543, the Wales and Berwick Act 1746 spelled out that any reference in past or future legislation to England should be interpreted as including Wales, unless the contrary was indicated.[284]

Things began to change, however, as a result of the disestablishment of the Church in Ireland in 1869, which opened up the possibility that the Welsh Church might be disestablished too. That depended on Wales being regarded as separate from England, at least in that respect, notwithstanding the assimilation of the two over the past three centuries – a difficult pill for the British Establishment to swallow. Nevertheless, on 18 September 1914, the same day as Home Rule would have been granted to Ireland but for the outbreak of the First World War, the Welsh Church Act received royal assent. [285] After centuries of dissent, the Church in Wales and Monmouthshire was disestablished from the Church of England. Although this did not take effect until 1920, it constituted the first constitutional break between England and Wales since the two had been united in the reign of Henry VIII. So Wales began its long hard road towards devolution.

The office of Minister of State for Welsh Affairs was established in 1951 and that of Secretary of State for Wales in 1964. Two years later, Plaid Cymru (the Welsh Nationalist Party) won its first seat at Westminster. A proposal for a Welsh Assembly was overwhelmingly rejected by a referendum in Wales in 1979. Eighteen years later that decision was reversed by a very slender majority, culminating in the creation of the National Assembly for Wales in 1998.[286] Since then, as with the Scottish Parliament, more and more powers have been devolved by Westminster, including limited powers to raise income tax. Even so, there is still pressure in some quarters for Wales to become fully independent, not least from Plaid Cymru.

Ireland

Ireland was never invaded by the Romans. Its people were Celtic, whose language was Goidelic (Q-Celtic), from which not only Irish but also Manx and Scots Gaelic developed. It was divided into five ancient kingdoms (known at times as 'fifths' and later as provinces) – Ulster in the north, Connacht in the west, Munster in the south-west, Leinster in the south-east and Mide (Meath) in the east – ruled over by a host of petty kings, princes or chiefs and, periodically, by a high king or overlord. However, as Ireland was progressively colonised, so the province of Meath merged with Leinster, leaving just the four provinces of Ulster, Connacht, Munster and Leinster.

Although the Romans never invaded, they did send Christian missionaries to Ireland, and the church which they founded there played a central role in the history of the colonisation of the island. The first recorded Christian missionary to arrive in Ireland was Palladius, but it was St Patrick who was forever to be remembered. Following the death of Palladius, Patrick was sent to Ireland by Pope Celestine I, arriving in 432 first in Wicklow, where he received a hostile reception, and then (reputedly at least) landing near Saul on the shore of Strangford Lough in what is now County Down.

Patrick founded his principal church in Ireland at Armagh in Ulster in 444 – a church which became, and remains to this day, the archdiocese of Ireland. It is ironic that the church which stands where Patrick's church once stood is now the Protestant Cathedral: the Catholic Cathedral, which is the seat of the Primate of All Ireland, was built on a neighbouring hill in the nineteenth century. Although Patrick's principal church was at Armagh, his remains are believed to have been buried beneath a rock outside Down Cathedral, not far from where he was reputed to have first landed on

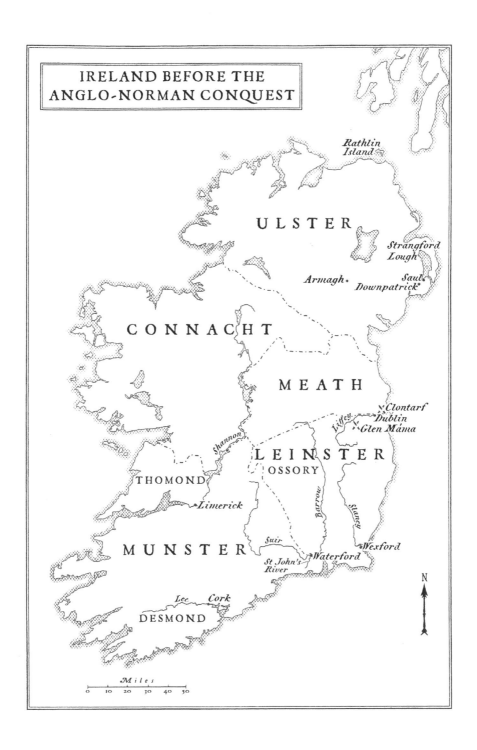

IRELAND BEFORE THE
ANGLO-NORMAN CONQUEST

Strangford Lough. (The present Down Cathedral was completed in 1818 and has exquisite neo-Gothic pews, chancel screen and organ case.)

It was the wealth of the churches in Ireland that became the principal target of the early Viking raids, the first recorded raid being on Rathlin Island off the coast of Antrim in 795, where the monastery was attacked, looted and burnt. Raids on a large scale began in 837, with the invasion of fleets of ships, one making landfall in the mouth of the Boyne and another in the mouth of the Liffey.

By 841 Vikings had established a settlement (a *loughport*, named after the stockade that surrounded their ships) at the confluence of the Poddle and the Liffey. Just upstream on the Poddle there was at that time a great black pool (*dubh linn*) from which the English name of Dublin was derived. A leader called Olaf founded the kingdom of Dublin a few years later. It was this Norse kingdom that was to play a significant part in the history of the conquest and colonisation of much of the British Isles over the next three centuries.

In 914 Vikings arrived in a great fleet of ships in the estuary of the Barrow and established a base at what became Waterford (from the Old Norse *vedrar fjord* – wether (as in gelded ram) fjord) and followed a few years later with Wexford (*waes fjord* – the fjord on the mudflats) on the estuary of the Slaney, Cork on the estuary of the Lee and Limerick on the estuary of the Shannon, all of which together with Dublin were to play an important part in what was to follow.

Before the arrival of the Vikings there were no towns, no roads and no coinage; the unit of value was the cow. The Vikings changed that, establishing their settlements as towns and introducing currency principally in the form of silver ingots and coins. The Norse King Sihtric II was responsible for the minting of silver coins in Dublin at the end of the tenth century.

The encroachment of the Vikings was brought to a halt by Brian Boru, King of Thomond (the north-westerly part of Munster). Following the sack of Limerick in 967 and the death of his brother Mathgamain in 976, Brian began progressively to conquer the rest of Ireland. Starting with Munster, he then defeated the Dublin Norse and their allies the Leinstermen at the Battle of Glen Máma in 999 and received the submission of Mael Sechnaill, who brought with him much of the north of the country, in 1002. Finally, in answer to an appeal by Mael Sechnaill for help against the continuing depredations of the Dublin Norse and the Leinstermen, Brian marched on Dublin. On 23 April 1014 he engaged the Dublin Norse and the Leinstermen in a pitched

Above: *Conway Castle* by Thomas Girtin, 1800. Conwy was one of many magnificent castles built by Edward I on the coast of Wales to subjugate the Welsh. Edward was himself besieged there briefly in 1295 until relieved by sea. It saw the surrender of Richard III to Henry Bolingbroke (later Henry IV) in 1399. Two years later it was captured and held for a while during Owain Glyn Dŵr's rebellion.

Below: *Caernarfon Castle* by John Varley, c. 1745. Like many of Edward I's castles in Wales, Caernarfon was built by a Savoyard master mason called Jacques de Saint-Georges d'Espéranche (known in English as James of St George), who introduced Savoyard designs: concentric fortifications and, in the case of Caernarfon, polygonal towers. The decorative bands of darker masonry were perhaps copied from the walls of Theodosius at Constantinople.

Right: *Princes Edward and Richard in the Tower* by John Everett Millais, 1878. The two Princes disappeared from the Tower of London after their uncle seized the throne, becoming Richard III, following the death of their father Edward IV in 1483. The elder of the two Princes was, or would have been had he been crowned, Edward V.

Left: Harlech Castle on the west coast of Wales. Another of the castles built by Edward I to subjugate the Welsh. This old photograph (c. 1860) shows the flat land at the foot of the castle from which the sea has receded since the castle was built but before the development which exists today.

Above: Baginbun Bay and Baginbun Head south-east of Waterford. Raymond FitzGerald (known as le Gros) landed in Baginbun Bay and set up camp on Baginbun Head in 1170 at an early stage of the Anglo-Norman conquest of Ireland. When the camp was attacked by the people of Waterford, those who had not already fled or been killed were thrown from the cliffs into the sea.

Below: *The Marriage of Strongbow and Aoife* by Daniel MacLise, c. 1854. The marriage took place in Christchurch Cathedral, Waterford between Richard de Clare (Strongbow), erstwhile Earl of Pembroke, and Eva (Aoife), daughter of Dermot MacMurrough, King of Leinster. It marked the first stage of the Anglo-Norman conquest of Ireland.

Above: King John's Castle,
King's Island in the River
Shannon, Limerick.
Completed in about 1212, it
is one of the best preserved
Norman castles in Europe.

Right: The Irish Pale: here
part of the 6-foot bank
with ditches either side in
County Kildare constructed
pursuant to an Act of the
Irish Parliament of 1488
to establish a defensible
boundary between the four
counties obedient to King
Henry VII (Kildare, Dublin,
Meath and Louth) and the
rest of Ireland.

Above: *Landing of William III at Carrickfergus, 14 June 1690* English School seventeenth century). The King's arrival was the prelude to his victory over James II on the River Boyne on 1 July 1690 and ultimately the crushing of the Jacobite cause in Ireland.

Below: *The Irish House of Commons* by Francis Wheatley, 1780. The Parliament House on College Green, Dublin, was the world's first purpose-built bi-cameral parliament, construction of which started in 1729. This scene, of Henry Grattan – standing on the right of the table in a red coat – urging the claim of Irish rights, was painted two years before the passing of the Acts which formed the first constitution of Ireland in 1782.

Right: *Henry Grattan* by Sir
Martin Archer Shee . Grattan
was a Protestant from an Anglo-
Irish family. He was a member of
the Irish Parliament from 1775
until its dissolution on the union
with Great Britain. He was the
architect of the constitution of
1782 which almost entirely freed
Ireland from the fetters of the
British Parliament. After the
union, which was an anathema
to him, he was a Member of the
Westminster Parliament until
his death in 1820. In the words of
Sydney Smith: 'No government
ever dismayed him. The world
could not bribe him. He thought
only of Ireland; lived for no
other object; dedicated to her
his beautiful fancy, his elegant
wit, his manly courage, and all
the splendour of his astonishing
eloquence.'

Above: Telford's Bridge over the Menai Strait looking towards Beaumaris (print after George
Arnald 1828). When completed in 1826, the bridge connected Anglesey with Telford's new road
to London (now the A5) and transformed the journey of Irish Members of Parliament between
their constituencies and Westminster.

Right: *Daniel O'Connell* by J.
P. Haverty, c. 1830. Scion of a
wealthy Irish Catholic family,
O'Connell was a bitter opponent
of the union between Great
Britain and Ireland and was
the successful protagonist
of Catholic emancipation
throughout the United Kingdom
in 1829, the latter prompting
George IV to complain:
'Wellington is the King of
England, O'Connell is King of
Ireland, and I am only the dean
of Windsor.' He was a Member
of Parliament from 1828 initially
for County Clare, then Dublin
City and finally for County Cork
until his death in 1847.

Below: Charles Stewart Parnell
and his mistress (later his wife)
Kitty O'Shea, 1880. Parnell
was a Protestant from a landed
Anglo-Irish family, often dubbed
'the uncrowned king of Ireland'.
He was a Member of Parliament
from 1875 initially for County
Meath and latterly for Cork City
until his untimely death in 1891
aged 45. He was the champion
of land reform and home rule
for Ireland but fell from grace in
1890 when he did not contest an
accusation of adultery with Mrs
O'Shea in divorce proceedings
brought by her husband. The
photograph of Parnell was given
to him by Mrs O'Shea soon after
they met and the photograph
of Mrs O'Shea was carried by
Parnell until his death.

Above: Eviction of 'Dr Tully', one of Lord Clanricarde's
tenants, at Woodford, County Galway, on 1 September 1888.
Francis Tully, a farmer and boat-builder known as Dr Tully,
campaigned for lower rents through collective bargaining. The
2nd Marquess of Clanricarde was the epitome of an absentee
landlord, never visiting his estates in Ireland and leaving
destitute thousands of tenants evicted for failure to pay their
rent during hard times. So unpopular was he that he needed
to call on a small army from the Royal Ulster Constabulary in
addition to his own bailiffs to carry out the evictions.

Right: A house straddling
the border between County
Fermanagh in Northern Ireland
and County Cavan in the Free
State, illustrating the absurdity
of the agreement reached in 1925
between the Governments of
the United Kingdom, Northern
Ireland and the Free State that
the border should follow the old
county boundaries which had
been established in the sixteenth
and seventeenth centuries,
notwithstanding that by 1925
they ran through towns, villages,
farms and even houses.

battle at Clontarf on the north side of what is now Dublin. Although he was too old to lead his troops into battle, he watched from his tent while they put their enemies to flight. But he never enjoyed the fruits of his victory. A Viking commander, named Brodar, in making his escape, recognised Brian and killed him in cold blood. Following their defeat, the Vikings confined their dominion to the coastal settlements which they had already established.

Brian's victory at Clontarf was followed by a period of relative stability, with the whole of Ireland recognisably ruled for the most part by a high king, albeit punctuated by internecine strife among the petty chiefs. Initially the high kings were scions of Brian's family. However, by the time of the Anglo-Norman conquest one and a half centuries later, Ruaidrí Ua Conchobair (Rory O'Connor) was high king, having succeeded his father in 1166.

The Anglo-Norman conquest

The story of the Anglo-Norman conquest of Ireland begins with the abduction of a princess. In 1152, Diarmaid MacMurchadha (Dermot MacMurrough), King of Leinster, abducted Devorgilla, the married daughter of the King of Meath, to 'satisfy his insatiable, carnal and adulterous lust'.[287] Although it took all of fourteen years to accomplish, in 1166 Rory O'Connor together with Devorgilla's husband and their supporters banished MacMurrough from Leinster in retribution for the abduction. Not to be outdone, MacMurrough sought help from the King of England, Henry II. At the time on campaign in Aquitaine, Henry was not in a position to provide troops but, having received from MacMurrough a bond of allegiance and oath of fealty, he gave to him letters patent permitting any vassal and liegeman of the King to help MacMurrough recover his lost territories.

Armed with the King's letters, MacMurrough proceeded first to Bristol and then to St David's on the most westerly tip of south Wales. While at Bristol he reached an agreement with Richard de Clare, known as Strongbow, the erstwhile Earl of Pembroke whose title and lands had been forfeited as a result of his support for Henry's adversary, King Stephen. In return for Strongbow's help in recovering his lands, MacMurrough promised his daughter, Eva (Aoife), in marriage and succession to his kingdom on his death. Then in St David's he promised the town of Wexford and its hinterland to two other Anglo-Norman knights, Robert FitzStephen and Maurice FitzGerald, in return for their help.

In August 1167 (or possibly 1168 – it is unclear), with the benefit of an easterly wind, MacMurrough sailed from St David's and landed at Glascarrig Bay on the Wexford coast, a few miles due east of his principal seat at Ferns, where he had built a castle (on the same site as the ruins of the Anglo-Norman castle which can be seen today) and founded the abbey of St Mary (the remains of which still stand in a meadow on the edge of the town). On Glascarrig Point an Anglo-Norman motte can be clearly seen, built subsequently to command the approaches from the sea and originally topped by a wooden fort and palisade. Having proceeded to Ferns, MacMurrough waited for the promised support from Wales, largely untroubled by O'Connor.[288]

In May 1169 FitzStephen sailed from Milford Haven with an army of knights, archers and foot soldiers and landed at Bannow Bay on the south coast, between Waterford and Wexford. Hearing of FitzStephen's landing, MacMurrough sent his illegitimate son, Duvenald, to join forces with him and together they attacked Wexford. Although the attack itself was repulsed, confronted by FitzStephen's superior forces, the town surrendered. True to his word, MacMurrough granted Wexford to FitzStephen and FitzGerald. The invading army then moved north towards Dublin, FitzStephen's horsemen winning a particularly gruesome victory on the plains of Ossory in what is now County Kilkenny on their way north, the severed heads of the vanquished being closely inspected by MacMurrough to identify those of his most hated enemies among them.

Concerned by the growing threat posed by MacMurrough, O'Connor mustered a great army with which to confront him. As things turned out, no battle was fought between them, a truce having been agreed on terms that MacMurrough should be allowed to recover Leinster, albeit on condition that he should acknowledge O'Connor as the High King of Ireland and should hand over his legitimate son, Conor, as a hostage with the tempting prospect of marriage to O'Connor's daughter should the peace last. There was also a separate and private agreement reached that, once MacMurrough had recovered Leinster, all his foreign allies would be sent home.

Maurice FitzGerald then landed at Wexford with reinforcements and from there proceeded to join forces with MacMurrough in subduing the area round Dublin.

In May 1170 Strongbow's advance party led by Raymond FitzGerald, aptly known as le Gros, landed in Baginbun Bay, south-east of Waterford,

THE ANGLO-NORMAN
CONQUEST OF IRELAND

ULSTER

Carrickfergus

Lough
Neagh

Downpatrick.

Faughart

Athankip

CONNACHT

MEATH

Liffey.

Dublin

Shannon

Kildare.

OSSORY

WICKLOW MOUNTAINS

Wicklow

THOMOND

LEINSTER

.Limerick

Barrow

Ferns

Glascarrig
Point

Cashel

Slaney

.Cashel

Suir

Wexford

MUNSTER

Waterford

Passage

Carrick

Bannow Bay

Beg-Eri

Baginbun Head

N

Callann

Lee

Cork

DESMOND

Miles

0   10   20   30   40   50

and set up camp in old fortifications on Baginbun Head to await the arrival of Strongbow and his main force. There is no sign of the fortifications today, only a Martello tower amidst (in May) a sea of thrift.

The town of Waterford at that time stood where the Viking Triangle stands today, with walls on all three sides and bounded on one side by the River Suir and on another by St John's River, just above their confluence with the River Barrow. With a view to making a pre-emptive strike, the people of Waterford mustered 3,000 men and advanced towards Strongbow's encampment on Baginbun Head. Notwithstanding the enormous disparity in numbers, they were beaten back, more than 500 of them being cut down and many others captured or thrown from the cliffs into the sea – and some cliffs they are too.

Finally on 23 August 1170, Strongbow himself arrived from Milford Haven with about 200 knights and 1,000 foot soldiers. They landed at Passage on the mouth of the River Barrow to the east of Waterford and joined forces with le Gros. Together they managed to breach the walls of Waterford and proceeded to storm the town. There they were joined by MacMurrough. True to his word, MacMurrough then gave his daughter, Eva, to Strongbow. The marriage was celebrated in Christ Church Cathedral, Waterford, and is the subject of a splendid painting by Daniel Maclise (originally commissioned to hang in the chamber of the House of Lords but now hanging in the National Gallery in Dublin).

From Waterford, MacMurrough marched north with the conquest of Dublin in his sights. Anticipating that the direct approach would be well defended, he proceeded through Wexford and from there went north, taking the high ground through the Wicklow Mountains. Before he reached Dublin, he was met by envoys from the Archbishop of Dublin offering a truce. However, before any truce was concluded, the walls of the city were stormed by men led by le Gros on one side and by Miles de Cogan on the other. Although many of the occupants were killed or captured, most of them managed to escape by boat, including their King, Ascall Mac Torcaill, taking with them much of their treasure and seeking refuge in the islands to the north. Having captured Dublin, MacMurrough knew no bounds and, breaking his truce with O'Connor, he invaded Meath, laying it to waste. But his breach of faith came at a terrible price – the life of his son, Conor, O'Connor's hostage for the observance by MacMurrough of his agreement to confine his ambitions to Leinster.

In May 1171 MacMurrough died at Ferns from some unknown disease. In accordance with MacMurrough's original promise and claiming also through his wife, Eva, Strongbow then declared himself King of Leinster and the other territories that MacMurrough had conquered. Henry II, concerned by this turn of events and by reports of the sale of free children from England into slavery in Ireland, imposed an embargo on the export of any goods from his dominions to Ireland. Deprived of much needed supplies and in an attempt to placate the King, Strongbow backed down. He sent le Gros as an envoy to Henry in Aquitaine with a letter acknowledging that he had only achieved what he had in Ireland by virtue of the King's licence and declaring that he held his territory in Ireland at the King's disposal.

That did not solve the problem of supplies immediately. Nor was it the only problem that confronted Strongbow. Shortly after MacMurrough's death, Ascall sailed into the Liffey with 60 ships bent on avenging the ignominy of his flight from Dublin the previous year. Miles de Cogan, then Governor of Dublin, marched his troops out of the city to meet him, but was driven back by Ascall's vastly superior numbers. However, de Cogan's brother, Richard, managed to lead a small body of men unobserved from the east postern gate and to attack Ascall's army in the rear. In the confusion that followed, Ascall's commander was killed and Ascall himself was captured trying to escape to his ship. Having been brought before Miles de Cogan as a prisoner to be held for ransom, Ascall showed such intemperate defiance that de Cogan ordered him there and then to be beheaded.

Although Ascall had been defeated, that was not the end of Strongbow's troubles. O'Connor together with the other Irish kings, knowing that Strongbow was short of men and supplies as a result of Henry's embargo and concerned at the threat to their own territories which Strongbow now posed, persuaded Godred,[289] King of Man, to blockade Dublin by sea; in the meantime O'Connor marshalled an enormous army and laid siege to Dublin. Dublin itself was poorly fortified at that stage and trapped within its walls were Strongbow, Maurice FitzGerald and le Gros, who had recently returned from his mission to King Henry. Notwithstanding that the defending force was grossly outnumbered, they sallied forth one afternoon, taking O'Connor (who was bathing in the Liffey at the time) and his army completely by surprise. Although O'Connor himself escaped, his army was routed, many being killed as they fled. Strongbow, having taken great quantities of booty, left a garrison in the city and marched with the remainder of his men towards Wexford.

Meanwhile, MacMurrough's son, Duvenald, had put about that Strongbow had robbed him of the inheritance to which he felt that he was entitled (notwithstanding that he was illegitimate) and had joined the disaffected people of Wexford in laying siege to FitzStephen and his modest force at nearby Carrick on Bannow Bay. Finding that FitzStephen was successfully harrying those laying siege and would not surrender, the Bishops of Wexford and Kildare were persuaded to trick FitzStephen into believing that Dublin had fallen, that Strongbow, Maurice FitzGerald and le Gros had been killed and that O'Connor's victorious army was fast approaching Carrick. On being offered safe passage for himself and his men back to Wales, FitzStephen fell for the trick and surrendered. News then reached his captors not only that the siege of Dublin had been raised but that it was Strongbow's army that was approaching, whereupon they set fire to Carrick and escaped to the island of Beg-Eri in what was then the harbour to the west, taking FitzStephen and their other captives with them. The island is no more, that part of the harbour having silted up, but at that time there was an abbey on it which had been founded by St Ivore.

On reaching Wexford, Strongbow received an invitation from King Henry to meet him at Newnham, near Gloucester, where he was making preparations for his own invasion of Ireland. At the meeting that followed and after some heated exchanges, Strongbow agreed to surrender Dublin and its hinterland, the coastal towns of Wexford and Waterford and all of the fortresses to the King, holding the remainder of his conquests (essentially Leinster) as a vassal of the King. Henry then proceeded via St David's to Milford Haven where he embarked his troops in 400 large ships and set sail for Ireland, landing near Waterford on 18 October 1171. From Waterford he toured the south of the country, receiving the submission of the Irish princes. He then marched his army north towards Dublin, receiving further submissions on the way. O'Connor, however, confident that he was safe in Connacht, refused at that stage to submit. As for FitzStephen, although released from the clutches of the men of Wexford, he was promptly held as a prisoner by the King, although that was possibly as a ruse to procure his release, because he was later freed and reinstated.

Early in the following year Henry called together a synod of all of the clergy of Ireland at Cashel. The Papal Legate presided over it and, with the approval of the King's representatives, a decree was issued for the better regulation of ecclesiastical matters in Ireland. Significantly the decree records the agreement of all the clergy that the King of England had been received as Lord and King of Ireland.[290]

Henry left Ireland precipitately, never to return, on 24 April 1172 to deal with an insurrection in England led by his three surviving elder sons (Henry, Richard and Geoffrey),[291] which had been brewing since the murder of Thomas à Becket two years earlier and had come to a head during his absence in Ireland. Before he left, the King granted Meath to Hugh de Lacy in fee, should he succeed in conquering it, and he also appointed him as Governor of Dublin.

Although initially peace was restored in England, there was open rebellion by the King's three sons the following year when they joined Louis VII of France with a view to deposing Henry in favour of the eldest of them, the young Henry. To defend his territories in France, Henry recalled de Lacy and his veteran troops from Ireland, leaving the government there for much of the time in the hands of Strongbow, ably assisted by le Gros. With the capture in July 1174 of King William of Scotland, who had opportunistically joined the rebel cause leading to his humiliation by the terms of the Treaty of Falaise in December that year, and with the capitulation of Louis VII by the Treaty of Montlouis on 30 September 1174, the rebellion was brought to an end.

While Henry's attention and much of his resources were focused on putting down the rebellion at home, there was, perhaps inevitably, trouble in Ireland. There were widespread uprisings against the Anglo-Norman occupation together with the settling of old scores among the Irish princes. Le Gros had returned to Wales following his father's death but, in answer to an urgent request from Strongbow, he had come back to Ireland with reinforcements – and incidentally fulfilled his wish of marrying Strongbow's sister, Basilia.

Having done much to re-establish the King's supremacy in the east of Ireland, in the autumn of 1175 le Gros led an expedition against Domnall O'Brien, whose kingdom of Thomond was centred on the Shannon estuary with its principal stronghold at Limerick. At this stage, paradoxically, O'Connor (King of Connacht and High King) now allied himself with le Gros. Around 1 October le Gros managed to ford the fast-flowing Shannon with his army and to storm Limerick, slaughtering many of the defenders and capturing not only the city but much booty besides. Having set up a garrison to defend the city, he left with the bulk of his army to return to Leinster. No sooner had he gone, however, than O'Brien laid siege to Limerick. Le Gros was then ordered by Strongbow to return and relieve the siege. By April 1176 he had reached the pass of Cashel, only to find that his way had been blocked by O'Brien, who had himself raised the siege and abandoned Limerick. Undaunted, le Gros and his men hacked their way through the pass and returned to Limerick victorious. Having repaired the damage to the city which had been caused by the siege, le Gros conferred separately with O'Connor and O'Brien, each of them giving hostages for their good behaviour and an oath of fealty to the King of England. In the event, O'Brien's oath proved worthless: following Strongbow's death in May 1176, the garrison had been withdrawn from Limerick as being too remote, whereupon O'Brien had set fire to the city and everything in it.

O'Connor, on the other hand, proved more worthy. On 6 October 1175, shortly after the capture of Limerick, his emissaries, no doubt unaware of events there, had concluded a treaty[292] with Henry at Windsor, by which O'Connor had agreed to become a liegeman of the King of England and to accept the direct jurisdiction of the King over Meath, Leinster and the other areas between Dublin, Wicklow, Wexford and Waterford held by the King's vassals in the King's name. In return, Henry had agreed to recognise O'Connor as the High King of the rest of Ireland. O'Connor was required however to procure the fealty to the King of those in possession of the land and the payment of tribute to the King in respect of it. In the event, the Treaty of Windsor turned out to be largely ineffective, not because of any breach of faith on the part of O'Connor, but because he was unable to control the other Irish kings.

It was at about this time that Henry ordered a moat to be dug and castles to be built to mark the boundary of Meath and Leinster, being the territory over which he had direct control, and which became known as the Pale (from the Latin *palus*, a stake – hence palisade). Although it is not clear whether the moat was dug at that stage, a bank bounded by ditches was constructed at some stage, the remains of which can still be seen in places today, and the castles were certainly built. Later the Pale came to refer to whatever area was under the direct control of the Crown as it waxed and waned.

The Papal Bull - *Laudabiliter*

Henry II's invasion and conquest of Ireland were said by some to have been justified by Papal authority, although Henry never claimed that himself. Apparently a Papal Bull (a document under seal, from the Latin *bulla*) had been issued by Pope Adrian IV and addressed to Henry in 1155 authorising the conquest in order to bring the supposedly Christian Irish into line with the tenets of the Church of Rome. The Irish Church had grown up very much on its own. It was a unique Gaelic institution, being non-territorial, non-episcopate and non-hierarchical. As a result it was a source of profound annoyance to the Pope.

No original of the Bull exists, notwithstanding the survival of the archives where one original at least would be expected to have been kept, but the text was quoted by Giraldus Cambrensis (Gerald of Wales), writing in 1188. John of Salisbury had visited Adrian IV in 1155 and, in his *Metalogicon* written in 1159, he says that, at the request of King Henry, the Pope had granted the King hereditary possession of Ireland and had handed to John a ring of investiture to give to the King. Although there is a letter to Henry dated 1172 known as a Privilege of Pope Alexander III which purports to confirm the Bull of 1155,[293] its authenticity has been questioned.

All of that said, until the nineteenth century the existence of the Bull was taken for granted by those expected to know, not least by Domhnall O'Neill in his appeal on behalf of the Irish chiefs to Pope John XXII in 1317 which cites the terms of the Bull to justify the intervention of the Pope to support Edward Bruce as King of Ireland in place of Edward II of England.[294] Had the existence of the Bull been in doubt, O'Neill would have been far better off to have said so, with a view to undermining any Papal support for the original conquest by Henry II. There are, however, two nice twists to this story: one, that Adrian IV was English (he was born Nicholas Breakspear), indeed the only Englishman ever to have been Pope, and might therefore have been inclined to support Henry's interest; the other, that Giraldus Cambrensis was seeking preferment from Henry within the English Church and would have been keen to show Henry in a good light.

The text of the Bull quoted by Giraldus Cambrensis opens with the word '*Laudabiliter*' – the name by which the Bull has come to be known. In translation the text includes the following passage:

Laudably and profitably your majesty considers how you may best promote your glory on earth ... You have signified to us, our well-beloved son of Christ, that you propose to enter the island of Ireland in order to subdue the people and to make them obedient to laws, to root out from among them the weeds of sin; and that you are willing to yield and pay yearly from every house the pension of one penny to St Peter, and to keep and preserve the rights of the churches in that land whole and inviolate. We therefore, regarding your pious and laudable design with favour, and graciously assenting to your petition, do hereby declare our will and pleasure, that, for the purpose of enlarging the borders of the Church, setting bounds to the progress of wickedness, reforming evil manners, planting virtue, and increasing the Christian religion, you do enter and take possession of that island, and execute therein whatsoever shall be for God's honour and the welfare of the same. And, further, we also strictly charge and require that the people of that land shall accept you with all honour, and dutifully obey you, as their liege lord ...[295]

Ostensibly, therefore, Henry would hold Ireland as a vassal of the Church of Rome and as Lord of Ireland. And it was by that title that he and his successors in Ireland were known until the problem created by the excommunication of Henry VIII in 1538.

Jean sans Terre and the lordship of Ireland

In May 1177, at a Council meeting at Oxford, Henry announced a new approach to make good the shortcomings of the Treaty of Windsor: he intended to grant the whole of Ireland to his youngest and otherwise landless son, John (Jean sans Terre, John Lackland), as Lord of Ireland. John at that stage was only ten years old, and to consolidate his position until he was of an age to govern the country himself, Henry made sweeping grants of land for colonisation by his staunchest supporters, principally the confirmation of the grant of Meath to Hugh de Lacy, of Desmond (in the south-west) to Robert FitzStephen and Miles de Cogan and of Thomond to Philip de Briouze. Importantly, those to whom the grants were made were required to do homage and swear an oath of fealty to John as well as to Henry himself. (In the event, the grant of Thomond fell through because de Briouze failed to subdue it.)

That same year saw the first incursion of Anglo-Normans into the north of Ireland and the conquest of the east of Ulster by the Herculean figure of John de Courcy. In February 1177 he set off from Dublin with only 22 knights and about 300 other soldiers, some of whom were disgruntled members of the Dublin garrison, gathering some allies on his way north. His first engagement was at Downpatrick, from which, against great odds, he eventually emerged victorious, reportedly having 'wielded his sword, with one stroke lopping off heads, with another arms', and pursuing his escaping enemy along the seashore so that many of them sunk under the weight of their armour in quicksands. That was made good by another victory at Downpatrick in July.[296] Although the following year de Courcy was defeated in two skirmishes, one in Fer-Li territory, north of Lough Neagh, which resulted in the loss of all but 11 of his men-at-arms and a retreat on foot in armour for 30 miles, and the other in Uriel territory to the south of Lough Neagh. He later secured a more lasting victory at what is now Newry Bridge.

To secure his position, de Courcy built the splendid keep and inner ward of the castle at Carrickfergus, which still stand today on their rocky outcrop commanding the approach to the harbour where William of Orange landed five hundred years later on his way to victory on the Boyne. In the end, de Courcy himself fell on hard times, losing Ulster to his rival, Hugh de Lacy, 1st Earl of Ulster (son of the Hugh de Lacy to whom Henry II had granted Meath), and living out his days in obscurity as a royal pensioner together with his wife, Affreca, the daughter of Godred Crovan (a great-granddaughter of the original Godred Crovan), King of Man.

A plan to send young Prince John to Ireland was shelved in 1183 with the death of his eldest brother, Henry. However, having turned eighteen and been knighted at Windsor, in April 1185 John set sail from Milford Haven in a fleet of 60 ships accompanied by 300 knights and a large force of foot soldiers and archers and landed safely at Waterford. The expedition was an unqualified disaster: John's potential allies were alienated by the loutish behaviour of his entourage, not least by having their beards pulled, and the army with which he expected to garrison his castles melted away because he failed to pay them properly. By the end of the year his forces were so depleted that he had no choice but to return to England.

In 1186 the third of King Henry's sons died, supposedly in a jousting tournament in Paris; he was Geoffrey, Duke of Brittany. Three years later

Henry himself died and was succeeded by John's only surviving brother, Richard I (the Lionheart). Then on 6 April 1199 Richard died without any legitimate children, having been wounded during the siege of the castle at Châlus. Although Geoffrey's posthumous son, Arthur, Duke of Brittany, had a claim to the throne, John took no chances and was crowned in Westminster Abbey on 27 May that year. Not only, therefore, was he Lord of Ireland but, notwithstanding that he had been born with three elder brothers, he was now King of England too. Thereafter the lordship of Ireland was held by the English Crown.

Initially John was too preoccupied with securing his realm in France to pay much attention to Ireland. To reward those men who had served him well in France, he made grants of land to them. In 1201 he gave the kingdom of Thomond to one such supporter, William de Briouze, the nephew of Philip de Briouze to whom it had previously been granted by King Henry. At Limerick, in the heart of Thomond, he built a great castle on an island formed by the Abbey River loop in the Shannon, known as King's Island. The castle was completed in about 1212 and much of it still stands today, being one of the best preserved Norman castles in Europe.

With the loss of his territories in France to King Philippe in 1204, John started to pay rather greater attention to Ireland. That same year he ordered the construction of a new stone castle at Dublin, intending that it should be the future seat of royal government. At the same time he made Dublin the only place in Ireland where coins could be minted (although – presumably against his wishes – coins continued to be minted in Limerick) and introduced into Ireland the same legal and administrative forms that applied in England.

A year later he struck a remarkable deal in respect of Connacht. The old King of Connacht, Rory O'Connor, had died in 1198 and been succeeded by his very much younger brother, Cathal. Cathal had lost a long-running struggle to hold on to his kingdom until, in December 1205, he agreed to surrender the whole of Connacht to King John. Part was set aside for the King and, of the remainder, one third was to be held by Cathal as a feudal tenant and the other two thirds as a suzerain kingdom, for which tribute would be paid, acknowledging John as the High King. Thus, at a stroke, Cathal became entitled to King John's protection from rivals and John (ostensibly at least) acquired sovereignty over Connacht.

The following year John ordered his Justiciar of Ireland (his deputy or chief minister) to begin shiring the south-west of the country, providing a structure of local government along the same lines as in England, with a view not only to better government but also to increasing his own control. In the meantime, his quixotic dealings with those to whom he had granted land led not only to chaos in the country but also at times to armed conflict, particularly with William de Briouze with whom an initial settlement was reached in 1208.

Two years later, dissatisfied with the recalcitrance of his principal vassals in Ireland, John mustered a vast army at Haverford in Wales. On 19 June 1210 his army set sail in a fleet of 700 ships and landed near Waterford the following day where it was joined by the Justiciar and forces friendly to the King. From there it marched first to Leinster, the tenant of which, William Marshal (the future Regent of England), had already made his peace with the King, and thence to Dublin. While there, on 28 June John received an offer of submission in respect of Meath from Walter de Lacy (the son of Hugh de Lacy), who uncharitably sought to blame his brother, another Hugh (Earl of Ulster), for the recent troubles. Nonetheless John banished Walter and advanced north into Meath, seizing all the castles and confiscating the lands. Faced with this advance, Hugh retreated further north to the principal de Lacy stronghold at Carrickfergus, burning some of the other castles on the way. Although Carrickfergus fell after a short siege, Hugh had escaped and, more importantly, he had escaped with William de Briouze's wife, Matilda, and her family to whom he had been giving shelter.

Matilda was in deep trouble with John because she had publicly voiced the widespread suspicion that John had been responsible for the murder in 1203 of his nephew, Arthur of Brittany, the son of Geoffrey, and thus the other claimant to the throne of England. She would also be a useful hostage to make amends for yet another rebellion raised by her husband. Together with Hugh, Matilda and her family fled first to the Isle of Man and from there to Galloway. Hugh and one of Matilda's sons, Reginald, managed to escape capture and fled to France. Matilda, on the other hand, was caught together with her other children. Although ultimately her husband agreed to a fine of 50,000 marks, he recognised that he would never be able to raise such a huge sum and so he too fled to France, leaving Matilda and the children to their fate – and some fate it was too. Learning of her husband's defection, she was defiant to the end and, with her son William, was starved to death.

Following King John's death in October 1216, William Marshal became

Regent for the young King Henry III. Under his aegis, Magna Carta (with necessary adaptations to the text) was applied to Ireland,[297] native Irish were precluded from public or episcopal office and peasants were imported from England and Wales to give effect to the agricultural revolution that he had instigated.

The colonisation by Anglo-Norman magnates continued briskly, such that by 1250 they had overrun three quarters of the country. However, it was at that stage that the tide of colonisation was not only stemmed but began to turn. In 1261 the colonists were defeated in battle at Callann, near Kenmare, and evicted from the far south-west of the country. Then in 1270 they were routed at the ford of Athankip, losing the north-west.

Notwithstanding that much blood had been shed in the process, the colonisation did bring with it the foundations of a centralised government administration, and in 1297 the first parliament (albeit an Anglo-Norman parliament) was summoned.[298]

The invasion by Edward Bruce

Although there had been an almost incessant struggle for supremacy between various Irish chiefs on the one hand and the Anglo-Norman colonists on the other, none of the battles led to a sufficient, let alone lasting, victory to either side. However, there was a sea change in 1315.

In response to a request from Domhnall O'Neill, the Irish King of Tír Eóghain (essentially County Tyrone), and other Irish chiefs to put a stop to the hated Anglo-Norman colonisation and with a view to building on his own victory over the English at Bannockburn, Robert the Bruce made plans for his brother, Edward, to invade Ireland. On 26 May 1315 Edward landed with 6,000 men near Larne on the north-east coast. Having joined forces with O'Neill and local supporters, within less than a year he had taken control of most of the country, the Irish chiefs agreeing to grant him the lordship of Ireland and calling him King. However, Edward's victories came at a price: the depredations of his army had by the beginning of 1317 led to famine, as a result of which support for him began to drain away. It was in that context that O'Neill despatched the Remonstrance of the Irish Chiefs to Pope John XXII seeking his help,[299] albeit to no avail.

On 14 October 1318, the Bruce dream came to a brutal end. At Faughart, near Dundalk, Edward Bruce faced a massive English army of 20,000 under the command of Sir John Bermingham. His Irish allies were unwilling to engage and Bruce, not wanting to wait for reinforcements and keen to win the victory for himself, led his paltry force of 2,000 Scots against the English onslaught. Defeat was almost inevitable, but made certain by the incompetent battle order of the Scots.

> The Scots were in three columns at such a distance from each other that the first was done with before the second came up, and the second before the third, with which Edward was marching, could render any aid. Thus the third column was routed, just as the two preceding ones had been. Edward fell at the same time and was beheaded after death; his body being divided into four quarters, which quarters were sent to the chief towns of Ireland. [300]

Nor was his death lamented by the Irish, as recorded in the *Annals of Clonmacnoise*:

> he was therein slaine himselfe as is declared to the great joy & comfort of the whole kingdome in generall, for there was not a better deed, that redounded better or more for the good of the kingdome since the creation of the world and since the banishment of Fine ffomores [notorious pirates] out of this land, done Ireland than the killing of Edward Bruce: for there raigned Scarcity of Victuals, breach of promises, ill performance of covenants, & the loss of men and women throughout the whole realme for the space of three yeares and a half that he bore sway. In soe much that men did commonly eat one another for want of sustenance during his tyme.[301]

The colonists take shelter

Although the Anglo-Norman colonists had defeated the Scots, the reach of their colonies was by this time in decline: their numbers were small, without support from their King they had limited resources, and many of their great magnates were going native. With a view to arresting the decline, in 1367 a Parliament of colonists passed an Act which required the colonists to distance themselves completely from the native Irish. The Parliament was presided over by Lionel, Duke of Clarence, a son of Edward III, who had been appointed as his father's deputy in Ireland some six years earlier. The Act is known as the Statute of Kilkenny, after the place where the Parliament sat.[302] It forbade intermarriage between English and Irish; it forbade the English from adopting or fostering Irish children; it forbade the sale of horses or armour to the Irish at any time or of victuals in time of war; it required the English to speak English, to use English names and to adopt the English mode of riding and dress according to their status; it required the English to adopt English common law; it forbade the playing of the Irish games of horlings (the precursor of hurling) and coiting, preferring that the English accustom themselves to drawing bows and throwing lances; it prohibited the appointment of any Irishman to a position in any cathedral or collegiate church; and, with a view to preventing the Irish from spying on the English, it forbade the English from receiving Irish pipers or story-tellers.[303] In the event the Statute was never fully effective, the colonists lacking the resources to enforce it. However, the one thing they did achieve was to drive a wedge between themselves and the Irish which has remained ever since. Indeed, although it had been forgotten by most, the Statute was only repealed in the Republic of Ireland in 1983.[304]

In a further attempt to halt the decline, Richard II invaded Ireland in the autumn of 1394. Having defeated Art MacMurrough, King of Leinster, he received the submission of many of the Irish kings, including Art MacMurrough himself on 7 January 1395 and Niall O'Neill (the younger) on 16 March 1395.[305] Believing that he had subdued Ireland, Richard returned to England, only to be bitterly disappointed: no sooner had he left than hostilities broke out once more. It was during those hostilities that in 1398 Richard's appointed heir, Roger Mortimer, 4th Earl of March, was killed in a skirmish. To avenge his death, Richard returned the following year, but to no avail: before he had achieved his aim, he was forced to return to England post-haste to try and rescue his throne from the usurping Henry Bolingbroke, Duke of Lancaster. In that endeavour he failed miserably, Henry being crowned as Henry IV on 13 October 1399 and Richard dying in prison a few months later.

The Wars of the Roses

By the end of the fourteenth century, the English colony in Ireland had shrunk dramatically. Whereas 150 years earlier it had embraced three quarters of Ireland, now it extended little further than Dublin and its hinterland, still known as the Pale, albeit that the towns, many of which had been established by the colonists, were generally sympathetic to the Crown.

Richard, Duke of York and Earl of Ulster, a great-grandson of Edward III, arrived at Howth, just north of Dublin, in July 1449. He was accompanied by his pregnant wife, Cecily – the Rose of Raby – and a large entourage. He had come to take up office as Lieutenant for the Lancastrian King, Henry VI – an office to which he had been appointed primarily to prevent him from stirring up trouble at home over rivalry for the throne of the weak and failing King. In October Cecily gave birth to a son (her third), George (later Duke of Clarence), who was baptised in Dublin amid scenes of jubilation with the Earls of Ormond and Desmond as his sponsors. By the time that Richard left the country a year later, he had forged the first firm link between Ireland and the Yorkist cause.

When the Yorkist army was routed at Ludlow in 1459, Richard fled to Ireland, where he was received with open arms. Such was his support among the English colony in Ireland that a year later their Parliament declared that only the laws adopted by it applied in Ireland and that English writs summoning people to answer charges in England did not run in Ireland, thus freeing Richard from responding to any summons to answer charges of treachery in England.[306] Unwisely from his perspective, Richard returned to England that same year and was killed at the Battle of Wakefield. However, his death was avenged by the Yorkist victory at Towton in 1461, following which Richard's eldest son, Edward, seized the throne, becoming Edward IV.

Edward died in 1483 and was succeeded by his brother, Richard III. It was Richard who was killed at Bosworth Field two years later, losing his crown to his Lancastrian rival, Henry Tudor, who became Henry VII.

Following his victory at Bosworth, Henry seized a ten-year-old boy and imprisoned him in the Tower of London. The boy was Edward, Earl of Warwick, son of George, Duke of Clarence, who had been christened in Dublin in 1449. With George's death some years earlier and with the death of Richard III at Bosworth, Edward had become one of Henry's Yorkist rivals to the throne of England. Edward had, however, managed to escape from the Tower and had disappeared, fuelling speculation as to his whereabouts.

On 5 May 1487 a fleet of ships with 2,000 Yorkist mercenaries arrived in Dublin. They were accompanied by Richard III's nephew and designated heir, the Earl of Lincoln, and by a boy who claimed to be Edward, Earl of Warwick (not to be confused with Edward V, the elder of the two Princes who had disappeared from the Tower). The boy who had arrived in Dublin was in fact Lambert Simnel. He had been tutored by an Oxford priest, Richard Symonds, and passed off as the Earl. Having been acknowledged as the Earl of Warwick by the 8th Earl of Kildare, the Lord Deputy of Ireland, he was crowned as Edward VI in Dublin Cathedral on 24 May that year. With the boy as their figurehead, forces were raised by Lincoln under the command of Kildare's brother, Sir Thomas FitzGerald, and invaded England, sweeping rapidly through Lancashire and Yorkshire. However, their hopes of seizing the throne from Henry were dashed on 16 June 1487. The Yorkist army had taken up a position on high ground in a loop of the River Trent near Stoke Field, a few miles to the south-west of Newark, when they were attacked by Henry's army under the command of the Earl of Oxford. In a bloody encounter, the Yorkists were all but wiped out: among the dead were both FitzGerald and Lincoln. So it was that the Wars of the Roses finally came to an end. Surprisingly, the boy was spared and apparently became a royal servant. Even more surprisingly, given the part that he had played, Kildare was not only spared but continued in office as Lord Deputy.

Notwithstanding Henry's victory at Stoke Field, the Yorkist threat to his throne did not go away. Four years later another imposter popped up in the form of Perkin Warbeck, claiming to be the younger of the two Princes who had disappeared from the Tower during the reign of Richard III. In 1491 he had arrived in Cork to sell silks, where he was prevailed upon by Yorkist sympathisers to impersonate the Prince, gaining the support of the Earl of Desmond. Two years later, influential figures in London were drawn into the plot, among them Sir William Stanley. Then in 1494 Warbeck's partisans managed to stir up a rebellion in Ireland and, with ships and soldiers supplied by the Holy Roman Emperor, Maximilian, he attempted an invasion of England, landing at Deal on 3 July. However, before most of his force had disembarked, his advance party was overwhelmed by local levies. Rather than attempt to land with the remainder of his force, he sailed away, first to Youghal and then to Waterford, where he joined Desmond in an unsuccessful siege of the town. After an abortive campaign in Cornwall, Warbeck was caught and was hanged at Tyburn in 1499.

The Tudor conquest

No doubt alarmed by the renewed threats to his realm in Ireland, Henry VII appointed Sir Edward Poynings, a well-trusted supporter, as Lord Deputy in place of the Earl of Kildare. On 1 December 1494, summoned by Sir Edward, the Irish Parliament assembled at Drogheda. During the course of that session, the Parliament passed several Acts of fundamental importance to tighten the King's control, or at least his control of the four counties which were obedient to him, Kildare, Dublin, Meath and Louth. Most of those Acts were to be a thorn in the flesh of the Irish for centuries.

Two of the Acts are known somewhat indiscriminately in the singular as Poynings' Law. The first was passed in 1494 and provided that the Irish Parliament could not meet until its proposed legislation had been approved not only by Ireland's Lord Deputy and Privy Council but also by England's monarch and Privy Council; and moreover that any Act to the contrary should be deemed void.[307] At a stroke, therefore, the Irish Parliament was deprived of the autonomy which it had enjoyed until then. The second, passed in the same session albeit in 1495, provided that any English statute for the common good should apply automatically to Ireland and that any Act to the contrary would be void.[308] This compounded the effect of the first of the two laws.[309] An Act in almost identical terms to the second of those two was passed by the English Parliament in the same year.[310] As two English humourists put it 'The Irish could have a Parliament of their own, but the English were to pass all the acts in it.'[311]

However, the Irish Parliament went much further than the so-called Poynings' Law. In the same session it confirmed the isolationist Statute of Kilkenny, except for that part requiring the English to speak English or to adopt the English mode of riding;[312] it required Englishmen according to their means to have an English bow and sheaf of arrows and those of greater substance to have a horse for their defence;[313] and, importantly, it redefined and fortified the Pale. What remained of the Pale having been identified six years earlier as comprised of the four obedient counties (Kildare, Dublin, Meath and Louth),[314] one of the Acts required the occupants of the marches of those counties to build and maintain a double ditch bounding a bank 6 feet high along the march.[315] (A good stretch of the bank with a deep ditch either side can still be seen running north from a sharp bend in the road about quarter of a mile north-west of Clonfert Pet Farm near Maynooth.)

Another of the Acts required the proper upkeep of the King's chief castles of Dublin, Trim, Leixlip, Athlone, Wicklow, Greencastle, Carlingford and Carrickfergus, and that there should be an able man born in England as the constable of each of them.[316]

Although the Irish Parliament had been emasculated by Poynings' Law, effective control of the powerful Irish chiefs was not achieved until the reign of Henry VIII, and that can be laid at the door of two individuals both of whom were later beheaded: one was Thomas FitzGerald, 10th Earl of Kildare; and the other was Anne Boleyn.

In 1534 the Lord Deputy of Ireland and head of the powerful FitzGerald family, the 9th Earl of Kildare, had been summoned to London to answer various charges of peculation. He had appointed his son, Thomas, as his deputy for the period while he was away. Unfortunately for him and even more unfortunately for Thomas, his family had many enemies who spread a rumour that the Earl had been beheaded in London. This provoked Thomas on 11 June 1534 to ride to St Mary's Abbey in Dublin where the King's Council was meeting. He was accompanied by a large retinue of horsemen sporting silk fringes on their helmets, for which he was named 'Silken Thomas'. He entered the council chamber and there renounced his allegiance to the King. His friend, the Lord Chancellor, Archbishop Cromer, sought to dissuade him, but to no avail. He threw down the sword of state and rushed out taking his men with him. News of this event was too much for his sick father who, contrary to the rumour, was still alive, but it precipitated his end, leaving Thomas as the 10th Earl of Kildare.

Other Irish chiefs then joined Thomas's standard. Together they entered Dublin and laid siege to the castle, albeit unsuccessfully. Sir William Skeffington, who had by this time been appointed Lord Deputy for the specific purpose of putting down the rebellion, was ill and initially did nothing effective to prevent its spread, leaving much of the country to havoc and ruin. However, in March the following year he besieged Maynooth Castle, the greatest of the FitzGerald strongholds. It was defended by 100 men but, after a siege of only nine days, it was taken by storm, except for the great keep. The surviving 37 defenders of the keep were under the command of a man named Parris. Fearful that their defence would fail, Parris struck a deal with Skeffington by which he agreed to betray Thomas and surrender in return for a reward and pardon. Although the 37 then surrendered, the pardon they received was death, known forever afterwards as the 'Maynooth

Pardon'. With the fall of Maynooth, support for the rebellion began to ebb away. Hoping for mercy, Thomas offered to surrender on condition that his life was spared, a condition which the new Lord Deputy, Lord Grey, purported to accept. But, as with Maynooth, it was a hope too far. In October 1535 he was sent as a prisoner to the Tower of London and, together with his five uncles who had been tricked by Lord Grey into attending a banquet and then arrested, he was hanged and beheaded at Tyburn in 1537. With the failure of the rebellion, Lord Grey set about restoring peace to Ireland and, although there was much fighting, ultimately most of the chiefs submitted to him. The notable exceptions were Desmond and O'Brien.

The subjugation of Ireland was taken a step further when, in 1537, the King assented to an Act of the Irish Parliament which made English the official language of Ireland, made the teaching of English compulsory and, most significantly, prohibited the wearing of traditional Irish dress.[317]

While all of this was going on, there was another drama unfolding. In 1525 Henry had become infatuated with Anne Boleyn and embarked on a course which would lead to his break with Rome. Wanting to marry Anne, in 1527 he sought a divorce from his wife, Catherine of Aragon, on the ground that she was his deceased brother's widow, but Pope Clement VII refused. Henry's solution was to break with Rome. In England that break came in a series of Acts[318] culminating in the Act of Supremacy of 1534, an English Act by which he was declared to be the 'Supreme Head on Earth of the Church of England'.[319] That was followed in Ireland by the Irish Act of Supremacy of 1537[320] declaring that he was the 'only Supreme Head in Earth of the whole Church of Ireland'.[321] Other than the changes which were necessitated by the substitution of the King for the Pope as head of the Church on earth, there was no great sea change in the beliefs or rituals of the Church of Ireland or indeed of the Church of England, as was made plain by the Ten Articles of 1536.[322]

The sea change, which was to have such momentous consequences in Ireland, began in the reign of Henry's successor, Edward VI,[323] and, following the brief Counter-Reformation of Bloody Mary's reign, culminated in the adoption of the Thirty-Nine Articles in England in 1571 and in Ireland in 1634. The fundamental differences between the Thirty-Nine Articles and the doctrines of the Roman Catholic Church are to be found in the rejection of transubstantiation, clerical celibacy, purgatory and the possibility of indulgences. It was the last of those four that had driven

Martin Luther to pin his ninety-five theses to the door of All Saints' Church in Wittenberg in 1517, sparking the Reformation in Europe. Ironically, it was the Reformation in Europe which had led Pope Leo X to confer the title of *Fidei Defensor* – Defender of the Faith – on Henry VIII in 1521, a role which Henry signally failed to fulfil.

Inevitably the break was unacceptable to Rome and on 17 December 1538 Henry was excommunicated by Pope Paul III. The Papal Bull issued that day confirmed an earlier Bull of 30 August 1535 excommunicating Henry, the effect of which had been suspended in the hope that Henry would return to the fold of Rome, a hope that had been sorely disappointed. The excommunication posed a serious constitutional problem because from the outset in the reign of Henry II, or at least since the reign of King John, Ireland had been held by the English Crown as a fief of the Holy See.[324] The simple solution adopted by Henry was to become himself the sovereign of Ireland. That he achieved ostensibly by an Act of the Irish Parliament, the passing of which was a remarkable event in itself.

On 12 June 1541 Parliament was assembled in Dublin. In order to lend greater importance to its deliberations, a number of the leading Irish chiefs were induced to attend, a rare occurrence in itself not least because many of them did not understand English. The King had instructed the Lord Deputy, Sir Anthony Sentleger, to treat them well and to offer them the prospect of peace and reconciliation. The Earl of Ormond translated the speeches of the Lord Chancellor and the Speaker. Without opposition the Crown of Ireland Act was then passed, by which the King, his heirs and successors became the Kings of Ireland 'to have, hold, and enjoy the said stile, title, majestie, and honours of King of Ireland, with all maner preheminences, prerogatives, dignities and all other the premisses unto the King's highnesse, his heyres and successours for ever, as united and knit to the imperial crown of England'.[325]

There was general rejoicing at the outcome and the King showered many of the Irish chiefs with titles, O'Neill becoming the Earl of Tyrone, O'Brien the Earl of Thomond and Burke the Earl of Clanrickarde.

Unlike his successors, Henry refused to expel the native Irish people from their lands to make room for new colonies, though often urged to do so by his officials. By the time of his death in 1547 the country was at peace and English power over it stronger than it had ever been before. Tragically for Ireland, that peace was not to last.

When Henry VIII died, he was succeeded by Edward VI, his nine-year-old son by his third wife, Jane Seymour. Following the introduction in England of the first Book of Common Prayer in 1549, Edward (or, more accurately, his fractious Council) introduced a similar book in Ireland. It was formally introduced in Christ Church Cathedral, Dublin, on Easter Day 1551. It was particularly significant not only because it was the first printed book to be produced in Ireland but also because, like its precursor in England, it was in English. Latin was no longer the language of the Church of Ireland, making palpable the break with Rome.

Edward died young and was succeeded by his half-sister, Mary, in 1553. Mary was a staunch Catholic, the daughter of Henry VIII's first wife, Catherine of Aragon. She was the first Queen of England in her own right, and so too therefore the first Queen of Ireland. On 25 July 1554 she married Philip, the son of the Holy Roman Emperor, Charles V, who two years later succeeded his father as King Philip II of Spain. On his marriage to Mary, and for the period of their marriage, Philip became the King of England and of Ireland too.[326] Potentially to the great advantage of the Catholic population of Ireland, between them Philip and Mary repealed Henry's laws reforming the Church in Ireland. However, Mary's reign and her Counter-Reformation were short-lived, for she died childless in 1558. She was succeeded by her Protestant half-sister, Elizabeth, Henry's daughter by Anne Boleyn. Through Mary's death, not only did Philip lose the kingdoms of England and Ireland, but he lost them to a Protestant whom he was determined to subdue.

Losing little time, in 1560 Queen Elizabeth assented to two Acts ostensibly of the Irish Parliament, both of which were fundamental to the events that followed: one was the Act of Supremacy,[327] and the other was the Act of Uniformity.[328] The Act of Supremacy repealed Mary's Counter-Reformation Acts, obliged the people of Ireland to acknowledge that Elizabeth was the rightful Queen of Ireland and the supreme head on earth of the Church of Ireland and required all clergy and holders of public office to take an oath recognising that supremacy, the most important effect of which was to exclude from public office any Catholic unwilling to perjure himself (there were of course no public offices open to women at that time). The Act of Uniformity prescribed the use of the English Book of Common Prayer for all religious ceremonies, thus outlawing the practices of Nonconformist Protestants, most significantly those of the growing number of Scots Presbyterians.

In the meantime, the colonisation of Ireland by the appropriation and re-grant of land by the Crown had begun in earnest in the reign of Queen Mary. In 1557 the Irish Parliament passed an Act to rename Leix and Offaly as Queen's County (after Mary) and King's County (after Philip), to confiscate all of the land in those counties, to evict the native Irish from two thirds of it and to re-grant that part to Englishmen born in England or Ireland, marking the start of what came to be known as the Plantation of Ireland.[329] It was partially successful but the resistance of the dispossessed was a running sore which has never healed.

During Elizabeth's reign there had been a private attempt in 1571 to colonise the north-east coastal area of the O'Neills of Clandeboye and another around Carrickfergus by the Earl of Essex (Walter, the father of the Queen's favourite, Robert) on behalf of the Crown between 1572 and 1575. Both failed, the latter ending in shocking acts of betrayal and bloodshed on the part of Essex.

Originating from the territorial strife between the earls of Desmond and the earls of Ormond, James FitzMaurice FitzGerald, a first cousin of Gerald FitzGerald, the 15th Earl of Desmond, and captain general of his army, led unsuccessful rebellions against the Crown: the first, between 1569 and 1573, was against the attempts of the Crown to wrest control of Desmond territory in and around Munster; and the second, between 1579 and 1585, a continuation of the first and aided substantially by the Pope, was in addition against the lack of religious toleration. Both rebellions were brutally crushed by a combination of force of arms, cold-blooded executions and starvation of the local population by the destruction of their crops and livestock. Following the rebellions, the Desmond territories were forfeited to the Crown by Act of the Irish Parliament and in 1586 the Queen approved a plan for the plantation of Munster by English-born settlers.[330] In the event, however, that took years to implement.

The suppression of the Desmond rebellion led disaffected Catholics to look for an alternative sovereign for Ireland. In 1588 they lighted on Archduke Albert, the nephew of Philip II. However, the Nine Years' War that followed shortly after put an end to their aspirations.

The Nine Years' War

By 1592, fearful of a Spanish invasion, Queen Elizabeth's Government in Ireland, through her Lord Deputy, Sir William Fitzwilliam,[331] was attempting to bring the whole country under its control and several Irish chiefs had been worsted in the process. Among them, the O'Donnells of Tyrconnell in the north-west of Ulster and the O'Neills based principally in Tyrone in the centre of Ulster were determined to resist this encroachment on their territory. The chief of the O'Donnells was Hugh Roe O'Donnell and, by 1595, the chief of the O'Neills was Hugh O'Neill, 2nd Earl of Tyrone, who had previously been loyal to the Crown. O'Donnell and O'Neill were able to obtain both men and arms from the Scots, always keen to cause trouble to their English enemies. They also solicited the support of Philip II of Spain who had long been engaged in hostilities against England, of which the wrecking of the Spanish Armada in 1588 had formed part.

The first phase of what came to be known as the Nine Years' War began in 1593 and was focused principally on the largely unsuccessful attempts of the English to secure outposts in Ulster. After some initial success, on 7 August 1594 an English column sent to relieve the garrison at Enniskillen was ambushed and routed at a ford across the Arney River, later dubbed the Ford of the Biscuits after the hard tack scattered there during the engagement. Although subsequently relieved, Enniskillen was surrendered in May the following year. However, notwithstanding the terms of the surrender to the contrary, the garrison were massacred.

That same month, the first major engagement occurred. On 25 May Sir Henry Bagenal, Marshal of the Queen's army in Ireland and, incidentally, O'Neill's brother-in-law, marched out of Newry with 19 companies of foot and 6 troops of horse, numbering 1,750 men in all, to escort a convoy of supplies to Monaghan to relieve the garrison there. Bagenal's men were constrained to keep to the tracks, the outlying ground being boggy, broken or wooded, making the column particularly vulnerable to attack, something which suited O'Neill well. Having camped for the night and resumed their march, the column had reached Crossdall, about 4 miles from Monaghan, when it was attacked by O'Neill with a considerable force of well-trained men. Just as suddenly as O'Neill had attacked, he then withdrew, minimising his own losses. However, that was just a foretaste of what was to come.

Having reached Monaghan and relieved the garrison there, the following day, 27 May, Bagenal started on the return march to Newry, wisely taking a different route. However, O'Neill was not to be evaded so easily. For the best part of seven hours his forces harried Bagenal's column. The heaviest fighting took place when O'Neill ambushed it at a pass at Clontibret. After

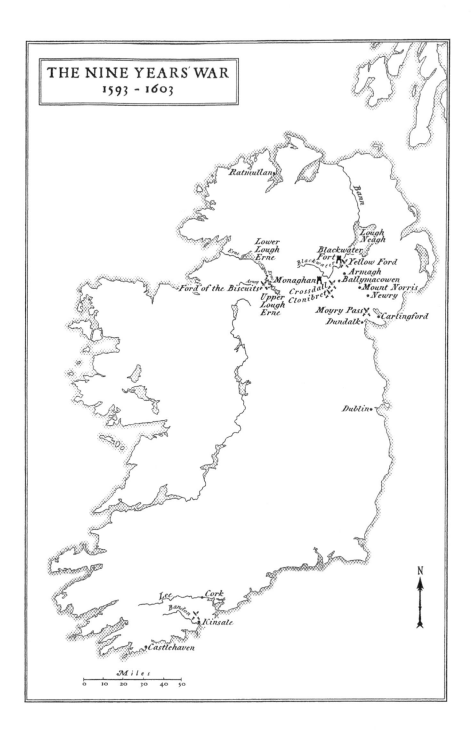

THE NINE YEARS' WAR
1593 – 1603

Ratmullan

Bann

Lower
Lough
Erne

Lough
Neagh

Blackwater
Fort

Blackwater

Yellow Ford

Erne

Arney

Monaghan

Armagh

Ballymacowen

Mount Norris

Ford of the Biscuits

Crossdall

Clonibret

Upper
Lough
Erne

Newry

Moyry Pass

Carlingford

Dundalk

Dublin

Lee

Cork

Bandon

Kinsale

Castlehaven

N

Miles

0   10   20   30   40   50

an unsuccessful attempt to kill O'Neill himself, the column finally forced a passage and limped its way to Ballymacowen for the night. By this stage both sides were exhausted and perilously short of powder. The following day the attacks were not renewed and the column reached the safety of Newry, having suffered substantial losses.

From the end of 1595 until the summer of 1597 little of significance happened. Then during that summer the Lord Deputy, Lord Burgh, succeeded in taking and destroying a fort which had been built by O'Neill on the Tyrone (west) bank of the River Blackwater about 5 miles north of Armagh and building a new earthwork fort nearby on the same side of the river. During the autumn the new fort was blockaded and attacked by O'Neill until an unexpected truce was concluded at the end of the year. The following summer when the truce expired the new fort was blockaded once more and the prospect of the garrison holding out became hopeless. Rather than suffer the loss of face of allowing the garrison to withdraw, it was decided that it should be relieved. To that end Bagenal was put in command of what was, by the standards of the day, an enormous force of about 4,000 foot and 300 horse. Having spent the night just north of Armagh, on the morning of 14 August 1598 Bagenal's army marched towards the beleaguered fort. The ground was difficult, just as it had been at Clontibret, part of the route lying across a ford through boggy ground which became known as the Yellow Ford. Worse still, O'Neill had constructed a well-fortified ditch and rampart to the south-east of the fort on the Armagh side of the Blackwater, which it would have been hard for Bagenal to outflank. The difficult ground and ultimately the rampart caused Bagenal's men to become so dangerously spread out that O'Neill was able to wreak havoc among them. Bagenal was mortally wounded when, having raised his visor, he was shot in the eye, after which the remnants of his shattered army turned tail and fled back to Armagh leaving the garrison of the fort to surrender. O'Neill had won a great victory and it prompted uprisings all over the country.

After an interval of two years following the death from Irish ague of Lord Burgh in 1597, Robert Devereux, Earl of Essex,[332] had been appointed as Lord Deputy. His attempts to suppress the uprising were ineffectual. Having agreed a truce with O'Neill in 1599, he returned to London without the Queen's permission, only to lose his head following an abortive rebellion against her two years later. He was succeeded by a man of a very different calibre, Lord Mountjoy.

However, even Lord Mountjoy got off to a shaky start. O'Neill had already blocked the approach from the Pale to Tyrone across the Blackwater by his successful defence at Yellow Ford. He now sought to block the gateway to Ulster through the Moyry Pass (the Northern Gap) through which lay the old road between Dundalk and Newry. The Pass is a narrow defile through rugged hills and the road at that time was 'a broken cawsey beset on both sides with bogs'.[333] In May 1600 Lord Mountjoy had marched north through the Pass unmolested, but he had been attacked by O'Neill from the rear on his return and a fierce but inconclusive fight in pouring rain had ensued. Then, in September, Mountjoy had set out from Dundalk with about 3,000 foot and 300 horse to re-establish the garrison at Armagh, which necessitated going through the Pass once more. On 20 September he pitched camp just south of the Pass. For the next ten days in atrocious weather exploratory approaches to the Pass were made and it was found to have been barricaded not just with one but with several well-fortified entrenchments, the scrub on the steep ground either side having been plashed (cut and laid as a hedge) to form together with the entrenchments almost impenetrable barriers. Between 2 and 9 October Mountjoy attempted to force the Pass but was beaten back on each occasion, suffering considerable losses; so too was an attempt to outflank the Pass over higher ground. On the 13th O'Neill suddenly, and for no apparent reason, withdrew, allowing Mountjoy to proceed. Mountjoy stopped 3 miles north of Newry, having given up his intention of occupying Armagh that year, building a fort at Mount Norris instead. Cautiously he returned to Dundalk by way of Carlingford and the coast road, avoiding the Pass altogether; even then he was ambushed and harried by O'Neill's men.

Up to that stage O'Neill had enjoyed success partly because he was an effective leader, partly because he had championed the Catholic cause against the hated Protestant invader and most importantly because he had fought a defensive war on ground of his own choosing. However by the end of the year his luck had begun to change. In October Neill Garbh O'Donnell, Hugh O'Donnell's cousin and one of his principal allies, had defected to the Crown. Although in December the Spanish had managed to send some arms, ammunition and money which O'Neill and Hugh O'Donnell had shared, Mountjoy's tentacles had been spreading further south; by the end of the year not a castle in Munster remained in O'Neill's hands; and by March 1601 Mountjoy had control of Monaghan and Wicklow too.

In January 1601, with the Treaty of Lyons, France made peace with Savoy, relieving Spain of any further need to provide support to the Savoyards and freeing up resources for O'Neill. On 3 September, after much argument and indecision in Spain, a Spanish armada of 33 ships sailed from Belém with about 4,400 fighting men on board under the command of their captain-general, Don Juan del Águila, bound for Kinsale on the Bandon estuary 17 miles south of Cork. The effective force was very much smaller than the 6,000 which had been stipulated for a landing on the Munster coast, and even that was thought by some to be too small. The armada arrived off the Irish coast on 27 September and prepared for landing the following morning; however that night a storm drove off 2 galleons and 6 accompanying craft, leaving Águila initially with only 1,700 fighting men. With them on 2 October Águila landed and took Kinsale. A week later his force had increased to 3,400, but the remainder of the ships scattered by the storm had been unable to return and had made for Spain, depriving Águila both of men and of vital stores and munitions.

Mountjoy soon heard of the arrival of the Spaniards and gave orders for troops to be withdrawn from elsewhere and to muster in Cork, where he himself arrived on 7 October. By the beginning of November Mountjoy had begun to lay siege to Kinsale, while O'Neill and O'Donnell had started to move south to join forces with the Spaniards. By the middle of December there had been a considerable build-up of forces on both sides. Reinforcements together with stores had arrived from Spain at Castlehaven (about 40 miles south-west of Kinsale) under the command of General Don Pedro de Zubiaur. More importantly for what was to come, both O'Donnell and O'Neill had reached the approaches to Kinsale after a remarkable winter march. The camps of both Mountjoy and his ally, the Earl of Thomond, were now potentially trapped between Kinsale and O'Neill's army. On 31 December both O'Neill and O'Donnell brought their armies up within view of their enemy, retired, pitched camp and waited, exploiting Mountjoy's difficulty in obtaining supplies.

On the night of 3 January 1602 (new style)[334] O'Neill and O'Donnell made their move, hoping to surprise their enemy at dawn. Having lost contact with O'Donnell during the night, O'Neill's army advanced but were spotted by Mountjoy's scouts and, for whatever reason, halted, thereby losing the initiative. They then withdrew to firmer ground beyond the Millwater Creek a few miles to the north-west of Kinsale at a point now marked by a memorial at the junction of the R605 and the L7244. There, having formed up to engage, they were charged by Mountjoy's cavalry. The charge caused O'Neill's horse to turn tail in disorder through their own infantry, leading to a rout by Mountjoy's forces. Although O'Donnell had finally caught up to the rear of O'Neill, he was unable to prevent the rout. As for Águila's men within Kinsale, they played no part, probably for want of adequate communication. This was the first occasion on which O'Neill had assumed the offensive and given battle on open ground away from his own country; and he had lost. It is ironic that, had he waited only a few days more, Mountjoy would have had to send his horses to Cork for want of forage, and it was the horses that had determined the outcome of the battle. Such are the fortunes of war.

Having told Águila that he could not help, O'Neill and the tattered remnants of his army fled north. O'Donnell managed to reach Castlehaven on 5 January and, abandoning his men, sailed with de Zubiaur for Spain in the hope of persuading the new King, Philip III, to provide reinforcements. But O'Donnell was to be disappointed and he died in Spain later that year. As for Águila, he surrendered on honourable terms, giving up all of the Spanish garrisons without a fight on 12 January.

With victory at Kinsale, Mountjoy set about bringing the long and costly war to a swift close. To that end he embarked on a ruthless subjugation of the native Irish, leading to famine and even cannibalism in Ulster. Although O'Neill had opened negotiations with Mountjoy within weeks of his defeat, the Queen did not actually authorise Mountjoy to negotiate until February 1603. The negotiations culminated in a treaty signed at Mellifont Abbey (the beautiful ruins of which still stand today) on 30 March 1603, six days after Elizabeth had died, as was known to Mountjoy, but not to O'Neill. The treaty was exceedingly generous to O'Neill: although he submitted to the Crown, he retained his lands and was reinstated with his earldom. Fortunately for Mountjoy, James I, who had succeeded to the English throne on Elizabeth's death, accepted what he had done.

In 1604 peace was agreed between England and Spain by the Treaty of London, thus ridding King James of the Spanish threat to his interests in Ireland, at least for the time being. In October the following year James issued a proclamation denouncing any presumption that he was prepared to allow religious toleration and ordering all Catholic clergy to quit Ireland by 10 December. The wisdom of that proclamation from his perspective was firmly reinforced by the attempt by Catholics to assassinate him when he attended the state opening of the English Parliament on 5 November: this was the Gunpowder Plot, led by Robert Catesby but remembered ever after by the name of the first of the plotters to be caught, Guy Fawkes. However, the solution to the King's control of Ireland lay not so much in rigorous suppression of Catholicism as in Protestant Plantation.

The Plantations – Protestants with horses

On 4 September 1607 O'Neill (now reinstated as 2nd Earl of Tyrone), Rory O'Donnell (brother of Hugh Roe O'Donnell and and newly created Earl of Tyrconnell) and some other Irish chiefs together with their families and some of their followers embarked at Rathmullan on the north coast of Ireland and sailed for the Continent – an event known to history as the Flight of the Earls. Fortuitously this enabled the King to seize their lands, accounting for much of Ulster, for outlawry and to embark on an aggressive process of colonisation, the ultimate effect of which was elegantly summed up by the playwright Brendan Behan in Act One of *The Hostage* (1958):

PAT. Will you shut up. As I was saying, he had every class of comfort until
   one day he discovered he was an Irishman.
MEG. Aren't you after telling me that he was an Englishman?
PAT. He was an Anglo-Irishman.
MEG. In the name of God, what's that?
PAT. A Protestant with a horse.
ROPEEN. Leadbetter.
PAT. No, no, an ordinary Protestant like Leadbetter, the plumber in the
   back parlour next door, won't do, nor a Belfast orangeman, not if he was
   as black as your boot.
MEG. Why not?
PAT. Because they work. An Anglo-Irishman only works at riding horses,
   drinking whisky and reading double meaning books in Irish at Trinity
   College.

Between 1608 and 1613 the land in five counties in Ulster (Armagh, Cavan, Donegal, Fermanagh and Tyrone) was redistributed by tenancies from the Crown.[335] The better and larger parcels were granted to Protestant settlers mainly from Scotland and England with the intention that the native Irish

should be evicted completely from their land; the remainder were granted
to favoured Irishmen, the Church and military officers who had served the
Crown during the Nine Years' War, all of whom were at least permitted to
take Irish tenants. The native Irish without tenancies found themselves
with nothing but the poorest land. Separate, but similar, arrangements were
made with the City of London in respect of the towns of Derry (renamed
Londonderry) and Coleraine together with the surrounding areas. There
was also piecemeal plantation of the counties of Waterford, Cork, Limerick
and Kerry with official indulgence rather than Crown assistance. Over a
rather longer period areas further south in Leitrim, Longford and Wexford
were colonised on a similar piecemeal basis, but in that instance with the
assistance of grants from the Crown. Two other counties in Ulster (Down
and Antrim) had been colonised privately over the intervening years. The
odd one out was Monaghan, which, although originally included in the plans
for the Plantation of Ulster, was never colonised in the same way.

Charles I succeeded his father in 1625. After protracted negotiations with
representatives of the Irish people, in 1628 through a special committee
of the English Privy Council he agreed, in return for an enormous sum of
money, to a package of 51 concessions, or 'graces'. The most important of
these were to give security of tenure of land to those who could show good
title over the past sixty years, to relieve Catholics of the requirement to
take an oath of supremacy, as opposed to an oath of allegiance, to confirm
the titles of the owners of land in Connacht and to restrain the oppressive
behaviour of the military.

Initially and to a limited extent the graces were implemented, albeit
slowly and halfheartedly. Then came the despotic rule between 1633 and
1640 of Thomas Wentworth as Lord Deputy, who, partly by bullying and
partly by trickery, succeeded largely in evading their implementation.
During his term of office, Wentworth procured verdicts by juries confirming
the King's title to much of the land in the counties of Roscommon, Mayo,
Sligo, Galway and Clare followed by re-grants to settlers, so continuing the
seemingly inexorable march of the Plantation. Moreover, he antagonised the
Protestant settlers by failing to stem the resurgent practice of Catholicism
and he antagonised the Scottish settlers by requiring them to take an
oath abjuring the Covenant on which their beliefs were founded (known
as the 'black oath'). Although Wentworth was promoted to the office of
Lord Lieutenant of Ireland in 1640 and was created Earl of Strafford, his

tenure was short-lived and was followed rapidly by his fall from grace, impeachment by the English Parliament in connection with his conduct in Ireland and finally his execution for treason on 12 May 1641.

The Eleven Years' War and Cromwell's conquest

Unsurprisingly discontent among the Catholics in Ireland, both Old Irish (i.e. Gaelic Irish) and Old English (i.e. those descended from the Anglo-Norman colonists), at the treatment they had received, not just from the Government generally since the Flight of the Earls but from Wentworth in particular, had been festering. It was exacerbated by the threat of invasion from Scotland as part of the ongoing struggle between the Scots Presbyterians and Charles I over the King's attempts to impose the Book of Common Prayer; and the last straw was a bad harvest in the summer of 1641. It all came to a head on 23 October 1641 when a small group of Catholic landowners, led by Sir Phelim O'Neill (nephew of Hugh O'Neill who had been defeated at Kinsale) and Rory O'Moore, supported by Old Irish and Old English alike, attempted a *coup d'état*. The aim of the *coup* had been to seize Dublin Castle and various other Government strongholds with a view to negotiation from a position of strength. Although the attempt failed, it unleashed a brutal uprising by the Catholics over which the leaders of the attempted *coup* lost control.

On 10 November the King appointed the Earl of Ormond (later the Marquess, and then the Duke, of Ormonde – the final 'e' the result of a mistake in the letters patent) to command the Government's army to crush the rebellion. To fund the army, the English Parliament devised an ingenious scheme with the Adventurers' Act passed on 19 March 1642, by which subscriptions were invited in return for land to be confiscated from rebels in Ireland should the suppression of the rebellion be successful.[336] The conflict escalated first with the landing of an army of Scots in support of the Protestant cause under the command of an experienced general, Robert Monro, at Carrickfergus on 15 April 1642; then with the arrival at Kinsale of English troops funded under the Adventurers' Act in July; and finally with the landing of two Irish Catholics, Owen Roe O'Neill (a great-nephew of Hugh O'Neill, 2nd Earl of Tyrone) and Thomas Preston. O'Neill landed in Donegal in July and Preston in Wexford in September. Both O'Neill and Preston were officers with long experience from the Spanish wars. Both brought with them

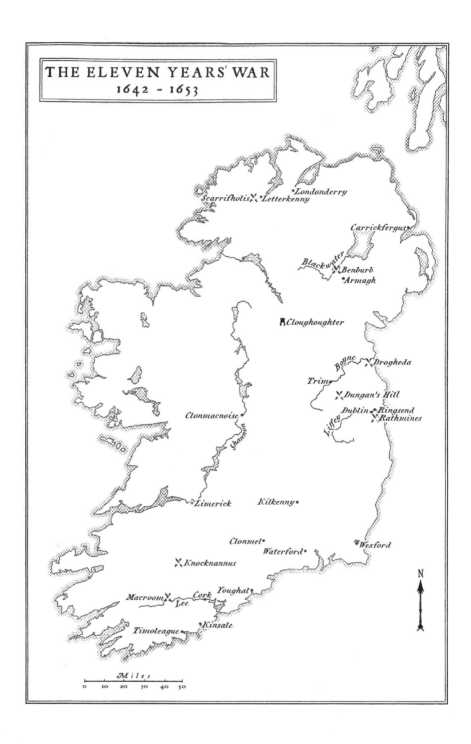

THE ELEVEN YEARS' WAR
1642 - 1653

other veterans, arms and ammunition. O'Neill was appointed commander of the Catholic army in Ulster and Preston in Leinster.

In the meantime there had been two other important developments. In May and June 1642, on the initiative of the Catholic clergy, the Confederate Catholic Association of Ireland was formed at Kilkenny, then in Catholic hands. Through its elected executive known as the Supreme Council, this became the organ of government of the united Catholic cause in Ireland for the next seven years. Then in August 1642 the first stage of the Civil War had broken out in England, putting pressure on King Charles to recall troops to England.

Following several inconclusive engagements between the opposing forces, a truce for one year was signed on 15 September 1643, giving the King an opportunity to recall troops and giving the Confederates an opportunity not only to negotiate with him but also to consolidate and train their army. The truce, however, was perceived by the Scots as a betrayal by the King of their cause to the Catholics. This set them not only against the Confederates but also in league with the English Parliament against the King, with the potentially disastrous consequence for Ormond that many of his troops, being Scots, deserted him for the Scots cause. On 13 November 1643 Ormond, now the Marquess of Ormonde, was appointed as Lord Deputy of Ireland, thus validating the truce which he had agreed in the name of the King.

Having been soundly defeated at the Battle of Marston Moor on 2 July 1644, King Charles was under even greater pressure to reach a negotiated settlement in Ireland but was trapped by the irresoluble differences between the existing, yet constitutionally valid, anti-Catholic laws on the one hand and the demands of the Catholic Confederates on the other. His difficulties were compounded by the arrival in Ireland on 12 October 1645 of the Papal Nuncio, Giovanni Battista Rinuccini, Archbishop of Ferno, bringing support for the Confederates and adding a further obstacle to any successful settlement. In the event Ormonde did succeed in negotiating an agreement with the Confederate Supreme Council on 28 March 1646, but it was rejected both by Rinuccini and by the Confederate General Assembly.

Although on 5 June 1646 the Confederate army under the command of O'Neill had won a great victory against General Monro at the Battle of Benburb, north-west of Armagh, nothing came of it essentially because Rinuccini dissuaded O'Neill from attempting to conquer Ulster. However, even if the victory had been better exploited, it would not have availed the Confederate cause because, with the ending of the first stage of the English Civil War two weeks later,[337] Oliver Cromwell was able to deploy the irresistible force of his New Model Army to crush the rebellion in Ireland once and for all.

On 7 June 1647 a contingent of 2,000 men of the New Model Army under the command of Colonel Michael Jones landed in Dublin, which Ormonde then ceded to him without a fight. Later that summer the English Parliament appointed Jones as commander of the New Model Army in Leinster and General George Monck as commander in Ulster. On 8 August Jones shattered Preston's army at Dungan's Hill near Trim in County Meath and in November the Earl of Inchiquin, having changed his allegiance for the second time, destroyed the Confederate army of Munster at Knocknanuss near Mallow in County Cork. Following an agreement concluded on 17 January 1649 between Ormonde on behalf of the King (only thirteen days before the King's execution) and the Confederates making concessions to the Catholics, the Royalists and Confederates made common cause, but they were on a hiding to nothing. An attempt by Ormonde (now ostensibly on behalf of Charles II) to take Dublin ended in disaster when his forces were routed following a surprise attack by Jones on 2 August at Rathmines (then just outside Dublin).

With Dublin secure, Cromwell himself was able to land unopposed at Ringsend at the mouth of the Liffey with 8,000 foot and 4,000 horse on 15 August 1649. To secure his lines of communication and supply with England, his first two targets were the east coast ports of Drogheda and Wexford. Drogheda fell on 11 September and, having refused to surrender, no quarter was given (as would have been customary at that time). Wexford fell a month later and most of the garrison and many of the inhabitants were massacred, notwithstanding that, unlike Drogheda, negotiations for surrender were on foot: if there were one single event for which Cromwell was, and continues to be, hated in Ireland, that was it. During the remaining campaign season of 1649, save for Waterford on the south coast, the strongholds of the coastal areas in the north from Londonderry eastwards, the east and the south as far west as Timoleague fell like dominoes, helped in part by dissent among the factions of the defenders. Here, at least, Cromwell honoured the conventions of war by giving quarter to those who surrendered. As for Waterford, it held out until its surrender on 10 August the following year, although bubonic plague took its toll in the meantime, including Colonel Jones the victor of Rathmines.

In December 1649, following meetings in Clonmacnoise, the Catholic bishops issued a proclamation of unity in the cause of their religion and of loyalty to the King. This provoked Cromwell the following month to issue a lengthy diatribe in response, attempting with astonishing disingenuity to justify his approach and stating squarely his political aims for Ireland: he declared that Englishmen had bought their interests in Ireland and that, notwithstanding that the Irish had equal justice before the law, they had risen to rebellion and massacre; he went on to declare that the practice of the Catholic faith would be prohibited, that the lands of the rebels would be forfeited, that the rebel leaders could expect no mercy, but – one saving grace – that private soldiers who had taken up arms would be treated honourably.[338]

Early in 1650 Cromwell moved north from Youghal and met up in Tipperary with a contingent under John Hewson from Dublin. Kilkenny, the headquarters of the Catholic Confederation, surrendered to them on 28 March. Then on 10 May Clonmel surrendered after an heroic defence by Hugh O'Neill (the nephew of Owen Roe O'Neill who had died in mysterious circumstances the previous year) which led to the loss of 2,000 of Cromwell's men. In the meantime Lord Broghill had put an end to any further organised resistance in Munster when on 10 April he wiped out a Catholic army near Macroom, leaving Cromwell's forces in a commanding position in every province except Connacht.

By that stage Cromwell was faced with a new threat, this time in Scotland. Although the Marquess of Montrose's uprising had been crushed at Carbisdale on 27 April and the Marquess himself had been executed a month later, the heir to the throne, the future Charles II, had on 1 May signed the Treaty of Breda,[339] essentially promising the Scots Presbyterians all that they were asking for and thus potentially bringing them into league with the Royalists against the English Parliament. In the face of that threat, Cromwell himself left Ireland on 26 May, leaving his son-in-law, Henry Ireton, in command.

A month later, the last cohesive field army opposing the English Parliamentarians was destroyed. Following the death of Owen Roe O'Neill the previous November, command of the Confederate army of Ulster had been given to Bishop MacMahon of Clogher. Unfortunately for the Confederates, the Bishop was, perhaps unsurprisingly at that date, no soldier and, contrary to the advice of his officers, on 21 June he committed them to battle at Scarrifholis near Letterkenny against troops from the New Model Army and Ulster Protestant settlers under the command of Sir Charles Coote. The outcome was a rout. Although the Bishop escaped from the field, he was later captured and hanged as a rebel.

The final twist for the Catholic cause came on 16 August 1650 when the future Charles II reneged on the agreement which had been reached by Ormonde on his father's behalf with the Confederates on 17 January the previous year.[340] In order to gain the support of the Scots against the English Parliament, Charles had had to deny all concessions to the Catholics in Ireland, robbing them of the last glimmer of hope. Thereafter the remaining pockets of organised resistance surrendered piecemeal, the last formal capitulation being at the island fortress of Cloughoughter on 27 April 1653. Cromwell's conquest was now complete.

Anticipating the completion of the conquest and to give final and brutal effect to it, on 12 August 1652 the English Parliament – known as the Rump Parliament following the purge of those hostile to the trial of Charles I – passed an Act for the Settlement of Ireland.[341] In essence the Act imposed a sliding scale of penalties, with death and forfeiture for those perceived to have been most closely involved in the rebellion; banishment and forfeiture for others who had borne high command, but with one third of their estates being allocated elsewhere in Ireland to their wives and children; forfeiture of the estates of other Catholics who had not been loyal to the Commonwealth, but with two thirds of their estates being allocated elsewhere in Ireland; and forfeiture of one fifth of the estates of anyone else who had not been loyal to the Commonwealth. Although in the event the Act was not fully enforced, it did result in a wholesale redistribution of land owned by Catholics and, with it, the loss of all political power.

On 2 March 1653 the English Rump Parliament voted that Ireland should in future be represented by thirty Members in the new Commonwealth Parliament. The Rump was dissolved on 20 April, but six nominated Irish Members sat in the Barebones Parliament when it opened on 4 July. However, the army forced the Barebones Parliament to surrender its powers to Cromwell and on 16 December Cromwell promulgated an Instrument of Government applicable to 'the Commonwealth of England, Scotland and Ireland' which provided for the supreme legislative authority to reside in the Lord Protector,[342] that the laws should not be altered except by Parliament,[343] that Parliament should be summoned to meet at Westminster on 3 September 1654,[344] that there should be thirty Irish representatives,[345] that none of them should be Catholic[346] and that there should be freedom to practise the Protestant, but not the Catholic, faith.[347] On 30 January 1654, somewhat inevitably, Cromwell was proclaimed in Dublin as Lord Protector. The first Protectorate Parliament, including thirty Irish Members, met for the first time on 3 September 1654. The Instrument of Government was given statutory effect by the second Protectorate Parliament two years later.

The Restoration, the Jacobites and the Williamite War

The Protectorate had its own problems and, in the event, it did not last long. Cromwell died on 3 September 1658 and with his death it began rapidly to unravel. His son, Richard, lasted as Lord Protector for less than a year. Following a struggle for power and a coup in which Sir Charles Coote played a prominent part, a new parliament in Ireland, known as the Convention Parliament, initially owing no allegiance either to the Commonwealth or to the Crown, was elected and in February 1660 declared its legislative independence. Then, reflecting events in England, on 14 May 1660 Charles II was proclaimed King in Dublin. Finally, on 23 April 1661 Charles II was crowned in Westminster Abbey as King of England, Ireland and France, being crowned subsequently as King of Scotland for a second time at Scone.

In November 1660 the King declared his intentions for the future settlement of Ireland, touching particularly on the redistribution of land. The Irish Parliament then met for the first time since the restoration on 8 May 1661 and the first Act which it passed was a lengthy and florid recognition that the King had lawfully succeeded to the throne of Ireland on the death of his father.[348] Later that summer they passed a new Act of Settlement largely giving effect to the King's declaration of the previous November.[349] Although the Act provided for the return of expropriated land to those who were found to be 'innocent', that in practice excluded most Catholics, and it was also dependent on other land being made available to those who were now to be dispossessed, but of which there was not enough to go round. Unsurprisingly, almost everyone felt hard done by.

Matters were then made worse by a series of Acts of the English Parliament designed to protect English markets from Ireland's principal exports. Ireland's economy depended at that time substantially on its pastoral land. Nevertheless, in 1667 the import of cattle, sheep and swine,

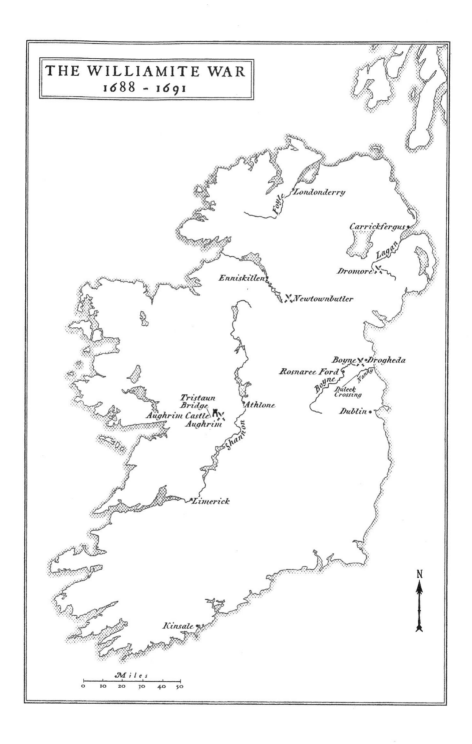

THE WILLIAMITE WAR
1688 – 1691

beef, pork and bacon from Ireland was prohibited for a period of seven years.[350] The prohibition was then reimposed in 1680 and extended to mutton, cheese and butter.[351] Attempts by Irish farmers to diversify were hamstrung two decades later by a prohibition of the export of wool and woollen products other than to England and Wales and even then subject to restrictions.[352]

Charles II died on 6 February 1685 and was succeeded by his brother, James. James II was a Catholic convert and his accession to the throne of Ireland inevitably raised the hopes and expectations of the Irish Catholics. In 1687 he appointed a Catholic, Richard Talbot, Earl of Tyrconnell (second creation), as Lord Deputy. Tyrconnell declared his intention of governing impartially, yet he set about the replacement of Protestant incumbents of offices of state or influence with Catholics. In the eyes of the Protestants, the problem was compounded when James's second wife, a Catholic, Maria d'Este, gave birth to a son and heir in 1688, raising the prospect of a Catholic dynasty in Ireland. It was the birth of this heir that precipitated the invasion of England by William of Orange, the husband of James's daughter, Mary, by his first wife, Anne Hyde, and the flight of James to France.

Matters came to a head on 7 December 1688 when thirteen apprentice boys closed the gates of Londonderry to a regiment raised by the Catholic Earl of Antrim which had been ordered by Tyrconnell to replace the largely Protestant garrison there: confronted by the closed gates, Antrim withdrew. Notwithstanding the setback in Londonderry, the Protestants in Dublin and further south were successfully disarmed by Tyrconnell and on 12 March King James landed at Kinsale. He was accompanied by a large French contingent under the command of the comte de Lauzun, all grist to the mill of Louis XIV of France as a means of distracting William from his own war against France as Stadtholder of the Dutch Republic. James then proceeded in triumph via Cork to Dublin.

Two days after James's arrival at Kinsale forces loyal to William were routed by Jacobites under the command of Richard Hamilton near Dromore, County Down. Then, on 18 April, James, at the head of a large Jacobite army, arrived at the walls of Londonderry and demanded the surrender of the city. The walls had been built some seventy years earlier in the reign of James I to provide a secure foothold for the Plantation of the region by Protestant settlers (they still stand almost completely intact today). Contrary to the wishes of the Governor, the inhabitants refused to surrender and the city was laid to siege. A boom was thrown across the River Foyle, downstream of the city, to prevent relief reaching the garrison by sea. Although it was effective for many weeks, on 28 July the boom was broken by two merchant ships and the city was finally relieved on 1 August. The day before the relief of Londonderry, Williamite forces had won a resounding victory over the Jacobites at Newtownbutler taking pressure off Enniskillen, the other seat of Protestant resistance in the north-west.

In the meantime, in May 1689 the Irish Parliament had been summoned by James and passed three Acts respectively recognising James II as the rightful sovereign of England and Ireland, declaring that the English Parliament had no jurisdiction in Ireland and that numerous named Williamites be attainted for treason.[353]

Little then happened until the following summer, 1690. Although a number of new regiments had been raised by William under the command of the Duke of Schomberg (an English dukedom, despite its name) and the Duke had taken Belfast without a fight, there was a stalemate followed by both sides withdrawing to winter quarters. In the spring preparations for the forthcoming campaign began, both armies being substantially reinforced. William's army was the larger, with 36,000 men, against James's 25,000.

William himself landed at Carrickfergus on 14 June (of which there is a splendid painting in the National Maritime Museum at Greenwich) and reached the north bank of the River Boyne about 2 miles upstream of Drogheda a fortnight later, there to face the Jacobites who had taken up a position within a loop of the river on the southern side. It was essential for James to hold the river to prevent William taking Dublin. However, his position was vulnerable in three respects: depending on the state of the tide, the river in the area was fordable in several places; although the Jacobites were on higher ground, being enclosed by the loop in the river they would be exposed to enfilading fire; and the line of retreat towards Dublin was blocked by the River Nanny 3 miles to the south, with only one practicable crossing at Duleek several miles away.

At dawn on 1 July William's right wing crossed the Boyne several miles upstream at the Rossnaree ford, drawing away a large part of James's army to engage them. Later in the morning, as the tide ebbed, the remainder of William's army managed to cross the river, initially at the ford at Oldbridge and later at Drybridge further downstream. Fierce fighting ensued against that part of the Jacobite army which had remained in the loop of the river, during the course of which Schomberg was killed. Ultimately, William's superior numbers gained the upper hand, sealing Ireland's fate. The survivors among the Jacobites managed to get away to Dublin via the crossing at Duleek, which was bravely defended by a detachment of French. However Dublin, together with the greater part of eastern Ireland, soon fell to William. James himself fled, sailing from Kinsale for France on 4 July.

In August 1690 William reached Limerick and laid siege to the Jacobite garrison in the Irish Town, which stands on the south bank of the Abbey River loop in the Shannon. However, the effectiveness of the siege was delayed by a successful Jacobite attack on a convoy bringing ammunition and heavy guns from Dublin, and, when the weather turned later that month, the siege was abandoned. At that stage, not only did William return to England, but Tyrconnell and the French contingent left Ireland for France. Left in command of the Jacobite forces in Ireland was the young Duke of Berwick, an illegitimate son of James II and future Marshal of France.

In January 1691 Tyrconnell returned to Ireland and in May a French general, the marquis de St-Ruth, arrived with reinforcements from France and took over command from Berwick. The Williamite campaign began with the successful storming of Athlone on 30 June under the command of a Dutch general, Baron van Ginkel, leaving the way clear to advance west of the Shannon into Connacht. St-Ruth then prepared for battle on the eastern slopes of a long ridge known as Aughrim or Kilcommadan Hill, 16 miles south-west of Athlone. At the foot of the ridge to the east was a bog with only two practicable crossing points: at the northern end was a narrow causeway near the ruined Aughrim Castle, and at the southern end the Tristaun Bridge. On the afternoon of 12 July Ginkel drew up his forces on the Urraghry Hill facing the Jacobites across the bog. After some inconclusive skirmishing, Ginkel contemplated retiring for the night, when it was observed that St-Ruth had been moving troops towards the southern end of the ridge to counter heavy attacks from across the Tristaun Bridge. This gave Ginkel the opportunity to try and force a passage at the more difficult northerly crossing by Aughrim Castle. Although there had been an unsuccessful attempt by Ginkel's infantry to attack across the bog, by 8 o'clock Major-General Mackay had succeeded in getting 4 battalions of Williamite infantry across the causeway at the northern end. Although initially repulsed, they were later joined by 14 squadrons of horse under the marquis de Ruvigny (later 1st Earl of Galway) and engaged St-Ruth's left wing. It was at this stage that disaster struck the Jacobites: St-Ruth was decapitated by a cannonball. Whether precipitated by St-Ruth's death or solely by force of arms, the Jacobite left wing was rapidly crushed by Mackay and de Ruvigny. Two hours later, Ginkel's forces at the southern end of the ridge gained the upper hand and, as night fell, the Jacobite forces were scattered, leaving about 4,000 dead and losing most of their equipment. Ginkel had won the day and the flickering flame of the Jacobite cause in Ireland had been extinguished.

The terms of the peace that followed were agreed in the Treaty of Limerick, signed on 3 October 1691 reputedly on the Treaty Stone in Limerick. On its face the treaty was surprisingly, and no doubt wisely, magnanimous towards the defeated Jacobite interests. It consisted of twelve Civil Articles and twenty-seven Military Articles.[354] The Civil Articles protected the rights of Catholics such as they had been in the reign of Charles II, protected the property of those who had taken up arms against the Crown provided that they took an oath of loyalty to the Crown, and granted a general moratorium in respect of damage suffered as a result of the hostilities. The Military Articles provided for the cessation of hostilities and gave those who had borne arms against the Crown the opportunity to return home, to join the British army or to proceed with honour abroad, with facilities for their transport to France should they so choose. The treaty was ratified by the King and Queen on 24 February the following year[355] and ultimately by the Irish Parliament (albeit in truncated form) in 1697.[356]

To cement his conquest, that same October William gave the royal assent to an Act[357] which, although abrogating any requirement in Ireland for the Elizabethan oath of supremacy, nevertheless substituted a requirement for all Members of the Irish Parliament to take an oath which in practice no Catholic could take, the effect of which was to prevent them from taking their seats whether in the House of Lords or in the House of Commons (as had been the case in England since the middle of the previous century). The obnoxious part of the oath entailed foreswearing the transubstantiation of the bread and wine in the celebration of the mass and acknowledging that the invocation of the Virgin Mary or other saints and the sacrifice of the mass were superstitious and idolatrous.

Although curiously the Act of 1691 was an English Act, it presaged a whole series of Acts of the Irish Parliament designed to secure the Protestant ascendancy in Ireland. In 1695 the first two of what became known as the

Irish Penal Laws were passed: one forbade Catholics from going abroad for education or from teaching in schools at home[358] and the other forbade Catholics not covered by the Treaty of Limerick from keeping weapons.[359]

The most significant of the Penal Laws was 'an Act to Prevent the Further Growth of Popery', which was passed in 1704 (early in the reign of Queen Anne):[360] it prohibited Catholics from buying land, inheriting land from Protestants or taking leases of more than thirty-one years; it also required land of deceased Catholics to be distributed equally among all of the sons or, failing sons, all of the daughters, of the deceased unless there was a single heir who was a Protestant. The overall effect was drastically to dilute Catholic land tenure and importantly the voting franchise which was dependent on it.

Before 1704 there had been nothing to prevent Catholics as such from voting in elections, provided that they were otherwise eligible whether as freeholders of land with a rental value of forty shillings (two pounds) or more, or as burgesses or freemen. However, the Act of 1704 prohibited Catholics from voting unless they took an oath of abjuration in terms similar to that prescribed by the 1691 Act – which in practice, therefore, prevented them from voting at all.[361] It was not until 1793 that Catholics were freed from that requirement.[362]

It would take a century and an armed insurrection to strike the worst of those shackles from the Irish Catholics.

First steps towards independence

The subjection of Ireland to the British Crown came starkly to the fore in 1719. Following the purported reversal of a decision of the Irish Court of Exchequer by the Irish House of Lords, the British Parliament passed an Act declaring that the kingdom of Ireland was 'subordinate to and dependent upon the imperial crown of Great Britain, as being inseparably united and annexed thereunto'; it also declared that the Irish House of Lords had no jurisdiction over the decision of any Irish court. It is known as the Declaratory Act 1719.[363]

In the event, the effect of the Declaratory Act was relatively short-lived. Spurred by the oratory, tenacity and integrity of Henry Grattan, a Protestant Member of the Irish House of Commons, Ireland took its first steps towards independence from the British Crown. In 1782 a series of Acts was passed by the Irish Parliament (each of which of course entailed the royal assent) and an Act of the British Parliament the following year which together formed the Irish constitution of 1782. In large part this new constitution gave independence to the Irish Parliament and the Irish judiciary. There were five Irish Acts in all, one of which repealed the Declaratory Act of 1719;[364] another, known as Yelverton's Act after the Member of the Irish Parliament who promoted it, largely repealed Poynings' Law of 1494, save that the holding of an Irish Parliament still required a licence from the British Crown;[365] a third applied English (and later British) statutes to Ireland relating to the settlement of forfeited land and to commerce and also happened formally to bring the Irish calendar into line with the English calendar;[366] a fourth gave jurisdiction to the Irish High Court of Parliament to review the decisions of other Irish courts;[367] and the last secured the independence of the Irish judiciary.[368] The British Act of 1783, known as the Renunciation Act,[369] made plain that the people of Ireland would be subject only to the laws of the Irish Parliament and that no British court could review the decision of any Irish court.

There followed a period of brief, but while it lasted unquestionable, prosperity in Ireland. Nevertheless, a decade later those first great strides towards independence were interrupted by armed insurrection and an attempt in 1800 by the Acts of Union to suppress it.

Insurrection and union

In 1789 revolution had broken out in France and on 1 February 1793 France had declared war on Great Britain. Encouraged by the revolutionary atmosphere and in the hope of help from France, trouble for the Government in Ireland erupted on two fronts: one was the demand by Catholics for agrarian reform; and the other was for the repeal of all of the disabling statutes which had turned Catholics into second-class citizens.

Since William III's conquest of the Jacobites, Irish policy had effectively been dictated by the British Parliament which, under pressure from English merchants and manufacturers, had so restricted Irish trade that the country had been forced to rely on agriculture, leaving the landlords, most of whom were Protestants, with a stranglehold on the Irish economy: Ireland was being systematically exploited as a colony by its largely absent landlords for its agricultural rents and produce, a situation made worse by the requirement to pay tithes to a Protestant Church to which only a fraction of the population belonged. In the 1790s, with a growing population, competition for tenancies had increased, the Catholics often outbidding their Protestant competitors because of their lower expectations of returns. This led the Protestants to form local armed bands, called the Peep o' Day Boys, who intimidated Catholics into leaving the land. To protect their interests, the Catholics in turn set up their own organisation known as the Defenders. As might have been expected, violence broke out and spread throughout much of the country. In September 1795 there was a serious affray between Defenders and militant Protestants near Loughall in north Armagh, known as the Battle of the Diamond, following which the Protestants established the Orange Society (named after William of Orange, the Protestant King William III), later known as the Orange Order, to promote their own interests.

On the political front, in 1791 a Protestant barrister named Wolfe Tone had been instrumental in the founding of a secret society of United Irishmen with the aim of achieving complete equality between all Irishmen of whatever creed. Among some members, at least, the aim developed into making Ireland a republic. Although the Catholics (as opposed to Presbyterians) won a large measure of equality in 1793 by virtue of an Act of the Irish Parliament known today as the Catholic Relief Act,[370] they continued in practice to be disqualified from sitting in either house of Parliament, from holding any of the principal offices of state, from serving as judges in the higher courts or, unless the owner of substantial property, from possessing arms or ammunition. The Presbyterians, on the other hand, continued to be wholly disabled by their inability to take the requisite oaths of allegiance and abjuration consistently with their beliefs.

By 1795 the situation was becoming dangerous, with outbreaks of violence spreading through the country. At the end of the following year, with the tide of war against Britain turning in France's favour, there was an attempt by a French fleet (with Wolfe Tone on board) to land in Bantry Bay. In the event it was thwarted by bad weather but it prompted greater vigilance on the part of the British navy and the strengthening of the forces at the disposal of the Irish Government. Armed with new powers under the Insurrection Act 1796,[371] which (among other things) made seditious oaths, such as those taken by the United Irishmen and the Defenders, a capital offence, and with the advantage of particularly effective intelligence from a network of well-paid informers, the Government strove to break up the United Irishmen by arresting its leaders and disarming its sympathisers. By the end of 1797 insurrection in Ulster had been ruthlessly crushed by General Lake, but there were numerous outbreaks elsewhere. On the night of 23 May 1798 there was an uprising in the counties round Dublin, directing attacks on local garrisons or unpopular households. Then on 5 June, following the defeat of a violent insurrection in New Ross, a large number of Protestants were trapped and killed in a barn a few miles away at Scullabogue.

During that summer other widespread uprisings had broken out, with atrocities on both sides which the Government only partially succeeded in repressing. Matters came to a head at Vinegar Hill. Vinegar Hill is a steep mound above Enniscorthy. It had become the main stronghold of the insurgents in County Wexford and from it they had already launched successful attacks on Wexford, Gorey and Bunclody. Determined to put an end to the insurrection, the Government despatched 20,000 troops under the command of General Lake, by this time the Commander-in-Chief in Ireland. His plan was to surround the hill and to annihilate the thousands of insurgents on it. The morning of 21 June 1798 began with an artillery bombardment and the encirclement of the hill. However, all did not go according to plan and a gap in the encirclement was left by General Needham's troops through which many of the insurgents managed to escape, at a point known to this day as Needham's Gap. Nevertheless, hundreds of the insurgents were killed, including many women and children, and the insurrection in County Wexford was crushed.

Between August and October 1798 three separate forces of United Irishmen were landed by the French navy at various points on the Irish coast. All three were intercepted and defeated by Government forces. One had enjoyed conspicuous success until overcome at Ballinamuck in County Longford on 23 September. Another was met by a British squadron off Lough Swilly in October, most of the French ships being captured. On board one of the captured ships was Wolfe Tone. He was immediately arrested, tried for treason and condemned to death. Although in the event he cheated the hangman by committing suicide, it was his death that came to personify the ideal of revolution and Irish independence.

The aims of the insurgents were doomed for want of effective leadership. Worse for them, the troubles of 1798 prompted the British Prime Minister, Pitt, to propose a radical, albeit not a novel, solution, that of union between the two kingdoms, with a view to suppressing any idea of independence, let alone a republic. Whereas the proposal was supported by the British Parliament throughout, it had a rough ride in the Irish Parliament, Grattan being among its most vocal opponents. Initially it was thrown out by the Irish House of Commons but by dint of generous compensation paid by the British Government for the loss of patronage over seats, bribery reputedly on a colossal scale (said to have been 4,000 guineas for a vote in the Irish House of Commons, and there were even annuities paid secretly by the British Government to some Members)[372] and the machinations both of Viscount Castlereagh, who had been appointed as Chief Secretary for Ireland in 1798, and of the Marquess Cornwallis, the Lord Lieutenant, a unionist majority was engineered in the Irish House of Commons despite vociferous objection from the opposition. Thus it was that on 1 August 1800 royal assent was given to an Irish Act for the Union of Great Britain and Ireland,[373] the operative provisions of which were in identical terms to those of a British Act[374] which had received the royal assent a month earlier.

Both Acts provided that, with effect from 1 January 1801, 'the kingdoms of Great Britain and Ireland should be united for ever after into one kingdom by the name of the United Kingdom of Great Britain and Ireland'; that the succession to the crown of the United Kingdom should follow that of the union between England and Scotland; that the United Kingdom should be represented by one parliament, with the Irish representation consisting of 4 bishops and 28 peers in the House of Lords and 100 Members of the House of Commons; that the Churches of England and Ireland should be united, but leaving the Church of Scotland as it was; that, subject to two limited exceptions, there was to be free trade between the two countries; that each country should retain its own currency but share the national debt proportionately; and that the laws in force should continue until changed by the new parliament. Under this new constitution, the Lord Lieutenant and the Chief Secretary formed the executive limb of the Government with responsibility for Ireland.

As with the union between Scotland and England nearly a century before, neither the Channel Islands nor the Isle of Man were included: they were not part of the kingdom of Great Britain; rather, they were dominions of the Crown.

Although representation at Westminster had been extended to Ireland, the time taken to travel between the two was a serious problem. The quickest route between Dublin and London was via the port of Holyhead off the west coast of Anglesey. However, in 1801 the journey took many days: the roads were appalling and there was no bridge across the treacherous Menai Strait between Anglesey and the mainland. It was not until 1815 that the engineer Thomas Telford had sufficient support even to make proposals to Parliament for improvements, let alone for work to begin. It was another eleven years before work was completed with the opening of Telford's magnificent suspension bridge over the Strait, connecting his new road to London (now the A5) with the road to Holyhead, and making the journey manageable.

There was one glaring omission from the Acts of Union: Catholics were still in practice disqualified from sitting in the new Parliament. This was true not only of Irish Catholics but also of English and Scots Catholics too. It would take until 1829 for that disqualification to be removed by the Roman Catholic Relief Act.[375] As a Member of the new House of Commons from 1805 until his death in 1820, Grattan was the principal protagonist for Catholic emancipation, against strong opposition from, among others, King George III, and, at times which mattered, by George IV both as Prince Regent (notwithstanding his long love affair with a Catholic, Maria Fitzherbert) and later as King. Although the Pope had recognised the legitimacy of the House of Hanover following the death of the Old Pretender in 1766, the opposition, particularly that of both Kings, was founded nevertheless on concerns about the divided loyalties of Catholics between the Crown and the Pope, on lingering concerns about the legitimacy of the Hanoverian dynasty, the principle that the Established Church and the state were indivisible and, importantly, on the Coronation Oath by which each King in turn had sworn to preserve the Established Church and all that that entailed.

After Grattan's death in 1820, Daniel O'Connell, a Catholic barrister, became the champion not only of the cause of Catholic emancipation but also of the independence of Ireland. He was elected to the House of Commons in 1828 as one of the Members for County Clare but was unable to take his seat by virtue of his unwillingness to take the requisite oaths of allegiance and abjuration. This brought matters to a head and, in the face of demonstrations throughout Ireland and in fear of rebellion, the Prime Minister (the Duke of Wellington) and the Home Secretary (Sir Robert Peel), notwithstanding their previous vehement opposition, recognised the political necessity for the Government to promote the emancipation of Catholics throughout the United Kingdom. Wellington having failed to win

George IV round, it took the King's mistress, the Marchioness Conyngham, her husband and the King's private secretary to persuade the by now nearly hysterical King to agree. A promise of relief was then included in the King's speech in February 1829 and, not without further resistance from the King, the Act received the royal assent on 13 April 1829.

The Act repealed most of the laws which penalised Catholics. It permitted Catholics to be elected to Parliament, both the Commons and as representative peers, and to vote in Parliament, provided that they took a prescribed oath of allegiance to the Crown, expressly acknowledging the legitimacy of the House of Hanover, and abjuring any temporal power of the Pope. Subject to taking the same oath, it also permitted Catholics to hold public office, except for the greatest offices of state, and to vote in Parliamentary elections.

Ironically, when O'Connell came to take his seat in the House of Commons he was caught out by the wording of the Act: the new oath only applied to Members elected after the Act came into force and therefore did not apply to him. Unsurprisingly, he refused to take the old oath and there was a by-election for his vacant seat in County Clare. In July he was elected once more – this time unopposed – and was finally able to take his seat when Parliament reassembled the following year.

There was, however, a nasty twist in the political price paid for the passage of the Roman Catholic Relief Act, and that was embodied in the Act that was passed immediately afterwards. The Parliamentary Elections (Ireland) Act 1829[376] restricted the entitlement to vote for representatives of Irish counties to the owners of freehold property in the county with a rental value of ten pounds or more, increasing it from the previous threshold, which continued to apply throughout the rest of the United Kingdom, of forty shillings (two pounds). The effect was to disenfranchise a large number of Irish previously entitled to vote, particularly Catholics, fuelling further resentment against Britain. That disparity continued until 1885, when the franchise was made the same throughout the United Kingdom.[377]

Home Rule

Hardly had the Acts of Union been passed than agitation for their repeal began. Although the Acts of 1793 and 1829 had given some political power to Catholics in Ireland, it was the drive to repeal the Acts of Union themselves and to gain independence from Britain that eclipsed all other aspects of Irish history for the next hundred years.

The agitation had been led initially by Grattan and then, following his death, by O'Connell. By 1843 O'Connell's endeavours had gone so far that he was convicted of seditious conspiracy and imprisoned, although in the end the conviction was quashed on appeal the following year on technical grounds.[378] However, all of those endeavours were overtaken by the Great Famine of 1845–52 and the fallout from it.

By 1845 Ireland was one of the most densely populated countries in Europe and four fifths of the population lived on the land. Most of those four fifths were tenants without any security of tenure, who provided labour in lieu of rent and whose staple diet was the potato. Indeed but for the potato agriculture in Ireland could not have supported so large a population nor would the population have expanded as rapidly as it had. Tenants had little if any cash with which they could buy food and, even if they did have cash, the price of corn (the other staple) was inflated by the tariffs imposed on imports under the Corn Laws. Although there had been widespread potato crop failures on previous occasions, in 1845 the failure caused by blight (*Phytophthora infestans*) affected the whole country for the first time. It was exacerbated by food shortages throughout Europe caused both by blight and by the widespread failure of grain harvests which precipitated many of the revolutions in Europe in 1848 and saw publication of *The Communist Manifesto* by Marx and Engels. Peel's Government provided some relief by importing maize from the United States at the end of that year, but the real disaster struck when the potato crop failed in 1846, by which time Peel's Government was out of office and the new Government under Lord John Russell was not dependent on the Irish vote to extinguish the sparks of revolution either in Britain (which came to a head with the Chartist Movement in 1848) or in Ireland.

Although the new Government was prepared to provide employment on public works in Ireland, generally the works did not include improvement to the land, because that would have provided an unacceptable private benefit to the landowners, nor was the Government prepared to feed the people directly or to prohibit the export of food from Ireland to Britain. Even then, the money which tenants earned by their labour on public works was of little use to them because in the areas most severely affected by the blight there was no cash economy nor was there any system for the retail distribution of food. Consequently, the repeal of the Corn Laws, which took effect progressively from 1846, was of little benefit. The problem was compounded by an unwillingness on the part of British politicians to spend what they thought of as British taxpayers' money on Ireland (in marked contrast with West German politicians on the reunification of Germany in 1990). Although in 1847 the potato crop survived, only a small crop had been sown, seed potatoes being scarce. But that short respite was only to be followed by complete failure in 1848 and then by partial failure in 1849.

Confronted with dwindling income from those few tenants who paid rent and with responsibility for the rates of smaller tenants, many landlords took the opportunity to evict their tenants and consolidate their holdings (there being little sense of loyalty to the tenants, unlike the proprietors of some estates in the Highlands of Scotland during the Clearances). The only exception at that stage was in Ulster, where some tenants enjoyed a degree of security by virtue of a customary 'tenant right'.

Unsurprisingly, with a large part of the population starving, disease was rife and exacerbated by the crowded conditions both in the hovels where they lived and in the workhouses and the temporary fever hospitals to which many of them were driven by their circumstances. As a result of starvation, disease and emigration, by 1851 not only had the population of Ireland fallen by a quarter in six years but it had been significantly debased because the emigrants were in large part those with the initiative to emigrate and the means to pay for their passage. In the longer term the emigration changed the face of politics in the United States.

Although land tenure had always had a central part to play in Irish politics, the Great Famine brought home to British politicians the desperate need to do something about it; but, as so often, too little was done too late and the discontent that it fostered drove the movement for Home Rule. In 1858 the secretive Fenian Brotherhood was formed with the object of overthrowing British rule in Ireland, using the *Irish People*, a Dublin weekly publication, for its propaganda. That in turn gave rise to the formation of the National Association in 1864 promoting land reform and disestablishment of the Church of Ireland, although it did not directly address the cry for independence from Britain. Then the following year several of the leaders of the Fenian Brotherhood were arrested, tried and convicted of treason-felony, giving considerable publicity to their cause.

Two years later, after some violent incidents provoked by Fenians in

England, public awareness of their cause and sympathy for it began to grow. This prompted the Prime Minister, Gladstone (an ardent evangelical Protestant), as a start to take up the cause of disestablishment of the Church, which he achieved as a result of political pragmatism on the part of the otherwise hostile majority in the House of Lords (a pragmatism of which a majority of the House of Lords had lost all sight come the *dénouement* in 1911). The Irish Church Act 1869 was an important milestone on the road to Home Rule not only because it signalled the beginning of the end of the Protestant ascendancy in Ireland but also incidentally because it gave tenants for the first time not only the right to buy their holdings but also the right to do so on favourable terms, albeit that the right was confined to the tenants of Church land.[379]

In 1870 Gladstone was able to follow this up with the first of his Land Acts.[380] Given the preponderance of landed interests in both Houses of Parliament, its passage was a remarkable achievement and a tribute to Gladstone's political skill. The Act gave tenants security in the form of tenant right where a custom to that effect could be proved or, where the lease was for less than thirty-one years (which for most Catholics it would have been following the Penal Law of 1704), compensation for disturbance in the event of eviction other than for non-payment of rent as well as compensation for improvements. It also established a favourable loan scheme for the purchase of holdings where the landlord was willing to sell. However, the Act did not work in practice: the custom was difficult to establish; the compensation which the landlords were required to pay was insufficient to deter them from evicting tenants or, therefore, to persuade them to grant leaseholds of more than thirty-one years even if the tenant could be persuaded to jettison the common belief that he was entitled to occupy his holding in perpetuity provided that he paid the rent;[381] the landlords were unwilling to sell; and, most importantly, there was no limit to the rent which the landlord could demand.

The same year as Gladstone's first Land Act, the Home Government Association was formed by an Irish Protestant named Isaac Butt with the sole purpose of establishing a federal union between Ireland and Great Britain under which Ireland would have its own parliament once more and thus a degree of Home Rule. Three years later the Association was superseded by the Home Rule League, the sole aim of which was to achieve Home Rule. After unexpected success among its members in the general election of 1874, the Home Rule League was reorganised as a distinct political party. By the time of the next general election in 1880, Charles Stewart Parnell, one of the Members for County Meath, had become the leader of this new party and, following the agricultural depression which had reached disastrous proportions in Ireland the previous year, Parnell had also become the president of the newly formed Land League, thus linking Home Rule with land reform. In the general election Gladstone's Liberal Government was returned to power and 61 Home Rule candidates from Ireland won seats.

Agriculture in Ireland had been severely depressed as a result of bad weather and poor harvests between 1877 and 1880 and the availability of cheap American grain following the opening up of the prairies in north America with new railroads and the rapid development of dependable steamships. Inevitably many tenants defaulted on their rent, leading more often than not to eviction. The evictions were commonly brutal, such little furniture as there was being thrown out of the house and the tenant sent packing with nowhere else to go. Battering rams were used to break into the homes of those tenants who dared to resist, piteous photographs of which can be seen to this day. Fear of resistance and hostility from neighbours frequently led to evictions being supported by large numbers of armed police and in some instances even of troops.

One of the most tyrannous of the landlords in that respect was the Earl of Leitrim, who was assassinated by three of his tenants on 2 April 1878. Following the election in 1880, Parnell suggested to a meeting of disaffected tenants that the most effective way to protest at their treatment was not to murder their landlords but to ostracise them. Thus it was that in the autumn of that year Captain Boycott, the agent responsible for evicting some of the tenants of the Earl of Erne, found himself one of the first victims of Parnell's suggestion: at the instigation of the tenants, all of his servants and employees walked out, leaving him to fend for himself, giving the word 'boycott' to the English language.

The political pressure from the Land League enabled Gladstone in 1881 to pass his next Land Act,[382] which not only gave substantial effect to the 'three Fs' of fair rent, fixity of tenure and freedom of the tenant to sell his right of occupation, but also improved the terms on which loans for purchase were made available to tenants. Caught between those agitating for war on the landlords come what may and those sufficiently satisfied by the Act to lose interest in Home Rule, Parnell temporised, criticising the Act and discouraging tenants from making use of it at least for the time being. This was interpreted by the Chief Secretary, William 'Buckshot' Forster, as an attempt to wreck the Act and Parnell was interned in Kilmainham Gaol under one of the Coercion Acts[383] which had been passed earlier that year. However, the internment of Parnell backfired: there were further outbreaks of violence and the Land League successfully persuaded many tenants to withhold their rents until all of their grievances had been met. The following spring a compromise was reached under which Parnell and other internees were released, coercion was to be relaxed, tenants in arrears of rent protected and the Land Act amended.[384] In return, Parnell was to use his influence to calm the country and to secure acceptance of the amending Act.

Incensed by the compromise, Forster (along with the Lord Lieutenant, Lord Cowper) resigned and was succeeded as Chief Secretary by Lord Frederick Cavendish. However, Cavendish's appointment was all too short, for on 6 May 1882, the day when he took up office, both he and his permanent under-secretary, Thomas Burke, were stabbed to death with surgical knives in Phoenix Park by assassins calling themselves the Invincibles. Parnell was horrified. The murders and his wholehearted denunciation of them, together with a radical extension of the franchise, enabled him in due course to lead a new political party, known as the Irish National League, to win a critical number of seats in the general election of 1885 which saw Gladstone returned to power for the third time but with Parnell's Irish Nationalists holding the balance of power.

In the 1885 election Wilfred Scawen Blunt, the colourful owner of Crabbet Park in Sussex, a Roman Catholic and a staunch advocate of Irish Home Rule, failed to win the English seat for which he had stood as a Conservative. The following year he travelled all over Ireland to see things for himself and was deeply shocked by what he found. As a substantial landlord and as a supporter of Home Rule, he found a receptive audience almost everywhere he went. With Dr Duggan, the Bishop of Clonfert on the vast Clanricarde estates in County Galway, he learnt that the landlord, the miserly Marquess of Clanricarde, never visited his estates, refused to renew leases which had fallen in and, to evict tenants unable to pay the extortionate rents demanded, found it necessary to use a small army from the Royal Irish Constabulary in addition to his own bailiffs, such was the hostility that he provoked. When one of his agents was assassinated while driving to church, he sent his infamous message to the tenants saying 'If you think you can intimidate me by shooting my agent, you are mistaken.' As Dr Duggan told Blunt, whenever asked what England had given Ireland, he would say simply 'the poor house'.[385]

The following year Blunt returned to Ireland to beat the drum for Home Rule once more. As a deliberately provocative act, he spoke at a meeting at Woodford on the Clanricarde estates, courting arrest by defying a proclamation by the Lord Lieutenant forbidding the meeting under the recently enacted Crimes Act.[386] Sure enough, Blunt was arrested and in due course sentenced to two months in prison. Having been bailed pending an unsuccessful appeal, he was held first in Galway Gaol and later moved to Kilmainham Gaol in Dublin where he served the rest of his sentence. The whole escapade and the publicity that it attracted did much to highlight the plight of Irish tenants and to further the cause of Home Rule, but greatly antagonised several of Blunt's aristocratic friends.

Although in the period before the First World War the condition of Irish tenants was progressively and radically improved by numerous Acts of the Westminster Parliament,[387] they did not solve the seemingly intractable problem of Home Rule. The first of several Home Rule bills was proposed by Gladstone in 1886 but, with a split within his Liberal party, it was rejected by the House of Commons. Parliament was then dissolved and the Conservatives under the Marquess of Salisbury were swept to power in the ensuing general election.

Having effectively admitted in divorce proceedings to adultery with Mrs O'Shea, Parnell fell from grace, his party was split and Parnell himself died of pneumonia at the age of forty-five in October 1891. Nevertheless, at the general election the following year Gladstone formed his fourth ministry, with the Irish Members holding the balance of power once more. When Parliament reassembled in 1893 Gladstone introduced his second Home Rule Bill, managed with difficulty to steer it through the Commons, but let it drop after it was defeated by the huge landed and intransigent majority in the Lords. Faced with defeat, Gladstone resigned and was succeeded by the Earl of Rosebery. However, Rosebery was defeated in the next general election in 1895 and the Conservatives returned to power, first under Salisbury and then under Arthur Balfour until 1905. In the meantime the split in the Irish Home Rule faction, which had resulted from Parnell's dalliance with Mrs O'Shea, had been mended and in 1900 John Redmond emerged as their leader.

The Liberals were returned to power in 1905 and it was on their watch that the great constitutional crisis of 1910–11 occurred, fundamentally changing the prospects for Home Rule. The crisis had originated from the Finance Bill in 1909 which was designed to raise additional revenue in part by increasing income taxes on the rich and in part by imposing taxes on various interests in land, both of which would have adversely affected the interests of the entrenched landowning and Conservative majority in the House of Lords. After a long and troubled passage through the Commons (including 544 divisions), it was rejected out of hand by the Lords, contrary to the convention (known as the 'financial privilege') which had been adopted by the Commons in 1671 and extended in 1678 to constrain the demands of Charles II for funds. This rejection by the Lords forced a general election in January 1910 which focused not only on whether the Commons should retain absolute control over national finance (known as 'Money Bills') but also on the wider question of the power of the Lords to amend or veto any Bill which had been passed by the Commons. The Liberals won the election, but with a reduced majority, and Herbert Asquith (who had succeeded Campbell-Bannerman as Prime Minister in 1908) resumed office.

By November that year, Asquith had proposed his Parliament Bill to curtail the powers of the Lords and had obtained in questionable circumstances a promise in secret from King George V to appoint a sufficient number of Liberal peers to ensure that the Bill would be passed by the Lords. By June 1911 the Bill had passed through all its stages in the Commons and had received its second reading in the Lords; however, it looked likely to be frustrated by amendments proposed by Unionist peers, including a requirement for a referendum on important constitutional changes such as Home Rule for Ireland. In the face of the proposed amendments, Asquith went public on the King's promise. At the suggestion of the King, the amendments were referred back to the Commons, but were rejected. The *dénouement* came with the debate in the Lords in soaring temperatures on 9 and 10 August. As a result of a large number of Unionist abstentions, the votes of most of the bishops and the brave support of a few Unionists, the Bill was passed by a majority of 17.

On 18 August 1911 the Parliament Act received the royal assent.[388] Although the Act contemplated a radical restructuring of the House of Lords so that it would consist of elected, rather than hereditary, Members (which continues to be the position under the Act today, although it has yet to be given effect),[389] for the time being it curtailed the power of the Lords to reject any Bill passed by the Commons: for public Bills other than Money Bills (and thus of direct relevance to Home Rule) the consent of the House of Lords would no longer be required after the Bill in question had been rejected by the Lords three times and two years had elapsed between the second and third readings in the Commons. Not only had the House of Lords been removed as an otherwise immovable obstacle to Home Rule, but critically Redmond held the balance of power in the Commons, making Home Rule almost inevitable.

Nevertheless, there was uncompromising resistance from the Conservatives led by Balfour, playing the Orange card, and by the Ulster Unionists. In 1910 the latter had chosen Sir Edward Carson, a former Conservative solicitor-general, as their leader. In September 1911, a month after the passing of the Parliament Act, Carson announced to a vast meeting of Unionists in Belfast that, if Home Rule became law, they would ignore it and set up their own government in Ulster. Then in April 1912 the new Conservative leader, Andrew Bonar Law, an Ulster Presbyterian, joined Carson at a great demonstration in Belfast and made plain that his support for Ulster's resistance to Home Rule would be unstinting. Two days later, Asquith introduced his Home Rule bill in the House of Commons providing for a form of devolved government in Ireland.

Although in the light of the Parliament Act the fate of the Bill was inevitable, there was not only vehement opposition in Parliament but, more ominously, the opposing factions in Ireland progressively took up arms, the Unionists under the banner of the Ulster Volunteers and the Home Rulers as the Irish Volunteers.

By March 1914, such was the threat of armed insurrection in Ulster that the Government set about strengthening the armed forces there. When the General Officer Commanding in Ireland, Sir Arthur Paget, expressed concern about the sympathies of some of his officers, he was instructed by the Secretary of State for War that officers required to suppress disorder in support of the civil power should not be permitted to resign their commissions but should, if they refused to obey orders, be dismissed, with the saving that officers domiciled in Ulster should be excused such duties. (It is symptomatic of the persistent insensitivity of Government that this saving did not apply to non-commissioned officers or other ranks.) Notwithstanding the instructions which he had received, Paget told his officers that active operations were about to commence against Ulster and that Ireland would shortly be in a blaze, without explaining that their role would be confined to supporting law and order. He then took the unprecedented step of asking the officers likely to be involved for an assurance of their willingness to serve against the Ulster Volunteers, only to find that 58 cavalry officers stationed at the Curragh would prefer to be dismissed. In the event those officers retained their commissions and obeyed their orders – the so-called Curragh mutiny was no such thing. Nevertheless, public confidence had been badly damaged.

In the hope of achieving a compromise, Asquith proposed that any of the nine counties of Ulster could opt to delay the implementation of Home Rule in that particular county for a period of six years. Whereas Redmond reluctantly accepted the proposal, it was rejected outright by Carson. The Home Rule Bill was not amended to include the proposal, but received its third reading in the Commons on 25 May (which was more than two years since the second reading). It was then, as expected, rejected by the Lords. In July King George V, who was personally convinced of the necessity for Home Rule, attempted to mediate by convening meetings between the two factions under the chairmanship of the Speaker of the House of Commons at Buckingham Palace, but it came to nothing, with both Redmond and Carson falling out over the fate of Tyrone. Then on 4 August the United Kingdom declared war against Germany, derailing the whole endeavour.

Although the Bill became law as the Government of Ireland Act 1914,[390] receiving the royal assent by virtue of the 1911 Act on 18 September 1914 notwithstanding the rejection by the Lords, its effect was immediately suspended by the Suspensory Act 1914[391] for the duration of the war or at least twelve months.

The Easter Rising

At first the majority of nationalists were content to wait for the war to end, but there was a minority who saw the war as an opportunity to exploit to their advantage, leading to a split in the Volunteer movement between the majority, who came to be called the National Volunteers, and the minority as Irish Volunteers under the command of Eoin MacNeill. Whereas MacNeill wished to follow a cautious defensive policy, there was within the minority a group led principally by Patrick Pearse which had resolved on achieving independence from Britain by force of arms before the war had ended. This militant minority did what they could to obtain arms and ammunition from Germany with Sir Roger Casement, an Irish-born British diplomat, acting as their go-between. But they had no prospect of success without the support of the remainder of the Irish Volunteers.

As a result of misleading MacNeill, Pearse managed to arrange for an armed rising by all of the Irish Volunteers to begin on Easter Sunday, 23 April 1916, in the guise of commonplace military manoeuvres. However, Pearse's plans began to fall apart on 20 April when a German ship carrying arms destined for the Volunteers was captured by the British off the coast of Kerry. The following day, after discovering that he had been misled, MacNeill countermanded the order for manoeuvres. At the same time, Casement, who had been put ashore from a German submarine, had been captured by the British.

Notwithstanding these setbacks, Pearse went ahead with his plan. Without causing any initial surprise, the Irish Volunteers paraded in Dublin on Easter Monday, but then took possession of the General Post Office, from the steps of which Pearse proclaimed the establishment of a republic. Stirring stuff it was too.

> In every generation the Irish people have asserted their right to national freedom and sovereignty; six times during the past three hundred years they have asserted it in arms. Standing on that fundamental right and again asserting it in arms in the face of the world, we hereby proclaim the Irish republic as a sovereign independent state, and we pledge our lives and the lives of our comrades-in-arms to the cause of its freedom, of its welfare, and of its exaltation among the nations.[392]

Hopelessly unprepared, the British then scrambled reinforcements to put down the rising and, following sporadic fighting, Pearse surrendered unconditionally on the Saturday. Martial law having been declared by the Government, Pearse and other leaders of the rising were tried by court martial, condemned and shot, stirring up outrage among the Irish.

Founded on a highly questionable reading of the Treason Act 1351,[393] Casement was hanged as a traitor a few months later. He had been indicted for 'adhering to the King's enemies' in Germany contrary to the Act of 1351. The Act declared (in Norman French) that it was (in translation) treason to 'be adherent to the King's enemies in his realm, giving to them aid or comfort in the realm or elsewhere'. On a plain reading of the Act, adherence to the King's enemies in Germany did not constitute adherence to the King's enemies in his realm and did not therefore constitute treason within that provision. If it had been otherwise, the words 'in his realm' would have been either redundant or incomplete. Indeed, given that the Act was declaratory and at the time that it was passed acts committed abroad were not triable in England, the meaning of that part of the Act was plain. Both the trial court and the Court of Criminal Appeal, however, pushed that simple point aside and relied on unreasoned expressions of opinion to the contrary, most of which simply begged the question.[394]

Following the Easter Rising, there was what might have been seen as a further blow to Irish independence. Although done to make communication more efficient in wartime, Dublin Mean Time was abolished. Dublin Mean Time had been 25 minutes behind Greenwich Mean Time but, with effect from 1 October 1916, it was brought into line.

The War of Independence and the creation of the Irish Free State

Although attempts were made by the Government to negotiate a political settlement, nothing had been achieved by the end of the war. In the general election on 14 December 1918, a month after the armistice, the coalition Government, now led by David Lloyd George, was re-elected, but 73 of the Irish seats were won by Sinn Féin, the Irish republican party which had been formed in 1905 and was now led by Eamonn de Valera. When Parliament assembled at Westminster in the new year, those Sinn Féin members who were not in prison refused to take their seats.[395] Instead, they met in Dublin and proclaimed themselves to be the Parliament of the Irish Republic (Dáil Eireann), of which de Valera was then elected president. The proclamation recited, no doubt with some justification, 'English rule in this country is, and always has been, based upon force and fraud and maintained by military occupation against the declared will of the people'.[396]

Among those who were in prison was Constance Markievicz, who was, surprisingly for a member of Sinn Féin, the daughter of the Protestant owner of a large estate in County Sligo, Sir Henry Gore-Booth. She was the first woman ever to be elected to the Westminster Parliament, although she never took her seat. She had originally been condemned to death for her part in the Easter Rising, but, taking account of her sex, her sentence had been commuted to life imprisonment. In the event, however, she had been released in 1917 under the general amnesty granted that year, but at the time of her election had been jailed once again, this time for campaigning against conscription.

Following the proclamation of the republic, the Irish Volunteers were reconstituted as the Irish Republican Army (known as the IRA) under the direction of Michael Collins. Law and order were enforced by the British Government through the Royal Irish Constabulary, against whom surprise attacks were launched by the IRA. The ensuing difficulty of recruiting for the Constabulary in Ireland led the Government to recruit in England. Because there was a shortage of uniforms for the new recruits, they were supplied with ex-army uniforms (khaki) and police caps (darkest green) and belts (black), giving rise to their nickname the Black and Tans. To the Constabulary the Government also added an Auxiliary Division consisting largely of young ex-officers. The violence escalated, with attacks and reprisals on both sides exacerbated by sectarian violence against Protestants in the south and Catholics in Ulster.

In an attempt to find a political solution, in 1920 the Westminster Government passed (although, of course, in the absence of the Sinn Féin members) the Government of Ireland Act[397] which divided Ireland in two, Northern Ireland consisting of six of the nine counties in Ulster and Southern Ireland consisting of the remainder of the country.[398] Each was to have its own parliament and a constitution otherwise similar to that under the 1914 Act, leaving the Westminster Parliament supreme[399] albeit still with Irish representatives[400] and all legislation still subject to royal assent.[401] Notwithstanding the Act, hostilities continued and it was not until 6 December 1921 that a peace treaty was finally concluded between representatives of the Government of the United Kingdom and representatives of the Dáil.

The treaty was negotiated on behalf of the Dáil by five delegates with power to conclude a treaty albeit subject to approval from Dublin.[402] It is unclear whether the British delegation knew of the latter restriction. At all events and after weeks of negotiation, Lloyd George, by whom the British delegation was led, presented the Irish with an ultimatum: either all of them agreed that night to sign the draft agreement which was then on offer or there would be war within three days. Having agonised over their decision for some time, the Irish delegates agreed to sign, curiously without insisting on reference back to Dublin. After some minor amendments to the draft, the agreement was finalised and signed in the early hours of 6 December.

Unsurprisingly some of the Dáil cabinet contended that the Irish delegates had not had authority to sign the treaty on the terms which they did without reference back to Dublin, complaining that too much had been conceded. However, the controversy was ultimately resolved by a vote in the Dáil and the treaty was then ratified, following which de Valera resigned in protest and Arthur Griffith (who had been the chairman of the Irish delegation) was elected as president in his place, Collins (another of the delegates) becoming chairman of the provisional government cabinet (effectively the prime minister). In his speech to the Dáil in support of the treaty on 7 January 1922, Griffith aptly invoked Thomas Carlyle, saying: 'I have thought of this many times while listening to the criticism of the treaty – he describes the fly that crawled along the front of the Cologne cathedral and communicated to all the other flies what a horribly rough surface it was, because the fly was unable to see the edifice.'[403]

The treaty[404] applied to the whole of Ireland but gave the option to Northern Ireland to separate from the South and to continue with the constitution with which it had been provided under the 1920 Act.[405] Subject to that, Ireland, referred to as the Irish Free State, was to have the same status within the British Empire as the Dominion of Canada,[406] the Members of its Parliament being required to swear an oath of allegiance not only to the constitution of the Free State but also to the King.[407] In the event that Northern Ireland opted to separate, the boundary with the South was to be determined by a commission representing the Free State, Northern Ireland and Great Britain.[408] The treaty was given effect by an Act of the United Kingdom Parliament[409] followed by the Constitution of the Irish Free State, the terms of which were set out in Acts of the respective Parliaments.[410] As was long since contemplated, on 7 December 1922 the Northern Irish Parliament opted to separate.

But that was not the end of the conflict, even for the time being. Not only was there sectarian violence in Northern Ireland between Catholics on the one hand, supported by the IRA, with a view to ending partition, and Protestants on the other, but there was also a fallout between the faction within the IRA which supported the treaty with the United Kingdom and the

faction led by de Valera which was determined that Ireland should become a
republic.[411] The fallout culminated in civil war which saw the assassination
of Collins, achieved nothing but bitterness and resulted tragically in the
destruction of the Irish Public Record Office with its enormous archive
of historical documents. It was only ended by de Valera's declaration of a
ceasefire on 24 May 1923.

With the ending of the civil war, attention was turned once more to the
delineation of the boundary between Northern Ireland and the Irish Free
State. In 1924 a Boundary Commission was appointed notwithstanding
the refusal of the Northern Ireland Government to co-operate. There
was speculation that the Free State would get parts of south Down and
Fermanagh and that the North would get part of east Donegal. Then, on
7 November 1925, the *Morning Post* published a leak (which happened
to be broadly accurate) that the Commission would recommend that the
border should be shortened by about 50 miles, that 286 square miles should
be transferred from the North to the Free State and that 77 square miles
(including part of east Donegal) should be transferred to the North. The
leak embarrassed the Government of the Free State and by common consent
not only was the Commission's report suppressed (in the event until 1969)
but on 3 December 1925 the three Governments agreed that the border
should follow the old county boundaries. Given that those boundaries had
been established in the sixteenth and seventeenth centuries, it comes as
no surprise that they made little sense: such were the changes since then
that the border now ran through the middle of towns, farms and even
individual houses, taking no account of religious or political sympathies. Of
all the ironies, the border left the seat of the Roman Catholic Primate of All
Ireland in Armagh, in other words in the Protestant North. It represented
yet another tragic failure to understand, let alone address, the problems to
which the colonisation of Ireland had given rise.

The final break, or almost the final break, with the United Kingdom
came in 1937 when de Valera achieved, or more accurately almost achieved,
his long hoped-for goal of turning the Free State into a republic – the
republic of Ireland or Éire. Following a referendum, the Dáil adopted a new
constitution[412] which affirms that Ireland is an independent sovereign state
(Article 1), declares (significantly) that the national territory consists of the
whole of the island of Ireland, its islands and territorial seas (Article 2) and
provides for the application of the law to the whole of the territory excluding

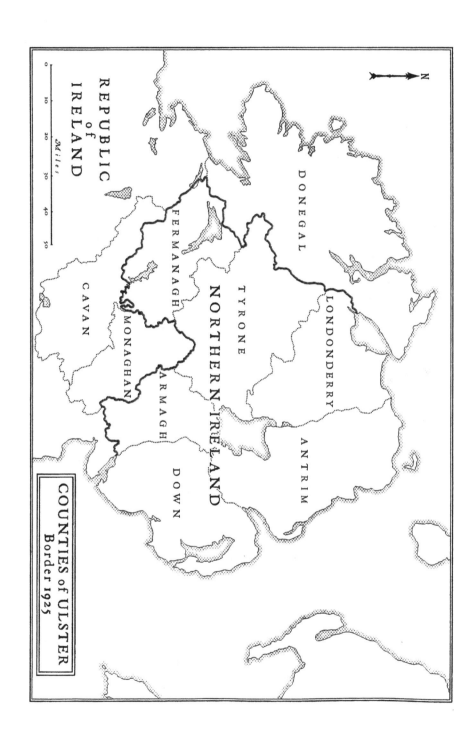

COUNTIES of ULSTER
Border 1925

REPUBLIC of IRELAND

DONEGAL

FERMANAGH

CAVAN

MONAGHAN

ARMAGH

TYRONE

NORTHERN IRELAND

LONDONDERRY

ANTRIM

DOWN

N

Northern Ireland 'Pending the re-integration of the national territory'
(Article 3). However, by virtue of the Good Friday Agreement of 1998,
Articles 2 and 3 of the 1937 Constitution were replaced by a new Article 3.1
which refers to an aspiration to peaceful union with Northern Ireland by
consent of a majority of the people, both north and south – an aspiration
which continues to this day.

Ironically, the Constitution of 1937 did not mention the word 'republic'.
It named the State 'Éire' or 'Ireland', not the Republic of Éire or the Republic
of Ireland, and, by Article 29.4.2, preserved the power of the King to appoint
the diplomatic and consular representatives of the State and to conclude
international treaties on its behalf. That was a power which the Parliament
of the Free State had conferred on the King the previous year[413] and it was left
intact. It was not until 1949 that the Dáil declared the State to be a republic,
which it named 'the Republic of Ireland', and abolished the remaining power
of the King.[414]

However, that was not the only vestige of empire that remained after
1937, albeit only briefly. On the evening of 11 July 1938 the Union Flag was
lowered and, after HMS *Acasta* and the last British troops had sailed away,
the new national flag of Ireland was raised on Spike Island in Cork Harbour[415]
marking the beginning of the end of the British imperial presence in what
was in reality the Republic of Ireland in all but name. Cork, like Berehaven
(in Bantry Bay) and Lough Swilly which were handed over later that year,
was one of the three British naval establishments which had remained in the
Free State and latterly Éire.[416] Under Article 7 of the 1921 Treaty it had been
agreed that they were to remain available to the British in time of peace,
together with such other harbours as the British Government might require
for defence in time of war or strained relations with any foreign power.
Whereas these three 'treaty ports' were regarded by the British as of vital
importance to the defence of the western approaches to Britain, particularly
in the light of experience during the First World War, Article 7 constituted a
fundamental impediment to any wish on the part of the Free State to remain
neutral in the event of any future war and thus a restriction of its sovereignty.
De Valera had been determined to put an end to this and finally had his way
on what turned out to be the eve of the Second World War. On 25 April 1938,
six weeks after the annexation of Austria by Nazi Germany, a further treaty
had been agreed and subsequently ratified by both Governments by which,
among many other things, Article 7 of the 1921 Treaty was abrogated and

the three treaty ports were to be handed over to the Government of Éire by the end of the year.[417] In the Second World War not only was Éire neutral but fortuitously it turned out that, after the fall of France and the subsequent German domination of waters to the south of Éire, the British were better off using Iceland for the defence of their shipping than they would have been had they retained their rights to the treaty ports.

The Troubles and the Good Friday Agreement

With the severance of the the last remaining links between Éire and the British Crown, the six counties of Northern Ireland now stood alone. Although the constitution of Northern Ireland prohibited laws which were discriminatory on religious grounds,[418] in practice until 1969 the Catholic population were gravely disadvantaged politically and also as respects employment, policing and social housing. Politically there was an inbuilt Protestant majority, partly as a result of the gerrymandering of constituency boundaries and partly as a result of the business votes available to the largely Protestant owners of businesses. Although many of the political disadvantages were removed in 1969,[419] their legacy together with the numerous other discriminatory practices to which the Catholics were subjected led to what became known as the Troubles.

The Troubles began in earnest with the Derry March on 5 October 1968 and reached their nadir with the Battle of the Bogside in the middle of August 1969 and then with the shooting of protesters by British troops on Bloody Sunday, 30 January 1972. In 1972 the Northern Irish Parliament was suspended and the province was governed directly by Westminster. However, the violence and bloodshed continued largely unabated until the Good Friday Agreement was concluded on 10 April 1998.

The Good Friday Agreement (officially known as the Belfast Agreement) was concluded between the British Government, the Irish Government and representatives of most of the political factions involved in the Troubles. At its heart was the agreement that the constitutional status of Northern Ireland would be determined by plebiscite and in the meantime that the Republic would give up its territorial claim to Northern Ireland. It was ratified by referendum both north and south of the border. Even then, however, it took another decade for the worst of the violence to be halted. In the end what had started with English conquest and colonisation has ended, so far at least, with the modern ideal of self-determination. With the growing proportion of Catholics to Protestants in Northern Ireland, reunification may not be far off.

Epilogue

✠

When Lord Palmerston referred to the protection of British subjects by the 'strong arm of England', he no doubt unwittingly reflected the subordination of Scotland, Wales and Ireland to English domination. Ironically the same mistake was made in Nelson's famous signal to the fleet at the Battle of Trafalgar: 'England expects that every man will do his duty', notwithstanding that the fleet was British and that among the sailors in the fleet a large proportion were Scots, Welsh and Irish.

The circumstances in which Scotland, Wales and Northern Ireland were united with England to form the United Kingdom were unlikely to make them easy bedfellows: having been worsted on most occasions in the seemingly endless hostilities over the centuries, the Scots were then overwhelmed economically and driven to form an uneasy union by agreement; the Welsh were conquered, their language was suppressed and for almost all purposes until recently Wales was treated as no more than an adjunct of England; and the Irish were not only conquered but ruthlessly colonised too, their produce being exploited, just like that of any other colony, to the advantage of the English. The desire of many in Scotland, Wales and, to a lesser extent, Northern Ireland for independence from England comes as no surprise. What is striking, however, is the absence of any obvious desire on the part of the people of the Channel Islands or of the Isle of Man for independence from the Crown, suggesting perhaps that the looser union – in substance a federal union – and in particular the far greater independence from Westminster, including taxation, has worked out better.

Whether the piecemeal devolution of power by Westminster to the Scots, the Welsh and the Northern Irish would ever be sufficient to stem the tide of independence is questionable. Had there been a looser union from the outset, such as that with the Channel Islands and the Isle of Man, and had they enjoyed greater economic strength, history might have taken a rather different course. Indeed, had the First World War not intervened, Ireland would have enjoyed Home Rule and probably so too would Scotland and Wales. Would that have prevented the partition of Ireland and would it have quieted the cries for independence? We shall never know.

One of the fundamental problems is that the population of England greatly exceeds that of Scotland, Wales and Northern Ireland and, as a result of the understandable aim of making parliamentary constituencies roughly the same size, England has the whip hand at Westminster. A clearly defined federal union, with an English Parliament for English laws, might well solve that problem and satisfy those who yearn for complete independence. However, the vested interests of the English Members of Parliament and the British approach of patch and mend, rather than that of adopting a more radical solution, is likely to perpetuate an uneasy union for the time being. But for how long? It was, after all, the failure of Parliament to address the question of Home Rule for Ireland in sufficient time that led to the unhappy events of the twentieth century.

Time alone will tell whether all parts of the British Isles will remain British or whether they will secede. If they did secede, would that be for the greater good? Demography might suggest otherwise.

Endnotes

1. For statutory purposes the term is 'British Islands', which, before the formation of the Republic of Ireland, included the whole of Ireland (see the Interpretation Act 1978, Schedule 1 to that Act and paragraph 4(2) of Schedule 2).
2. In 1850 the British navy had blockaded Greek ports in support of a claim for compensation against an obdurate Greek Government by a British Jew called Don Pacifico, who had lost his property during anti-semitic riots in Athens. In his speech Palmerston spoke in terms of the 'Government of England' and 'the strong arm of England'.
3. The Statute of Kilkenny 1367, much of which was confirmed in 1494 (by 10 Hen. 7 c. 8) and not repealed until 1983.
4. 4 Hen. 4 c. 30, which remained in force for over two centuries.
5. The Act of Proscription 1746 (19 Geo. 2 c. 39), which was not repealed until 1782.
6. This ceremony was performed, for example, when Niall O'Neill the younger submitted to King Richard II on 16 March 1395, as recorded in a treaty between them of that date, with the picturesque difference that, as the treaty recounts, O'Neill swore his oath in the Irish language which was then 'rendered into English' by an interpreter (*Irish Historical Documents*, pp. 64–65).
7. The ceremony is still derived from the form prescribed by the Coronation Oath Act 1688 (1 Gul. & Mar. c. 6).
8. 1 Ann. c. 1, section 5.
9. The Russian Orthodox Church has stuck resolutely to the Julian calendar. The Greek Orthodox Church (among a few others) adopted the Gregorian calendar in 1923, save for fixing the date of Easter.
10. Bond, *Handy-Book of Rules and Tables*, pp. xvii–xviii, n.
11. 24 Geo. 2 c. 23, *English Historical Documents*, vol. 7, no. 61.
12. 21 & 22 Geo. 3 c. 48.
13. Take, for example, the English statute cited as 27 Hen. 8 c. 26. The first number identifies the parliamentary session during which the statute was enacted by reference to the number of years since the monarch acceded to the throne, and there may be two such numbers where the session spanned more than one year; the second number (the regnal number – the name of the monarch being Latinised and abbreviated) identifies the monarch if more than one of the same name; and the third number identifies the number of the statute enacted during that session, known as a chapter or, in Latin, as *capitulum*, abbreviated to 'cap' or 'c'. Since 1896 the date has been included in the title to all statutes. In addition, new and short titles were given by the Short Titles Act 1896 to all extant statutes enacted since 1351.
14. The other Celtic language was Goedelic (Q-Celtic) which survives variously as Irish, Scots and Manx Gaelic.
15. *Anglo-Saxon Chronicles*, p. 55.
16. *Anglo-Saxon Chronicles*, pp. 55, 57.
17. In the seventh century the two distinct kingdoms of Bernicia and Deira merged to form Northumbria. Bernicia stretched between the Forth and the Tees and Deira

between the Tees and the Humber.

18. *Annales Monastici*, II, *Annales Monasterii de Wintonia (AD 519–1277)*, ed. H. R. Luard (London: Longman, Green, Longman, Roberts, and Green 1865), p. 7.
19. *Anglo-Saxon Chronicles*, p. 104.
20. *William of Malmesbury*, pp. 74–75.
21. *William of Malmesbury*, p. 76.
22. *Egil's Saga*, ch. 51.
23. *Egil's Saga*, chs 50–54.
24. Dumville, *Wessex and England*, p. 171.
25. *William of Malmesbury*, p. 103.
26. *Chronicle of John of Worcester*, vol. 2, p. 461.
27. *William of Malmesbury*, p. 103.
28. The assumption of the title of 'Duke', as opposed to Count, of Normandy began in the tenth century but was not consistent, even William the Conqueror more often than not styling himself 'Count' (Crouch, pp. 18–20, 60–61).
29. *Anglo-Saxon Chronicles*, p. 151.
30. *Anglo-Saxon Chronicles*, p. 151.
31. *William of Malmesbury*, p. 109.
32. *Orkneyinga Saga*, p. 26.
33. *Anglo-Saxon Chronicles*, p. 162.
34. *Anglo-Saxon Chronicles*, p. 198.
35. *William of Malmesbury*, p. 152.
36. *Allen Brown's English Castles*, p. 31.
37. Davis, 'A Contemporary Account of the Battle of Tinchebrai'.
38. *Bishop of Sodor and Man v Earl of Derby* (1751), 2 Vesey Senior 337, at p. 351.
39. Treaty of Mantes, 9 July 1193, Roger of Howden, *Chronica*, vol. 3, pp. 216–17.
40. Roger of Howden, *Chronica*, vol. 3, p. 203; Gillingham, *Richard I*, p. 248, particularly at n. 92.
41. *Roger of Wendover*, vol. 1, p. 473.
42. Another explanation of the origin of the name is that Geoffrey planted broom as cover for hunting.
43. *Roger of Wendover*, vol. 1, pp. 509–10.
44. 25 Oct. 1154.
45. 19 Dec. 1154.
46. *King John*, Act IV, scene III.
47. By this stage New, or Little, Andely had been built at the very foot of the castle mound. Together with Grand Andely, the two settlements became known as Les Andelys.
48. The charter by which the surrender was effected refers indiscriminately to the kingdom of Ireland and to the lordship of Ireland. Ireland may already have been a vassal state of the Holy See by virtue of the Papal Bull of *Laudabiliter* of 1155.
49. *English Historical Documents*, vol. 3, no. 17.
50. Ireland may already have been a vassal state of the Holy See by virtue of the Papal Bull of *Laudabiliter* of 1155.
51. *English Historical Documents*, vol. 4, no. 376.
52. Otto was the son of John's sister Matilda and a grandson of Henry II. He had been elected as Holy Roman Emperor in 1208 following the assassination of his predecessor, Philip of Swabia.
53. *Roger of Wendover*, p. 397.
54. Smith, 'The Treaty of Lambeth 1217', pp. 562–79.
55. *English Historical Documents*, vol. 3, no. 41.
56. *Minquiers and Ecrehos Case*, p. 56.
57. *English Historical Documents*, vol. 4, no. 4.
58. *English Historical Documents*, vol. 4, no. 21(ii).
59. *English Historical Documents*, vol. 4, no. 39.
60. *English Historical Documents*, vol. 5, no.113.
61. The reference to Great Britain in the Treaties was a misnomer, Great Britain only coming into existence with the Act of Union between England and Scotland in 1707.
62. Articles 48–49 of the Annex to the Hague Convention Respecting the Laws and Customs of War on Land 1907.
63. In the seventh century Bernicia merged with Deira to form Northumbria.
64. 'Chronicle of the Canons of Huntingdon', *Early Sources of Scottish History*, vol. 1, p. 271.
65. *Scottish Annals*, p. 81.
66. *Scottish Annals*, p. 81.
67. The terminology in historical references to Cumbria, Cumberland and Strathclyde is, to, put it mildly, confused. See Fiona Edmonds, 'The Emergence and Transformation of Medieval Cumbria', *Scottish Historical Review*, vol. 93, 2, no. 237, pp. 195–216.
68. As a result of her first marriage to the Emperor Heinrich of Germany, she was also known as Maude or Maud.
69. *Scottish Annals*, p. 195.

70. *Scottish Annals*, p. 239, *Sourcebook of Scottish History*, vol. 1, p. 77.
71. *English Historical Documents*, vol. 2, no. 26. For the version which was read out at York Minster in August 1175 see *Scottish Annals*, pp. 260–63.
72. *Sourcebook of Scottish History*, vol. 1, pp. 79–80; *Early Sources of Scottish History*, vol. 2, pp. 322–23.
73. *Early Sources of Scottish History*, vol. 2, pp. 372–77; *Scottish Annals*, pp. 328–29.
74. This is referred to in the Treaty of York as 15,000 silver marks.
75. *English Historical Documents*, vol. 3, no. 31; *Sourcebook of Scottish History*, vol. 1, pp. 82–83; *Early Sources of Scottish History*, vol. 2, pp. 502–3.
76. The chronicles refer to a previous payment of £13,000.
77. Chapter 59 of Magna Carta reads in translation as follows: 'We will do toward Alexander, King of Scots, concerning the return of his sisters and his hostages, and concerning his franchises, and his right, in the same manner as we shall do toward our other barons of England, unless it ought to be otherwise according to the charters which we hold from William his father, formerly King of Scots; and this shall be according to the judgment of his peers in our court.'
    However, the *Annals of Dunstable*, vol. 3, p. 58, record that Alexander's sisters were still in the custody of Henry III in 1220 (*Scottish Annals*, p. 335).
78. *Early Sources of Scottish History*, vol. 2, pp. 655–56, n. 4; *Sourcebook of Scottish History*, vol. 1, pp. 21–23.
79. *Early Sources of Scottish History*, vol. 2, p. 654.
80. Adopting modern nomenclature, they were McDonald of Dunyvaig, McLean of Duart, McDonald of Sleat, McLeod of Harris, McKinnon of McKinnon, McLean of Coll, McDonald of Moidart, McLean of Lochbuie and MacQuarrie of Ulva.
81. *Sourcebook of Scottish History*, vol. 3, pp. 263–73.
82. *Sourcebook of Scottish History*, vol. 1, p. 105.
83. *English Historical Documents*, vol. 3, no. 65; *A Sourcebook of Scottish History*, vol. 1, pp. 107–9.
84. *Sourcebook of Scottish History*, vol. 1, pp. 109–11.
85. *Sourcebook of Scottish History*, vol. 1, pp. 113–14.
86. *Sourcebook of Scottish History*, vol. 1, pp. 114–15, *Chronicle of Lanercost*, pp. 81, 260. This document was the first of those known as the Ragman Rolls.
87. *Sourcebook of Scottish History*, vol. 1, pp. 116–17.
88. *Sourcebook of Scottish History*, vol. 1, pp. 121–26.
89. *Sourcebook of Scottish History*, vol. 1, pp. 136–39.
90. *Chronicle of Lanercost*, pp. 259–62; *Sourcebook of Scottish History*, vol. 1, p. 139.
91. *Chronicle of Lanercost*, pp. 278–82; *English Historical Documents*, vol. 4, no. 9.
92. *Sourcebook of Scottish History*, vol. 1, pp. 144–45.
93. *Chronicle of Lanercost*, pp. 330–32.
94. *Sourcebook of Scottish History*, vol. 1, pp. 146–48; *English Historical Documents*, vol. 4, no. 37.
95. *Sourcebook of Scottish History*, vol. 1, pp. 150–51; Duncan, *'Honi soit qui mal y pense'*, pp. 135–38.
96. *English Historical Documents*, vol. 5, no. 44.
97. *Sourcebook of Scottish History*, vol. 1, pp. 157–60.
98. *Sourcebook of Scottish History*, vol. 2, pp. 54–56.
99. *Sourcebook of Scottish History*, vol. 2, p. 57.
100. Derry, *History of Scandinavia*, p. 79.
101. Whereas the Treaty of Perth 1266 had provided for the application of Scottish law to the Hebrides, there was no comparable provision in the pledge to secure the dowry of Princess Margaret in 1468. (See Linklater, *Udal Law*, p. 10.) Although in 1611 an order of the Scottish Privy Council imposed Scottish law on the islands, it did not have the effect of displacing udal law in respect of land tenure (ibid.).
102. *Sourcebook of Scottish History*, vol. 2, pp. 57–58.
103. Linklater, *Udal Law*, p. 8.
104. Not to be confused with the castle and ramparts built further downstream in the sixteenth century, much of which with later embellishments survives today.
105. Ridpath, *Border History*, p. 293.

106. Ridpath, *Border History*, p. 296.
107. *English Historical Documents*, vol. 4, no. 194.
108. *Acta Regia*, p. 314.
109. Ridpath, *Border History*, pp. 306–7.
110. *Sourcebook of Scottish History*, vol. 2, pp. 58–60.
111. Burne, *Battlefields of England*, pp. 157–58.
112. Burne, *Battlefields of England*, pp. 159–60.
113. *Sourcebook of Scottish History*, vol. 2, pp. 67–70.
114. *Sourcebook of Scottish History*, vol. 2, pp. 123–24.
115. *Sourcebook of Scottish History*, vol. 2, pp. 133–36.
116. Michel, *Les Ecossais en France*, vol. 1, pp. 520–21.
117. *Sourcebook of Scottish History*, vol. 2, pp. 148–49.
118. 35 Hen. 8 c. 1.
119. *English Historical Documents*, vol. 5(a), no. 30.
120. *Sourcebook of Scottish History*, vol. 2, pp. 171–75.
121. *Sourcebook of Scottish History*, vol. 2, pp. 177–78.
122. The Papal Jurisdiction Act 1560, A1560/8/4.
123. The Confession of Faith Ratification Act 1560, A1560/8/3.
124. *Sourcebook of Scottish History*, vol. 2, pp. 175–78.
125. *Sourcebook of Scottish History*, vol. 2, p. 191–94.
126. Nicolson, *Leges Marchiarum*, p. 6; Ridpath, *Border History*, p. 98.
127. The annexation of Berwick-upon-Tweed was formally recognised by section 3 of the Wales and Berwick Act 1747 (20 Geo. 2 c. 42). Although it has been suggested that Berwick-upon-Tweed is still at war with Russia following the declaration of the Crimean War in 1854, there is no substance to the suggestion, there being no specific reference to Berwick-upon-Tweed either in the declaration of war or in the peace treaty of 1856.
128. Robb, *The Debatable Land*, p. 84.
129. Ridpath, *Border History*, p. 393.
130. Bain, *Calendar of the State Papers relating to Scotland*, p. 190; Mack, *The Border Line*, pp. 88–89.
131. Mack, *The Border Line*, pp. 15–40.
132. Mack, *The Border Line*, pp. 42–45.
133. Although today the line is marked with precision on Ordnance Survey maps, that is not determinative (Ordnance Survey Act 1841, section 12 (4 & 5 Vict. c. 30) and *Halsbury's Laws of England*, vol. 34, para. 1001).
134. *Sourcebook of Scottish History*, vol. 3, pp. 441–43.
135. *Sourcebook of Scottish History*, vol. 3, pp. 443–44.
136. *Sourcebook of Scottish History*, vol. 3, p. 440.
137. *Sourcebook of Scottish History*, vol. 3, pp. 453–55.
138. *Halsbury's Laws of England*, vol. 20, para. 62. It was the fear that the successor to the Scottish throne might not be the same as the successor to the English throne and, more complicated still, that one of them might be Catholic which was one of the underlying drivers of the union in 1707.
139. Cassavetti, *The Lion and the Lilies*, p. 73.
140. 1607/3/12.
141. 4 Jac. 1 c. 1.
142. The 1637 Book of Common Prayer was adopted by the Scottish Episcopal Church after the Glorious Revolution of 1688 and later formed the basis of the American Book of Common Prayer.
143. *Sourcebook of Scottish History*, vol. 3, pp. 95–104.
144. *Sourcebook of Scottish History*, vol. 3, pp. 122–25.
145. Gardiner, *History of the Great Civil War*, pp. 138, 186, 188.
146. *Sourcebook of Scottish History*, vol. 3, pp. 134–39.
147. The King was taken from Shoreham on the south coast of England to Fécamp in Normandy by a Brighthelmstone coal brig called *Surprise*. After his restoration, he purchased the brig and re-named her the *Royal Escape*. There is a fine painting of her in the Royal Collection by Willem van de Velde the Younger.
148. *Sourcebook of Scottish History*, vol. 3, p. 248; *English Historical Documents*, vol. 5(b), no. 393.
149. *Sourcebook of Scottish History*, vol. 3, pp. 248–50; *Halsbury's Laws of England*, vol. 20, para. 62.

150. *English Historical Documents*, vol. 5(b), no. 381.

151. *Journals of the House of Lords*, vol. 11, pp. 7–8, 1 May 1660.

152. *English Historical Documents*, vol. 6, no. 39.

153. 1 Gul. & Mar., sess. 2, c. 2.

154. *Sourcebook of Scottish History*, vol. 3, pp. 200–207.

155. *Sourcebook of Scottish History*, vol. 3, pp. 207–8.

156. Sunset on 17 July 1689 at Killiecrankie was at 20.21 GMT.

157. *Sourcebook of Scottish History*, vol. 3, p. 222.

158. *Sourcebook of Scottish History*, vol. 3, p. 221.

159. *Sourcebook of Scottish History*, vol. 3, p. 222.

160. *Sourcebook of Scottish History*, vol. 3, p. 223.

161. *The Laws of Scotland: Stair Memorial Encyclopaedia*, vol. 5, pp. 343–45.

162. At least since the time of the marriage of Mary Queen of Scots with the Dauphin of France in 1558, Scotland, unlike England, had enjoyed freedom of trade with France, the Scots having all the same privileges as the French and vice versa (Michel, *Les Ecossais en France*, vol. 1, pp. 520–21). Those privileges continued until 1663 (Keith, *Commercial Relations of England and Scotland*, pp. 145–46).

163. 'October 1651: An Act for increase of Shipping, and Encouragement of the Navigation of this Nation', in *Acts and Ordinances of the Interregnum, 1642–1660*, ed. C. H. Firth and R. S. Rait (London: Stationery Office 1911), pp. 559–62.

164. 12 Car. 2 c. 18. The Act specifically included Ireland, the Channel Islands and the town of Berwick-upon-Tweed.

165. 14 Car. 2 c. 11 (1662), 15 Car. 2 c. 7 (1663), 22 Car. 2 c. 13 (1670) and 7 & 8 Gul. 3 c. 22 (1696).

166. 1681/7/36, *Sourcebook of Scottish History*, vol. 3, pp. 329–30.

167. 1693/4/107.

168. 1695/5/104, *Sourcebook of Scottish History*, vol. 3, pp. 339–41.

169. In giving the royal assent to the Scottish Act, the Lord High Commissioner may well have exceeded the authority which had been granted

to him by the King (Keith, *Commercial Relations of England and Scotland*, p. 168).

170. *Sourcebook of Scottish History*, vol. 3, pp. 341–42.

171. *Sourcebook of Scottish History*, vol. 3, pp. 342–43.

172. *English Historical Documents*, vol. 6, no. 339.

173. *English Historical Documents*, vol. 6, no. 345.

174. 12 & 13 Gul. 3 c. 2.

175. 1703/5/193.

176. Ridpath, *Border History*, pp. 269–70.

177. 1704/7/68.

178. See the terms of the Act approved by the Scottish Parliament in Ridpath and Fletcher, *An Account of the Proceedings of the Parliament of Scotland ... on the 6th of May 1703*, pp. 241–49, at p. 246, and Scott, *Andrew Fletcher and the Treaty of Union*, ch. 11.

179. The English East India Company was the new one which had been founded under a charter dated 5 September 1698 by English investors disappointed by being prevented from investing in the Scottish Company.

180. The decision of the Court of Exchequer was by a majority of four to one.

181. There does not appear to be any record of the fate of the appeal. In 1710 the Scottish Company petitioned Parliament (by that stage the British Parliament) for compensation, presumably under the terms of the Treaty of Union (India Office Records/H/30).

182. 3 & 4 Ann. c. 7, *Sourcebook of Scottish History*, vol. 3, p. 477.

183. 1705/6/194.

184. *Sourcebook of Scottish History*, III, p. 480.

185. Union with England Act 1707, 1706/10/257.

186. Union with Scotland Act 1706, 6 Ann. c. 11.

187. It therefore preserved the udal law relating to land tenure in Orkney and Shetland which even today differs in some significant respects from that applicable in mainland Scotland. (See Linklater, *Udal Law*.)

188. *The Laws of Scotland: Stair Memorial Encyclopaedia*, V, pp. 343–45.

189. This was decided by the *Court of*

Session in *MacCormick v Lord Advocate*
(1953) SC 396.

190. The same convention has been adopted
in other nation states. Note that before
the union of England and Scotland
this problem did not arise. James VI of
Scotland was James I of England, not
James VI.

191. *English Historical Documents*, vol. 6,
no. 348.

192. *London Gazette*, no. 5247, 31 July–3
Aug. 1714.

193. 1 Geo. 1 Stat. 2 c. 54, sections 1 and 6.

194. 1 Geo. 1 Stat 2. c. 55.

195. Maclean, *Bonnie Prince Charlie*, p. 108.

196. Cassavetti, *The Lion and the Lilies*, p.
251.

197. 19 Geo. 2 c. 39, sections 1, 13 and 17,
and extended by 20 Geo. 2 c. 51.

198. 20 Geo. 2 c. 43, section 1.

199. The Representation of the People
(Scotland) Act 1832 (2 & 3 Gul. 4 c. 65).

200. The Representation of the People
(Scotland) Act 1868 (31 & 32 Vict. c. 48).

201. The Representation of the People Act
1884 (48 & 49 Vict. c. 3).

202. The Redistribution of Seats Act
1885 (48 & 49 Vict. c. 23).

203. 1998 c. 46.

204. *Early Sources of Scottish History*, vol.
2, p. 100.

205. Ward, *Isle of Mann*, pp. 8–9.

206. *Sodor and Man Diocese*; Moore,
History of the Isle of Man, bk 2, ch. V, p.
354.

207. *Calvin's Case* (1608) 7 Coke Report 1a,
at p. 21a.

208. *Sourcebook of Scottish History*, vol. 1,
p. 138.

209. Although there are indications to the
contrary, the Scots did not subsequently
win control of the island (see Thornton,
Scotland and the Isle of Man.

210. Rymer, *Foedera*, vol. 2, pt 2, p. 868.

211. *Rotuli Parliamentorum* 33 Ed. 1.

212. *Sourcebook of Scottish History*, I, p.
147; *English Historical Documents*, vol.
4, no. 37.

213. Train, *Historical and Statiscal
Account*, pp. 150–53.

214. Moore, *History of the Isle of Man*, bk 1,
ch. VII.

215. *English Historical Documents*, vol. 4,
no. 219.

216. 7 Hen IV.

217. As also recited in the preamble in to
The Isle of Man Purchase Act 1765 (5 Geo.
3 c. 26).

218. *English Historical Documents*, vol. 5(a),
no. 283.

219. Rotuli Littrerarua Patentum 7 Jac. 1.

220. 3 Oliver's Monumenta 99.

221. 7 Jac. 1 c. 4.

222. Moore, *History of the Isle of Man*, bk 2,
ch. II, Apx C.

223. Moore, *History of the Isle of Man*, bk
2, ch. III.

224. 12 Car. 2 c. 11.

225. Walpole, *The Land of Home Rule*, ch.
IX.

226. (1751) 2 Vesey Senior 337.

227. 5 Geo. 3 c. 26.

228. 5 Geo. 3 c. 39.

229. 45 Geo. 3 c. 123.

230. An Act to empower the Commissioners
of His Majesty's Treasury to purchase a
certain Annuity in respect of Duties and
Customs levied in the Isle of Man, and
any reserved sovereign rights in the said
Island belonging to John Duke of Atholl
(6 Geo. 4 c. 34).

231. The Isle of Man Customs, Harbours,
and Public Purposes Act 1866 (29 & 30
Vict. c. 23).

232. The Isle of Man Act 1958 (6 & 7 Eliz.
2 c. 11).

233. See for example the Isle of Man
Act 1979 which is an Act of the United
Kingdom Parliament giving effect to an
agreement between the two governments
relating, among other things, to the share
of customs revenues.

234. Cognate with the Vlachs in the
Balkans.

235. David Nash Lord, *Early British
Kingdoms* (www.earlybritishkingdoms.
com/bios/beuno.html).

236. Reflected in the core of Jenkins, *The
Law of Hywel Dda*.

237. *Acts of Welsh Rulers 1120–1283*, no.
233.

238. *English Historical Documents*, vol. 3,
no. 16.

239. *Acts of Welsh Rulers 1120–1283*, no.
276.

240. Article 56, *English Historical
Documents*, vol. 3, no. 20. Any dispute in
that respect was to be determined by the
law of Wales for land in Wales, the law of
the Marches for land in the Marches and

the law of England for land in England.

241. Article 58, *English Historical Documents*, vol. 3, no. 20.

242. *Acts of Welsh Rulers 1120–1283*, nos 240–42.

243. *Acts of Welsh Rulers 1120–1283*, nos 270, 271, 272–74.

244. The terms of the agreement are contained in two letters patent of Dafydd ap Llywelyn reproduced in *Acts of Welsh Rulers 1120–1283*, nos. 300 & 301.

245. *Acts of Welsh Rulers 1120–1283*, no. 284.

246. *Acts of Welsh Rulers 1120–1283*, no. 331.

247. *Acts of Welsh Rulers 1120–1283*, nos 342, 349

248. *Acts of Welsh Rulers 1120–1283*, no. 358.

249. *Acts of Welsh Rulers 1120–1283*, no. 363.

250. The terms of the Treaty were set out in several documents; *Acts of Welsh Rulers 1120–1283*, nos. 402–5.

251. *English Historical Documents*, vol. 3, no. 66(a).

252. *English Historical Documents*, vol. 3, no. 48.

253. *English Historical Documents*, vol. 3, no. 55.

254. Article II.

255. Articles III–XIV.

256. Article I.

257. 28 Edw. 3 c. 2.

258. 2 Hen. 4 c. 12, 16–20.

259. The 5th Earl of March was a first cousin twice removed of Richard II.

260. 4 Hen. 4 c. 26–34.

261. *Richard III*, Act V, scene IV.

262. 27 Hen. 8 c. 26.

263. 34 & 35 Hen. 8 c. 26.

264. Salop (Shropshire), Hereford and Gloucester (Articles XI, XII and XIII).

265. Flint, Anglesey, Caernarfon, Merioneth, Cardigan, Carmarthen, Pembroke and Glamorgan (34 & 35 Hen. 8 c. 26 Article II).

266. Monmouth, Brecknock (Brecon), Radnor, Montgomery and Denbigh (Article III).

267. Articles XXVIII and XIX. This number of representatives continued until the Great Reform Act of 1832, when it was increased, partially at least as a result of the bloody Merthyr Rising in 1831

(Davies, *A History of Wales*, pp. 365–67).

268. Article II.

269. By the nineteenth century this had led to the concentration of land in the hands of a very few landowners and was the cause of considerable discontent.

270. Articles XIV–XVIII.

271. Article XXVII.

272. Article XXX.

273. Article XXXI.

274. Article XX.

275. Article XX (among others) was repealed by section 35(1) of the Welsh Language Act 1993.

276. 34 & 35 Hen. 8 c. 26.

277. Article IV.

278. Article V.

279. Articles II, V, XCI and CI.

280. Local Government Act 1972, Schedule 4.

281. 5 Eliz. c. 28.

282. 1 Gul. & Mar. 1 c. 27 section 2.

283. 11 Geo. 4 & 1 Gul. 4 c. 70, section XIV.

284. 20 Geo. 2 c. 42, section 3.

285. 4 & 5 Geo. 5 c. 91.

286. The National Assembly for Wales was created by the Government of Wales Act 1998 (1998 c. 38).

287. *Annals of Clonmacnoise*, pp. 199–200. See also *Annals ... of the Four Masters*, M1152.10, and Giraldus, p. 184.

288. *Annals ... of the Four Masters* state that there were skirmishes between O'Connor and MacMurrough at this stage (M1167.12 and M1167.13).

289. Grandson of Godred Crovan.

290. The only direct record of the content of the decree is contained in Giraldus at pp. 233–34. However, it is corroborated by three letters sent by Pope Alexander III dated 20 September 1172 (*Irish Historical Documents*, pp. 19–22).

291. The first son, William, had died as a child.

292. *Irish Historical Documents*, pp. 22–24.

293. *Irish Historical Documents*, pp. 20–22.

294. *Irish Historical Documents*, pp. 38–46.

295. Giraldus, pp. 261–62.

296. 24 June 1177 old style.

297. *Irish Historical Documents*, pp. 28–31.

298. *Irish Historical Documents*, pp. 32–33.

299. *Irish Historical Documents*, pp. 38–46.

300. *Chronicle of Lanercost*, pp. 225–26.

301. *Annals of Clonmacnoise*, p. 282.

302. *Irish Historical Documents*, pp. 52–59.

303. Articles 2, 3, 4, 6, 13 and 15.
304. Statute Law Revision Act 1983, section 1, and Schedule pt 1.
305. *Irish Historical Documents*, pp. 64–67.
306. Declaration of Independence of the Irish Parliament 1460 (*Irish Historical Documents*, pp. 72–76).
307. 10 Hen. 7 c. 4.
308. 10 Hen. 7 c. 22.
309. It is ironic that Poynings' Law of 1495 was not repealed in the Republic of Ireland until 2007 (by the Statute Law Revision Act 2007). It is still effective in Northern Ireland today.
310. English statute 10 Hen. 7 c. 22.
311. Donaldson, *Some Comparative Aspects of Irish Law*, p. 43.
312. 10 Hen. 7 c. 8.
313. 10 Hen. 7 c. 9.
314. 3 Hen. 7 c. 1, which was only repealed in 2007.
315. The text of the Act was never printed but can be found in *Tracts Relating to Ireland*, vol. 2, 1843, p. 4, n.
316. 10 Hen. 7 c. 14.
317. 28 Hen. 8 c. 15.
318. The Ecclesiastical Appeals Act 1532 (24 Hen. 8 c. 12) declared the independence of the 'empire' of England from the See of Rome.
319. 26 Hen. 8 c. 1.
320. 28 Hen. 8 c. 5.
321. Although the break with Rome facilitated the adoption of Protestantism by both the Church of England and the Church of Ireland, it did not itself constitute any fundamental change other than that of the head of the Church on earth.
322. *English Historical Documents*, vol. 5, no. 112.
323. *English Historical Documents*, vol. 5, no. 130.
324. Had the Papal Bull of *Laudabiliter* existed as reported in Giraldus, pp. 261–62, then Ireland would have been held as a fief of the Holy See since the reign of Henry II.
325. 33 Hen. 8 c. 1. It is remarkable that neither the Crown of Ireland Act 1542 nor the Act of Supremacy 1537 was repealed in the Republic until the enactment of the Statute Law Revision (Pre-Union Irish Statutes) Act 1962.
326. By virtue of Queen Mary's Marriage

Act 1554 (1 Mar. Sess. 3 c. 2).
327. 2 . 1 c. 1.
328. 2 Eliz. 1 c. 2.
329. 3 & 4 Phil. & Mar. c. 2.
330. *English Historical Documents*, vol. 5(a), no. 372.
331. As Governor of Fotheringhay Castle, Sir William Fitzwilliam had overseen the execution of Mary Queen of Scots in 1587.
332. Son of Walter Devereux, 1st Earl of Essex.
333. Hayes-McCoy, *Irish Battles*, p. 132.
334. Both Spain and the Irish under O'Neill and O'Donnell had adopted the Gregorian calendar by this stage; 23 December 1601 in the Julian calendar.
335. The terms of the tenancies were set out in the Conditions to be observed by the British undertakers of the escheated lands in Ulster 1610 (*Irish Historical Documents*, pp. 128–31).
336. 16 Car. I c. 33.
337. The Treaty of Oxford was signed on 20 June 1646.
338. *A Declaration of the Lord Lieutenant of Ireland For the undeceiving of a deluded and seduced People etc.* (reprinted London 21 March 1650).
339. The Treaty of Breda 1650 is not the same as the Declaration of Breda 1660, although the subject matter was similar.
340. Known as the Declaration of Dunfermline.
341. Scobell, *A collection of acts*, vol. 2, pp. 197–200.
342. Article I.
343. Article VI.
344. Article VII.
345. Article IX.
346. Article XV.
347. Article XXXVII.
348. 13 Car. 2 c. 1.
349. 14 & 15 Car. 2 c. 2.
350. 18 Car. 2 c. 2.
351. 32 Car. 2 c. 2.
352. 10 & 11 Gul. 3 c. 10.
353. *English Historical Documents*, vol. 6, nos 287–89.
354. *English Historical Documents*, vol. 6, no. 293.
355. *English Historical Documents*, vol. 6, no. 294.
356. *English Historical Documents*, vol. 6, no. 295.
357. An Act for the Abrogating the Oath

of Supremacy in Ireland and Appointing other Oaths, 3 Gul. & Mar. c. 2, *English Historical Documents*, VI, no. 296, *Irish Historical Documents*, pp. 180–83).

358. An Act to Restrain Foreign Education, 7 Gul. c. 4.

359. An Act of the better securing the Government, by dissenting Papists, 7 Gul. 3 c. 5.

360. 2 Ann. c. 6.

361. In 1728 a loophole was plugged by 1 Geo. 2 c. 9 which disqualified Catholics from voting unless they had taken the oath of abjuration at least six months before voting, so preventing them from acquiring sham freeholds.

362. By virtue of the Catholic Relief Act 1793, 33 Geo. 3 c. 21.

363. 6 Geo. 1 c. 5, *English Historical Documents*,7, no. 197, *Irish Historical Documents*, p. 186.

364. 22 Geo. 3 c. 53, *English Historical Documents*, vol. 7, no. 206, *Irish Historical Documents*, pp. 186–87.

365. 21 & 22 Geo. 3 c. 47, *English Historical Documents*, vol. 7, no. 207.

366. 21 & 22 Geo. 3 c. 48, *English Historical Documents*, vol. 7, no. 208.

367. 21 & 22 Geo. 3 c. 209, *English Historical Documents*, vol. 7, no. 209.

368. 21 & 22 Geo. 3 c. 210, *English Historical Documents*, vol. 7, no. 210.

369. 23 Geo. 3 c. 28, *English Historical Documents*, vol. 7, no. 212, *Irish Historical Documents*, pp. 187–88.

370. An Act for the Relief of His Majesty's Popish, or Roman Catholick Subjects, 33 Geo. 3 c. 21, *English Historical Documents*, XI, no. 456, *Irish Historical Documents*, pp. 198–202).

371. 36 Geo. 3 c. 20, *Irish Historical Documents*, pp. 204–8.

372. Hague, *William Pitt the Younger*, p. 383.

373. 40 Geo. 3 c. 38 (*Irish Historical Documents*, pp. 208–13).

374. 39 & 40 Geo. 3 c. 67, *English Historical Documents*, vol. 11, no. 142.

375. 10 Geo. 4 c. 7, *English Historical Documents*, vol. 11, no. 459, *Irish Historical Documents*, pp. 247–50.

376. 10 Geo. 4 c. 8, *English Historical Documents*, vol. 11, no. 284.

377. By the Representation of the People Act 1884, 48 & 49 Vict. c. 3, *English*

Historical Documents, vol. 12(2), no. 30.

378. *O'Connell v R* (1844) 11 Cl. & Fin. 155.

379. 32 & 33 Vict. c. 42, *English Historical Documents*, vol. 12(2), no. 81. The Irish Church Act was followed in 1873 by the University of Dublin Tests Act 1873 which permitted Roman Catholics and Nonconformists to study and hold academic appointments (other than in the Divinity School) at Trinity College Dublin for the first time, putting a further nail in the coffin of the Protestant ascendancy.

380. The Landlord and Tenant (Ireland) Act 1870, 33 & 34 Vict. c. 46, *English Historical Documents*, vol. 12(2), no. 82.

381. A similar belief was held by the small tenants of Highland estates in Scotland during the Clearances of the nineteenth century (Devine, *The Scottish Clearances*, p. 300).

382. The Land Law (Ireland) Act 1881, 44 & 45 Vict. c. 49, *English Historical Documents*, vol. 12(2), no. 86.

383. The Protection of Persons and Property (Ireland) Act 1881 (44 & 45 Vict. c. 4).

384. The arrears of rent were subsequently paid under the Arrears of Rent (Ireland) Act) 1882 (45 & 46 Vict. c. 47).

385. Egremont, *The Cousins*, pp. 104–5.

386. The Criminal Law and Procedure (Ireland) Act 1887 (50 & 51 Vict. c. 20), which was not repealed in the Republic until 1983.

387. Notable among them were the Purchase of Land (Ireland) Act 1885 (the Ashbourne Act, passed by the Conservative Government in the hope of swaying the Irish vote in the forthcoming general election), the Irish Land Act 1903 (Wyndham's Act) and the Evicted Tenants Act 1907 (Birrell's Act).

388. 1 & 2 Geo. 5 c. 13, *English Historical Documents*, XII(2), no. 40.

389. The second recital to the Act provides 'whereas it is intended to substitute for the House of Lords as it at present exists a Second Chamber constituted on a popular instead of hereditary basis, but such substitution cannot be immediately brought into operation'.

390. 4 & 5 Geo. 5 c. 90.

391. 4 & 5 Geo. 5 c. 88.

392. *Irish Historical Documents*, p. 317.

393. 25 Edw. 3 c. 2.

394. Transcripts of the trial and judgments are to be found in Knott, *The Trial of Sir Roger Casement*.

395. Some of the Sinn Féin members were in prison and would have been unable to take their seats even had they wished to.

396. *Irish Historical Documents*, pp. 318–19.

397. 10 & 11 Geo. 5 c. 67 (*Irish Historical Documents*, pp. 297–303).

398. Antrim, Armagh, Down, Fermanagh, Londonderry and Tyrone together with the parliamentary boroughs of Belfast and Londonderry (section 1(2)). The other three were Cavan, Donegal and Monaghan.

399. Section 75.

400. Section 19.

401. Section 12.

402. Griffith (chairman), Collins (second in command), Brugha, Gavan Duffy and Barton.

403. *Irish Historical Documents*, p. 329.

404. No. 214 DE 2/304/1 (*Irish Historical Documents*, pp. 322–26).

405. Article 12.

406. Articles 1–2.

407. Article 4.

408. Article 12.

409. The Irish Free State (Agreement) Act 1922 (12 & 13 Geo. 5 c. 4).

410. The Constitution of the Irish Free State (Saorstát Eireann) Act 1922 in Ireland and the Irish Free State Constitution Act 1922 (Session 2) (13 Geo. 5 sess 2 c. 1) in the United Kingdom.

411. The pro-treaty faction were known as National, or Free State, troops and the republican faction as the Irregulars.

412. Pursuant to Article 48 of the 1922 Constitution.

413. Executive Authority (External Relations) Act 1936 (No. 58 of 1936).

414. The Republic of Ireland Act 1948 (No 22 of 1948) which came into effect on 18 April 1949.

415. *The Times*, 12 July 1938.

416. A fourth naval establishment at Belfast Lough had been included but, being in what became Northern Ireland, it remained within the United Kingdom.

417. British-Irish tripartite agreement on Trade, Finance and Defence (P no. 3104), no. 175, NAI DT S10389A.

418. Section 5 of the Government of Ireland Act 1920.

419. By the Electoral Law Act (Northern Ireland) 1968.

Bibliography

Acta Regia; being the Account which Mr. Rapin de Thoyras Published of the History of England ... grounded upon those Records which ... are collected in that Inestimable Fund of History Mr. Rymer's Foedera (London: James, John and Paul Knapton *et al.* 1733)

The Acts of Welsh Rulers 1120–1283, ed. Huw Price (Cardiff: University of Wales Press 2005)

Anderson, Alan Orr, *Early Sources of Scottish History 500–1286* (Edinburgh: Oliver and Boyd 1922)

---, *Scottish Annals from English Chroniclers AD 500–1286* (London: David Nutt 1908)

Andrew, W. J., *Numismatic Sidelights on the Battle of Brunanburh, AD 937* (London: Harrison and Sons 1933)

Anglo-Saxon Chronicles, transl. and ed. Michael Swanton (London: Phoenix Press 1996)

The Annals of Clonmacnoise; being annals of Ireland, from the earliest period to AD 1408. Transcribed into English AD 1627, transl. C. Mageoghagan, ed. D. Murphy (Dublin: Royal Society of Antiquaries of Ireland 1896)

Annals of the Kingdom of Ireland by the Four Masters (Cork: CELT 2008)

Annals of Ulster, Otherwise, Annala Senait, Annals of Senat: A Chronicle of Irish Affairs from AD 431–AD 1131; AD1155–AD1541, transl. and ed. B. MacCarthy (Dublin: H.M.S.O. 1895)

Arnot, Hugo, *A Collection and Abridgement of Celebrated Criminal Trials in Scotland from 1530 to 1784 with Historical and Critical Remarks* (Edinburgh: William Smellie 1785)

Bain, Joseph, ed., *Calendar of the State Papers relating to Scotland and Mary Queen of Scots 1547–1603*, vol. 1 (Edinburgh: H.M.S.O. 1898)

Barbour, John, *The Brus, from a collation of the Cambridge and Edinburgh manuscripts*, ed. C. Innes, bk 18 (Aberdeen: Spalding Club 1856)

The Battle of Brunanburh: A Casebook, ed. Michael Livingston (Exeter: University of Exeter Press 2011)

www.battlefieldsofbritain.co.uk/battle_glenshiel_1719.html

Beckett, J. C., *The Making of Modern Ireland 1603–1923* (New York: Alfred A. Knopf 1966)

Bond, John J., *Handy-Book of Rules and Tables for verifying Dates with the Christian Era* (London: George Bell & Sons 1875)

Boyle, David, *Blondel's Song: the Capture, Imprisonment and Ransom of Richard the Lionheart* (London: Viking 2005)

Bragg, Melvyn, *The Adventure of English: the Biography of a Language* (London: Hodder and Stoughton 2003)

Brierly, J. L., *The Law of Nations: An Introduction to the Law of Peace*, 6th edn, ed. Sir Humphrey Waldock (Oxford: Clarendon Press 1963)

Brown, Allen R., *Allen Brown's English Castles*, 3rd edn (London: Batsford 1976)

Brownlie's Principles of Public International Law, 9th edn, ed. James Crawford (Oxford: Oxford University Press 2019)

Buchan, James, *John Law: A Scottish*

Adventurer of the Eighteenth Century (London: MacLehose Press 2018)

Buck, A. R., 'The politics of land law in Tudor England, 1529–1540', *Journal of Legal History*, vol. 11, 2 (1990), pp. 200–217, DOI: 10.1080/01440369008531002

Bullock, H. A., *A History of the Isle of Man, with a comparative view of the past and present state of society and manners; containing also biographical anecdotes of eminent persons connected with that island* (London: Longman, Hurst, Rees, Orme, and Brown 1816)

Burne, Alfred H., *The Battlefields of England* (London: Greenhill Books 1996)

–––, *More Battlefields of England* (London: Methuen 1952)

Cannon, Henry Lewin, 'The Battle of Sandwich and Eustace the Monk', *English Historical Review*, vol. 27, no. 108 (Oct. 1912), pp. 649–70

Carey, Robert, *The Memoirs of Robert Carey, Earl of Monmouth, written by himself* (Edinburgh: Constable 1808)

Carr, A. D., *Medieval Wales* (New York: St Martin's Press 1995)

Cassavetti, Eileen, *The Lion and the Lilies: The Stuarts and France* (London: MacDonald and Jane's 1977)

Castor, Helen, *Joan of Arc: A History* (London: Faber and Faber 2014)

–––, *She Wolves: The Women Who Ruled England Before Elizabeth* (London: Faber and Faber 2010)

The Chronicle of John of Worcester, ed. R. R. Darlington and P. McGurk, transl. Jennifer Bray and P. McGurk (Oxford: Clarendon Press 1995), vol. 2

The Chronicle of Lanercost 1272–1346, transl. Sir Herbert Maxwell (Glasgow: James MacLehose and Sons 1913)

Clerigh, Arthur ua, *The History of Ireland to the coming of Henry II*, vol. 1 (London: T. Fisher-Unwin 1910)

Conlan, Fr Patrick, 'The Conlan Coin Collection', *North Munster Antiquarian Journal*, vol. 45 (2005), pp. 19–31

Cooper, John, *The Queen's Agent: Francis Walsingham at the Court of Elizabeth I* (London: Faber and Faber 2011)

The Coronation Oath (House of Commons Library Standard Note SN/PC/00435 2008)

Courtney, Sir Ilbert, *The Government of India: A Brief Historical Survey of Parliamentary Legislation Relating to India* (Oxford: Clarendon Press 1922)

Crouch, David, *The Normans: The History of a Dynasty* (London: Hambledon and London 2002)

Cruickshank, Charles Greig, *The German Occupation of the Channel Islands* (London/New York: Oxford University Press 1975)

Cullen, Seamus, *The Pale* (Reformation to Referendum: Writing a New History of Parliament)

Darby, H. C., 'The Marches of Wales in 1086', *Transactions of the Society of British Geographers*, vol. 11, no. 3 (1986), pp. 259–78

Davies, John, *A History of Wales* (London: Allen Lane 1993)

Davies, Norman, *The Isles* (Oxford: Macmillan 1999)

Davies, R. R., *The First English Empire: Power and Identities in the British Isles 1093–1343* (Oxford: Oxford University Press 2000)

Davis, H. W. C., 'A Contemporary Account of the Battle of Tinchebrai', *English Historical Review*, vol. 24, no. 96 (Oct. 1909), pp. 728–32

A Declaration of the Lord Lieutenant of Ireland For the undeceiving of a deluded and seduced People, etc. (London, 21 March 1650)

Derry, T. K., *A History of Scandinavia: Norway, Sweden, Denmark, Finland and Iceland* (Minneapolis: Minneapolis University Press 1979)

Devine, T. M., *The Scottish Clearances: A History of the Dispossessed* (London: Penguin Random House 2018)

The Dictionary of Welsh Biography down to 1940 (London: Honourable Society of Cymmrodorion 1959)

Donaldson, A. G., *Some Comparative Aspects of Irish Law* (Durham, N.C.: Duke University Press/London: Cambridge University Press 1957)

Douglas, D. C., 'Rollo of Normandy', *English Historical Review*, vol. 57, no. 228 (Oct. 1942), pp. 417–36

Duffy, Seán, and Harold Mytum, eds, *A New History of the Isle of Man*, vol. 3, *The Medieval Period 1000–1406* (Liverpool: Liverpool University Press 2015)

Dumville, David N., *Wessex and England from Alfred to Edgar: Six Essays on Political,*

Cultural, and Ecclesiastical Revival
(Rochester, N.Y.: Boydell Press 1992)

Duncan, A. M. M., '*Honi soit qui mal y pense*:
David II and Edward III, 1346–1352',
Scottish Historical Review, vol. 67, no. 184
(Oct. 1988), pt 2, pp. 113–41

Early British Kingdoms (Nash Ford
Publishing 1996–2017) [www.
earlybritishkingdoms.com/bios/beuno.
html]

Edmonds, Fiona, 'The Emergence and
Transformation of Medieval Cumbria',
Scottish Historical Review, vol. 93, no. 237
(Oct. 2014), pp. 195–216

Egil's Saga Skallagrímssonar, transl. W. C.
Green (London: E. Stock 1893)

Egremont, Max, *The Cousins: The
Friendship, Opinions and Activities
of Wilfrid Scawen Blunt and George
Wyndham* (London: Collins 1977)

Ellis, M. F. H., 'The Channel Islands and the
Great Rebellion', *Bulletin, Société Jersiaise*,
vol. 13 (1937), p. 193

Encyclopaedia Britannica, 14th edn (London:
Encyclopaedia Britannica 1929–37)

English Historical Documents, ed. D. C.
Douglas (London: Eyre & Spottiswoode
1953–77)

Falkiner, C. Litton, *Illustrations of Irish
History and Topography, mainly of the
seventeenth century* (London: Longmans,
Green 1904)

Farrant, R. D., *Mann: Its Land Tenure,
Constitution, Lords Rents and Deemsters*
(London: Oxford University Press 1937)

Ferriter, Diarmaid, *The Border: The Legacy of
a Century of Anglo-Irish Politics* (London:
Profile Books 2019)

*Foedera, conventiones, litterae et
cujuscunque generis acta publica …
cura et studio Thomae Rymer et Roberti
Sanderson* (London: Johanne Caley et
Fred. Holbrooke 1821)

Fraser, Antonia, *The King and the Catholics:
The Fight for Rights 1829* (London:
Weidenfeld & Nicolson 2015)

---, *Mary Queen of Scots* (London:
Weidenfeld & Nicolson 1994)

Fraser, George MacDonald, *The Steel
Bonnets: The Story of the Anglo-Scottish
Border Reivers* (London: Pan Books 1974)

Freeman, Edward A., *The History of the
Norman Conquest of England: its Causes
and its Results* (Oxford: Clarendon Press
1867–79)

Gardiner, S. R., *History of the Great Civil War*
(London: Longmans, Green 1896)

Gibbon, Alex, *The Mystery of Jack of Kent and
the Fate of Owain Glyndŵr* (Stroud: Sutton
Publishing 2004)

Gillingham, John, *Richard I* (New Haven/
London: Yale University Press 1999)

[Giraldus Cambrensis] *The Historical Works
of Giraldus Cambrensis: containing the
topography of Ireland*, transl. Thomas
Wright and Thomas Forester (London:
William Clowes and Sons 1923)

Glover, Julian, *Man of Iron: Thomas Telford
and the Building of Britain* (London:
Bloomsbury 2017)

Gordon, William M., *Scottish Land Law*
(Edinburgh: W. Green and Son 1999)

Graham, Eric J., *Seawolves: Pirates and the
Scots* (Edinburgh: Berlinn 2007)

Grant, R. G., *1848: Year of Revolution* (Hove:
Wayland 1995)

[Gray, Sir Thomas] *The 'Scalacronica' of Sir
Thomas Gray*, transl. Sir Herbert Maxwell
(Glasgow: J. MacLehose & Sons 1907)

Griffiths, John, 'The Revolt of Madog ap
Llywelyn, 1294–5', *Transactions of the
Caernarfonshire Historical Society*, vol.
16 (1955)

Hague, William, *William Pitt the Younger*
(London: HarperCollins 2004)

Halsbury's Laws of England, 5th edn, vols. 20
and 34 (LNUK)

Haskins, Charles H., 'Normandy under
Geoffrey Plantagenet', *English Historical
Review*, vol. 27, no. 107 (July 1912), pp.
417–44

Hayes-McCoy, G. A., *Irish Battles* (Harlow:
Longmans 1969)

Hewitt, Rachel, *Map of a Nation: A
Biography of the Ordnance Survey*
(London: Granta Publications 2010)

Higham, Nicholas J., and Martin J. Ryan, *The
Anglo-Saxon World* (New Haven/London:
Yale University Press 2013)

Hobhouse, Henry, *Seeds of Change: Six
Plants that Transformed Mankind*
(London: Pan Books 2002)

Holland, Tom, *Athelstan: The Making of
Modern England* (London: Penguin
Random House 2016)

Hollister, C. Warren, *Henry I* (New Haven/
London: Yale University Press 2001)

[History of Parliament] https://
historyofparliamentblog.wordpress.
com/2012/02/15/the-house-of-lords-and-

the-origins-of-financial-privilege-1671-and-1678/

Hudson, Benjamin T., 'Cnut and the Scottish Kings', *English Historical Review*, vol. 107, no. 423 (1 April 1992), pp. 350–60

Hull, Eleanor, *A History of Ireland and her People to the Close of the Tudor period* (London: Harrap 1926)

Hull, Lise, *The Welsh Marches* (https://toursofwales.co.uk/wandering-bard/the-welsh-marches-by-lise-hull-1995)

Hunter, Joseph, 'King Edward's Spoliations in Scotland in A.D. 1296 – the Coronation Stone – original and unpublished evidence', *Archaeological Journal*, vol. 13, 1 (1 Jan. 1856), pp. 245–55

Irish Historical Documents 1172–1922, ed. Edmund Curtis and R. B. McDowell (London: Methuen 1943)

Jamieson, A. G., ed. *A People of the Sea: The Maritime History of the Channel Islands*, (London: Methuen 1986)

Jenkins, Dafydd, *The Law of Hywel Dda: Law texts from Medieval Wales translated and edited* (Landysul: Gomer Press 1986)

Jenkins, Simon, *A Short History of Europe: From Pericles to Putin* (London: Penguin Random House 2018)

———, *Wales: Churches, Houses and Castles* (London: Penguin Group 2008)

Journal of the House of Lords, vol. 11 (1 May 1660)

Joyce, P. W., *A Concise History of Ireland* (New York, London, Bombay: Longmans, Green 1905)

Kaeuper, Richard W., *Bankers to the Crown: The Riccardi of Lucca and Edward I* (Princeton, N.J.: Princeton University Press 1973)

Kearney, Hugh, *The British Isles: A History of Four Nations* (Cambridge: Cambridge University Press 1989)

Keene, H. G., 'The Channel Islands', *English Historical Review*, vol. 2, no. 5 (Jan. 1887), pp. 21–39

Keith, Theodora, *Commercial Relations of England and Scotland, 1603–1707* (Cambridge: Cambridge University Press 1910)

Kelly, J. M., *Fundamental Rights in the Irish Law and Constitution*, 2nd edn (Dublin: Allen Figgis 1967)

———, *The Irish Constitution*, 4th edn (Dublin: Butterworths 2003)

Kennedy, Ludovic, *In Bed with an Elephant* (London: Bantam Press 1995)

Kermode, David G., *Offshore Island Politics: The Constitutional and Political Development of the Isle of Man in the Twentieth Century* (Liverpool: Liverpool University Press 2001)

Kinross, John, *Battlefields of England and Scotland* (Stroud: Amberley 2016)

Knox, Oliver, *Rebels and Informers: Stirrings of Irish Independence* (London: John Murray 1997)

Kostick, Conor. '"Laudabiliter": A New Interpretation by Professor Anne Duggan', *History Ireland*, vol. 13, no. 3 (2005), pp. 07–08 (JSTOR www.jstor.org/stable/27725258)

Knott, George H., ed., *The Trial of Sir Roger Casement* (Philadelphia: Cromarty Law Book Co. 1917)

Latimer, Paul, 'Henry II's Campaign against the Welsh in 1165', *Welsh History Review*, vol. 14, 4 (1989), pp. 523–52

Latimer, William T., 'The Battle of the Yellow Ford', *Journal of the Royal Society of Antiquaries of Ireland*, 5th ser., vol. 10, no. 1 (1900), pp. 34–39

Lemprière, Raoul, *History of the Channel Islands* (London: Robert Hale 1974)

Lenihan, Pádraig, *Confederate Catholics at War 1641–49* (Cork: Cork University Press 2001)

Linklater, Eileen, *Udal Law – Past, Present and Future?* (Glasgow: University of Strathclyde 2002)

Longford, Lord, *Peace by Ordeal: An Account, from First-hand Sources, of the Negotiation and Signature of the Anglo-Irish Treaty 1921* (London: Sidgwick & Jackson 1972)

Macdougall, Norman, *James III, a Political Study* (Edinburgh: J. Donald 1982)

MacGregor, M. D., 'The Statutes of Iona: text and context', *Innes Review*, vol. 52, no. 2 (2006), pp. 111–81

Mack, James Logan, *The Border Line from the Solway Firth to the North Sea, along the Marches of Scotland and England*, 2nd edn (Edinburgh: Oliver and Boyd 1926)

Maclean, Fitzroy, *Bonnie Prince Charlie* (London: Weidenfeld & Nicolson 1988)

———, *Scotland, A Concise History* (London: Thames & Hudson 1993)

Maginn, Christopher, 'Contesting the Sovereignty of Early Modern Ireland', *History Ireland*, vol. 15, no. 6 (Nov./Dec. 2007), pp. 20–25

Manx Society for the Publication of National Documents (Douglas: Manx Society 1858–93)

Mathew, Frank, *Ireland painted by Francis S. Walker R.H.A.* (London: Adam & Charles Black 1905)

McLynn, Frank, *France and the Jacobite Rising of 1745* (Edinburgh: Edinburgh University Press 1981)

Michel, Francisque, *Les Ecossais en France, les Français en Ecosse* (London: Trübner 1862)

The Minquiers and Ecrehos Case (France/United Kingdom), International Court of Justice, Judgment of 17 November 1953, report (Leyden: A. W. Sijthoffs)

Monasticon Hibernicum, or, the Monastical History of Ireland (London: William Mears 1722)

Moody, T. W., and F. X. Martin, eds, *The Course of Irish History* (Cork: Mercier Press 1967)

–––, F. X. Martin and F. J. Byrne, eds, *A New History of Ireland* (Oxford: Oxford University Press 1984–86)

Moore, A. W., *A History of the Isle of Man* (London: T. F. Unwin 1900)

Moore, David W., *The Other British Isles* (Jefferson, N.C.: McFarland 2005)

Morgan, Hiram, '"The Pope's New Invention": the introduction of the Gregorian Calendar in Ireland 1583–1782', paper given at 'Ireland, Rome and the Holy See: History, Culture and Contact', UCC History Department symposium at the Pontifical Irish College, Rome, 1 April 2006 (ucc-ie.academia.edu/HiramMorgan)

Morgan, O. Morein, *The Battles of Wales: the Unconquered Country of the Empire* (Liverpool: Salesbury Hughes 1920)

Morris, Marc, *King John: Treachery, Tyranny and the Road to Magna Carta* (London: Penguin Random House 2015)

Nicolson, William, *Leges Marchiarum or Border Laws, etc.* (London: Hamilton and Balfour 1747)

Norwich, John Julius, *Sicily: A Short History from the Greeks to Cosa Nostra* (London: John Murray 2015)

Ó Mearáin, Lorcan, 'The Battle of Clontibret', *Clogher Record*, vol. 1, no. 4 (1956), pp. 1–28

O'Neill, James, 'The Cockpit of Ulster: War along the River Blackwater 1593–1603', *Ulster Journal of Archaeology*, 3rd ser., vol. 72 (2013/14), pp. 184–99

Oliver, J. R., *Monumenta de Insula Manniae or a collection of National Documents relating to the Isle of Man* (Douglas: Manx Society 1860)

[Orderic Vitalis] *The Ecclesiastical History of Orderic Vitalis*, transl. and ed. Marjorie Chibnall (Oxford: Clarendon Press 1969–80)

Orkneyinga Saga: The History of the Earls of Orkney, transl. Hermann Pálsson and Paul Edwards (London: Penguin Books 1981)

Orpen, Goddard H., 'Site of the Battle of Glen-Mama', *Journal of the Royal Society of Antiquaries of Ireland*, 5th ser., vol. 36, no. 1 (31 March 1906), pp. 78–80

Oxford Dictionary of National Biography, ed. H. C. G. Matthew, Brian Harrison, Lawrence Goldman (Oxford: Oxford University Press 1903 et seq.)

Painter, Sidney, *William Marshall: Knight-Errant, Baron, and Regent of England* (Toronto: University of Toronto Press 1982)

Pégot-Ogier, Eugène, *Histoire des Iles de la Manche: Jersey, Guernsey, Aurigny, Serck* (Paris: E. Plon 1881)

Prebble, John, *The Darien Disaster* (London: Pimlico 2002)

Rankin, K. J., *The Creation and Consolidation of the Irish Border, Mapping Frontiers, Plotting Pathways: routes to North South cooperation in a divided island*, Working Paper no. 2 (2005)

Rapport, Mike, *1848 Year of Revolution* (London: Abacus 2014)

Reid, R. R., 'The Office of Warden of the Marches: Its Origin and Early History', *English Historical Review*, vol. 32, no. 128 (Oct. 1917), pp. 479–96

Ridpath, George, *The Border History of England and Scotland, deduced from the earliest Times to the Union of the Two Crowns* (Edinburgh: Mercat Press 1977)

–––, and Andrew Fletcher, *An Account of the Proceedings of the Parliament of Scotland, which met at Edinburgh on the 6th of May 1703 and was adjourned on the 15th of September following* (1704)

Robb, Graham, *The Debatable Land: The Lost World Between Scotland and England* (London: Picador 2018)

[Roger of Howden] *Chronica, Magistri Rogeri de Houedene*, ed. William Stubbs (London: Longmans 1870)

Roger of Wendover's Flowers of History, Comprising the History of England from the Descent of the Saxons to 1235, transl. J. A. Giles (London: Henry G. Bohn 1849)

Rose, Kenneth, King George V (London: Weidenfeld & Nicolson 1983)

Rowsell, Mary C., The Life-Story of Charlotte de la Trémoille Countess of Derby (London: Kegan Paul, Trench, Trübner 1905)

Scobell, Henry, A Collection of Acts and Ordinances of General Use, made in the Parliament, begun and held at Westminster, the third day of November, anno 1640: and since, unto the adjournment of the Parliament begun and holden the 17th of September, anno 1656 (London: Henry Hills and John Field 1658)

Scott, P. H., Andrew Fletcher and the Treaty of Union (Edinburgh: John Donald 1992)

Seward, Desmond, Richard III, England's Black Legend (London: Country Life 1983)

Simms, J. G., 'Irish Catholics and the Parliamentary Franchise, 1692–1728', Irish Historical Studies, vol. 12, no. 45 (March 1960), pp. 28–37

Simpson, Grant G., 'Why Was John Balliol Called "Toom Tabard"?', Scottish Historical Review, vol. 47, no. 144 (Oct. 1968), pt 2

Smedley, Edward, The History of France, from the Partition of the Empire of Charlemagne to the Peace of Cambray (London: Baldwin and Cradock 1836)

Smith, J. Beverley, 'The Treaty of Lambeth, 1217', English Historical Review, vol. 94, no. 372 (July 1979), pp. 562–79

Sodor and Man Diocese: History and Description (Clergy of the Church of England Database)

A Sourcebook of Scottish History, ed. W. C. Dickinson, Gordon Donaldson and Isabel A. Milne (Edinburgh: Nelson 1952–54)

Squatriti, Paolo, 'Offa's Dyke between Nature and Culture', Environmental History, vol. 9, no. 1 (Jan. 2004), pp. 37–56

Stair Memorial Encyclopaedia: The Laws of Scotland (Edinburgh: Lexis/Nexis 1987)

Stenton, F. M., Anglo-Saxon England, 3rd edn (Oxford: Oxford University Press 1977)

Stewart, Rory, The Marches: Border Walks with my Father (London: Jonathan Cape 2016)

Stubbs, William, The Constitutional History of England, in its Origin and Development, 6th edn, vol. 1 (Oxford: Clarendon Press 1897)

Taswell-Langmead, Thomas Pitt, English Constitutional History from the Teutonic Conquest to the Present Time, 11th edn (London: Sweet & Maxwell 1960)

Temple, Sir Richard Carnac, New Light on the Mysterious Tragedy of the 'Worcester' 1704–1705 (London: Ernest Benn 1930)

Thomas, Jeffrey L., Welsh Castles of Edward I (http://www.castlewales.com/edwrdcas. html)

Thornton, Tim, 'Scotland and the Isle of Man, c. 1400–1625: Noble Power and Royal Presumption in the Northern Irish Sea Province', Scottish Historical Review, vol. 77, no. 203, pt 1 (Apr. 1998), pp. 1–30

---, The Channel Islands, 1370–1640: between England and Normandy (Woodbridge: Boydell Press 2012)

Tracts relating to Ireland (Dublin: Irish Archaeological Society 1841–43)

Train, Joseph, An Historical and Statistical Account of the Isle of Man from the earliest Times to the Present Date; with a View of its Ancient Laws, Peculiar Customs, and Popular Superstitions (Douglas: Mary A. Quiggin 1845)

Ua Clerigh, Arthur, The History of Ireland to the Coming of Henry II, vol. 1 (London: T. Fisher-Unwin 1910)

Uttley, John, The Story of the Channel Islands (London: Faber 1966)

Walker, David M., A Legal History of Scotland (Edinburgh: Green 1988)

Walpole, Sir Spencer, The Land of Home Rule: an Essay on the History and Constitution of the Isle of Man (London/New York: Longmans, Green 1893)

Ward, William Perceval, Isle of Mann and Diocese of Sodor and Mann, Antient and Authentic Records and Documents Relating to the Civil and Ecclesiastical History and Constitution of the Island (London: J. G. and F. Rivington 1837)

William of Malmesbury's Chronicle of the Kings of England from the Earliest Period to the Reign of King Stephen, transl. J. A. Giles (London: Henry G. Bohn 1847)

Wood, Alan and Mary, Islands in Danger: the Story of the German Occupation of the Channel Islands (London: Evans Brothers 1955)

Woolf, Alex, From Pictland to Alba: 789–1070 (Edinburgh: Edinburgh University Press 2007)

Acknowledgements & Picture Credits

I could not have begun to write this book without the hard work and erudition of the authors whose works are listed in the Bibliography. Chief among them are those who devoted their time to transcribing and translating the manuscripts of early chronicles and state papers. To all of them I am greatly indebted. The mistakes, which I fear may be numerous, are mine alone.

My heartfelt thanks go to Emily Lane for her exacting editing, for coping with my many foibles and importantly for her encouragement; to David Atkinson for drawing the beautiful maps in the light of my often woefully inadequate instructions; to Katie Greenwood for conjuring up the pictures; to Jonathan Christie for his charming design of this book; and to everyone else at Unicorn under the wise and steady hand of Ian Strathcarron. My thanks too to the unfailingly helpful staff of the London Library; to Eleo Carson for her time and advice at the early stages; to Alison Cathie and Ariane Bankes for helping me to navigate what were for me the uncharted waters of publishing; to my son Ivar for his geographical research; to my daughter, Rose, and my son-in-law, John Gladstone, for reading and commenting on the draft of the text; and to Zara, my wife, for her remarkable navigational skills when accompanying me to some of the more obscure corners of the British Isles and the Republic of Ireland in search of battlefields, castles and other relicts of history.

Thank you to the following sources for providing the images featured in this book:

Alamy/Peter Barritt: Plate XIV (bottom); Image Professionals GmbH: Plate III; Mick Sharp: Plate XVI (bottom); World History Archive Plate IX (bottom); Bibliothèque nationale de France: Plate XIV (top); Mark Bloxham: Plate VII (centre); Bridgeman Images: Plate IX (top); Leeds Museums and Galleries (Lotherton Hall) U.K.: Plate XXI (bottom); Royal Collection Trust © Her Majesty Queen Elizabeth II, 2020: Plate XI; Royal Holloway, University of London: Plate XVIII (top); British Library: Endpapers, Plate IV, Plate V (top); Michael Harpur/eOceanic.com: Plate XIX (top); Historic Environment Scotland © Crown copyright HES: Plate XIII (top); Iain Milligan: Plate VII (top); Kyle Monroe: Plate VIII (centre); Marilyn Peddle: Plate I (top); National Galleries Scotland: Plate VIII (bottom); National Library of Ireland: Plate XXIV (top); National Maritime Museum, Greenwich, London: Plate XXI (top); PA Images/David Jones: Plate XVI (top); Shutterstock/David Falconer: Plate X (top); Jorisvo: Plate II (top); James T M Towill: Plate XII (bottom); Undiscovered Scotland: Plate XIII (centre); Yale Center for British Art: Plate XVII (bottom); Plate XVIII (bottom)

Every effort has been made to trace copyright holders and acknowledge the images. The publisher welcomes further information regarding any unintentional omissions.

Index Italic numbers indicate maps and pl. indicates illustrations.